CW01497287

UNBROKEN CHAINS

'Guilt over slavery and its inheritances rightly grips Europe and America. But this electrifying history of its brutality runs deeper and longer across Africa, still now, still hidden away. This erudite book is an eye-opening revelation and a transfixing read.'

— Polly Toynbee, *Guardian* columnist

'Expansive and sophisticated, Martin Plaut's book is absolutely essential reading for anyone seeking to understand the long history of slavery, and its ongoing life.'

— Kris Manjapra, author of *Black Ghost of Empire*

'An immense, bold undertaking, placing the dominant trans-Atlantic narrative as one part of a jigsaw that stretches across five millennia and involves the enslavement and trade in humans within Africa itself and across multiple oceans.'

— Mary Harper, author and BBC Africa Editor

'An important introduction to a controversial subject. As usual Martin Plaut pulls no punches and provides evidence from ancient Egypt to the modern day to make a compelling case against Africa's rich and powerful.'

— Hakim Adi, author of *African and Caribbean People in Britain*

'Martin Plaut has combined his journalist's eye with scholarship and depth of understanding of Africa to bring to life, through the words of the enslaved, a compelling analysis of the complexity and scale of African enslavement and its continuing impact on current African areas of conflict.'

— Mark Bowden, former UN Assistant Secretary General

'A powerful narrative that reads like a thriller. Martin Plaut's meticulous research provides a much-needed correction of the myths and misperceptions around a most sordid aspect of our common humanity.'

— Mukesh Kapila, author of *Against a Tide of Evil*

'In masterly fashion, *Unbroken Chains* sweeps from the trans-Saharan slave trade through indigenous slavery in Ethiopia and Nigeria to the Indian Ocean trade and slavery today. A must-read for anyone interested in African enslavement.'

— Christopher Saunders, University of Cape Town

'This important book covers the vast canvas of Africa's enslaved peoples, underlining that the abomination of slavery was not confined to the trans-Atlantic trade.'

— Sue Onslow, Visiting Professor, King's College London

MARTIN PLAUT

Unbroken Chains

*A 5000-Year History of
African Enslavement*

HURST & COMPANY, LONDON

First published in the United Kingdom in 2025 by
C. Hurst & Co. (Publishers) Ltd.,
New Wing, Somerset House, Strand, London, WC2R 1LA
© Martin Plaut, 2025
All rights reserved.

Distributed in the United States, Canada and Latin
America by Oxford University Press, 198 Madison Avenue,
New York, NY 10016, United States of America.

A Cataloguing-in-Publication data record for this book
is available from the British Library.

ISBN: 9781805264026

www.hurstpublishers.com

Printed and bound in Great Britain by Bell & Bain Ltd, Glasgow

CONTENTS

PREFACE

Any time while I was a slave, if one minute's freedom had been offered to me, and I had been told I must die at the end of that minute, I would have taken it—just to stand one minute on God's earth a free woman—I would.

Elizabeth Freeman, Massachusetts, 1781[1]

Can anyone doubt the intense longing for liberty among the enslaved peoples of our world? Elizabeth Freeman, who spoke so eloquently, won her case in the Massachusetts Supreme Court by arguing that the constitution of her new state made bondage illegal. That passionate desire for freedom drove men and women to break their chains; it continues to drive the fight against the enslavement of hundreds of thousands of Africans to this day.

I grew up in Cape Town. Enslaved men and women were mostly brought to South Africa by the Dutch, while others were captured by farmers. Slavery is part of our heritage, just as it is for everyone born in the American South, or among the plantations of the Caribbean or Brazil. One of the earliest sounds I recall was of the muezzin's call to prayer, echoing over the sleeping city. The 'Malay' community is central to the Cape's life, with roots deep within the slave tradition. Their lively festivals, spicy food and vibrant culture enriched our otherwise bland, restrictive, mainly Protestant heritage. They were a reminder, at the height of apartheid, that there was so much more to South Africa than the narrow, repressive life that the government attempted to impose on us.

I joined the University of Cape Town in 1968, but my studies were cut short. My participation in protests against the university's refusal to appoint a black lecturer meant I did not study, failed my exams and had to leave. I returned in 1973, having earned my fees. This time I worked diligently, while campaigning to rebuild black unions destroyed by the government in the 1960s. In 1976 I was on the streets of Johannesburg, in solidarity with the children of Soweto, before leaving for exile in Britain. London has been my home ever since. I became the British Labour Party's Africa secretary, representing the Party on the Anti-Apartheid Movement. In 1984 I joined the BBC World Service. Working on Africa, with African colleagues, for the next three decades was a joy and a privilege. I retired in 2013 having served for a decade as Africa editor of BBC World Service News. Since then, I have continued my engagement with the continent, writing books on South Africa and the Horn of Africa.

I came across the story of Dr Abdullah Abdurahman (1872–1940), the first black South African ever to win an election in the country, taking a seat on the Cape Town city council. From 1904 until his death, he represented the diverse community of District Six. I felt impelled to write his biography in an attempt to capture something of this extraordinary man.[2] Dr Abdurahman was the grandson of a slave, probably brought from Bengal. It troubled me that I knew so little about the slave trade across the Indian Ocean, which has been swamped by the Trans-Atlantic narrative, and so I decided to look at the subject in greater detail. As I began to investigate this history I came across a much wider canvas: slaves of the vast Sokoto Caliphate, or the fate of Oromo slaves from Ethiopia, captured and forced to march for weeks and months until they were sold in Arabia, and the men and women of Irish villages captured and taken to North Africa as slaves. Each is a fragment of the African story of enslavement that has not yet concluded. Slavery continues to this day, with refugees trapped in Libya's officially sanctioned detention centres still being sold to the highest bidder.

This book is—for the most part—the story of enslavement in Africa itself, not a record of the fate of slaves after they left Africa's shores. How well I have succeeded is for others to judge, but my deep gratitude is to my many friends who commented on my drafts. I owe special thanks to Zina Rohan and David Killingray. I want to express my gratitude to the staff at Hurst and to Sebastian Ballard for his marvellous maps. All errors are, of course, my own.

INTRODUCTION

Slavery over millennia

Seized and in chains. Whipped into the holds of fetid boats, never to see their African homes again. These are the images of slavery etched onto our minds—the scourge of Africa down the centuries. British ships, leaving Liverpool, London or Bristol to bring slaves to the Caribbean or the Americas, returning with sugar, tobacco and cotton, which was then sold as cloth. This was the notorious 'triangular trade', the backbone of Empire. When African slavery is discussed, this is what we recall. It is, of course, accurate, yet it is only a fragment of the story. Africa was by no means the only continent to be afflicted by enslavement, which has been an almost universal practice. However, no-one can question the cruelty Africa's people have had to endure.

My aim in writing this book is to provide a single source that attempts to cover the whole canvas of slavery in Africa. It will not generally dwell in detail on what happened to these men and women once they left the continent. The focus is on slavery on the continent itself. At the same time, I will try to dispel some of the myths that have grown up around the subject.

Popular culture tends to:

- assume that slavery was exclusively imposed from outside Africa;
- conflate slavery with colonialism;
- treat Trans-Atlantic slavery as the only form of African enslavement;
- believe that slavery ended in the nineteenth century.

Each of these assumptions is false, and there are others too. It is often thought that Britain was the largest slave trader across the Atlantic, yet this was not the case.

The Portuguese started first in the trade and finished last. They carried 5,848,265 Africans, mostly to Brazil. They accounted for nearly 47 per cent of all slaves who embarked on slave voyages. Britain was the next biggest European carrier, taking 3,259,440 Africans to the British West Indies and British North America.[1]

It is not possible to know with certainty how many Africans have been enslaved, but let us begin by attempting to estimate the scale.[2] Information available suggests that the figure exceeds 40 million— especially since the data used in Table 1 begins in 650 and ends in 1900, yet we know that slavery dates from at least 2900 BCE and that it continues to the present day. Statistics for Indian, Saudi Arabian and Iranian slaves have not been included as they are not precise enough. As recently as 2023, the UN special rapporteur on contemporary forms of slavery reported that 200,000 Malians were living 'under the direct control of their "masters"'.[3] These numbers are not included here, but they suggest that a figure nearer 50 million may not be an exaggeration.

Table 1: African Slavery, 650 CE–1900

Region	Dates	No. of Slaves
Indian Ocean	800–1900	12,580,000[4]
Trans-Atlantic	1501–1867	12,522,570[5]
Trans-Sahara	650–1800	9,387,000[6]
Sokoto	1860	4,000,000[7]
Ottoman	1800–1900	1,300,000[8]
Barbary Corsairs	1530–1869	1,000,000[9]
Iran	1800–1900	147,000[10]
Ethiopia	1935	300,000[11]
Total		41,236,570

African agency and troubling silences

African slavery was not the sole responsibility of foreign powers. The Ethiopian scholar Mekuria Bulcha put the issue succinctly: 'The notion that outsiders of white Christians from Europe and Muslim

Arabs from the Middle East and Asia imposed slavery on Africa has no basis in history.'[12] Africans themselves engaged in the trade for centuries before external powers intervened, and they continue to practice enslavement to this day. As the African American academic and broadcaster Henry Gates Jr argued: 'Erasing the role of black agents in the slave trade. That's just dishonest. It's bad history.'[13]

Investigating these questions comes up against several obstacles, while discussions of African slavery are characterised by troubling silences. This is not a question that is new to Britain. In 1814, Jane Austen included this exchange in her novel *Mansfield Park*:

> Did not you hear me ask him about the slave trade last night?
> I did—and was in hopes the question would be followed up by others. It would have pleased your uncle to be inquired of farther.
> And I longed to do it—but there was such a dead silence![14]

Recently, churches in Britain have begun to examine their role in the trade.[15] So too have other institutions, from universities to museums. Yet Muslim societies continue to resist engaging with the subject. 'Why is it so difficult to examine slavery in the Muslim world?' asked Yacine Daddi Addoun.[16] 'The overwhelming silence on the subject raises questions about how slavery has been perceived in the past and why silence seems to be necessary in the present.'[17] Just as concerning is the unwillingness of the leaders of Africa, through the African Union or Arab League, to address the continent's involvement in slavery, in the past and in the present.

The failure of African leaders to act in no way justifies the role that Europeans, Arabs, Indians, Iranians and Turks played in African slavery down the years. China imported Africans as novelties, while Crimean khans had African eunuchs in their harems.[18] This inescapable reality cannot be brushed aside, any more than the European role in creating the industrial revolution, which established the parameters within which modern slavery evolved. The intense discussion of the role of Europe and the United States in the Trans-Atlantic slave trade and the issue of reparations is to be welcomed. Why is there no similar debate under way in the Arabic and Muslim world? Why does India not question its African slave legacy, and why—for example—does Egypt not discuss its enslavement of Sudanese and Ethiopians down many centuries? Much the same question could be put to the Saudi or Omani authorities. Scholars also need to broaden their horizons. It is striking how few references there are in otherwise scholarly works to some central aspects of African enslavement.[19]

If we are to come to grips with this complex and deeply troubling subject, these issues need to be faced. Yet this is not just a tale of suffering: extraordinary people surface in this history, not all of them slaves. Men like Mansa Musa, the fourteenth-century West African ruler, who was so rich that his opulent generosity came close to wrecking the Egyptian economy. Ibn Battuta, a Maghrebi, was possibly the greatest explorer of all time, travelling three times the distance of Marco Polo's journeys on his trips to China and India and across Africa. Or Malik Ambar, who rose from Ethiopian servitude to become one of India's greatest military leaders. All played their part in shaping our past. The history of enslavement begins and ends on the banks of the Nile, although all of Africa, as far south as the Cape of Good Hope, is part of the narrative.

Slavery and colonialism

The belief that European colonialism of Africa can be conflated with slavery is glaringly inaccurate. From the beginning of the Portuguese slave trade in the 1440s until the age of colonialism initiated by the 'scramble for Africa' in the 1880s, only the fringes of the continent were under foreign settlement. Colonisation had taken place. The Portuguese held parts of Angola and Mozambique, Britain had taken coastal territory in South Africa, France had captured parts of North Africa, and Oman controlled areas of Africa's east coast, but colonialism's impact was limited. In 1870, only 10 per cent of Africa was under European control.[20] By the time of the First World War in 1914, the situation had been reversed: only Liberia and Ethiopia remained free. Colonial powers had seized 90 per cent of the continent, but by this time European slavery had long since ended.

It is not difficult to understand why this was the case. 'No continent was less inviting for European explorers,' wrote Thomas Pakenham in his monumental work on the subject.[21] 'It was nearly 400 years since the smooth round profile of Africa had decorated the charts of the Portuguese navigators. For the most of that time the interior—with notable exceptions to north and south—had remained as mysterious as the surface of the moon.' The British presence was a case in point.

> Until the last quarter of the nineteenth century Britain encountered very few African cultures, because the British presence was confined to small coastal enclaves, to intermittent expeditions or embassies into an unknown interior, or to the offshore influence of the Royal Navy.[22]

It was in these enclaves that the Europeans built forts from which to operate. They established these by reaching contracts with local elites, whose rulers, rather reluctantly, agreed to a limited presence from which trade could be conducted.

> Strictly speaking, the only European colony on the Western side of Africa before the end of the eighteenth century was Portuguese Angola. Elsewhere Europeans who settled to trade paid rent for their settlements to African rulers. Sovereignty was not surrendered. African rulers followed the precedent set in 1482, when the Portuguese were grudgingly permitted to build a fort at Elmina in return for a regularly paid rent.[23]

In this period the continent remained for the Europeans what it had been when they first circumnavigated it: 'a series of coasts— Barbary Coast, Windward Coast, Grain Coast … Swahili Coast, Somali Coast—surrounded by a vast enigmatic blank.'[24] Some coastal enclaves were the product of European raids, but outside powers generally required the assistance and support of local rulers to acquire the slaves they were seeking. As the eminent Africanist Basil Davidson argued: 'Raids soon gave way to alliances, for the Europeans could offer goods that African chieftains greatly desired: horses to begin with and then, increasingly, firearms and alcohol.'[25] African leaders around the continent co-operated by marching their captives to the sea, sometimes over vast distances. They were then packed into foreign vessels, seldom to return.

> The trade was thus an African trade until it reached the coast. Only very rarely were Europeans directly involved in procuring slaves, and that was largely in Angola. Particularly in savanna regions,

long-distance caravans brought slaves from hundreds of miles in the interior. In forest regions such as modern Ivory Coast 'stateless' communities passed on slaves like a baton in a relay aimed at the sea. Slaves generally appear to have been sold several times before reaching the point of shipment.[26]

It is frequently forgotten that for the most part the European colonial period lasted less than a century (from the 1880s to the 1960s), while African slavery can be traced back over at least 5,000 years. British, German, French, Dutch, Spanish, Portuguese and Belgian colonialism transformed African societies across the continent in the late nineteenth and early twentieth centuries. Their intervention was frequently brutal and bloody, but over a limited period.

European opposition to and disgust at slavery developed gradually, along with campaigns against the practice, but the movements eventually become irresistible. By the nineteenth century, the abolitionist campaigns had made huge advances. In 1807, Britain abolished the slave trade, but not the ownership of slaves. Then, in 1833, it passed the Slavery Abolition Act, ending slavery itself in most British colonies, and freeing more than 800,000 enslaved Africans in the Caribbean and South Africa, as well as a small number in Canada. Rather than encouraging the trade, London deployed naval taskforces off West and East Africa to try—not always successfully—to halt slavery. This was in stark contrast to the role of other slave traders, including the Arabs, the Ethiopians or the rulers of North Africa, whose routes across the Sahara continued to extract the slaves they desired. Where were the local campaigns to end the practice?[27] The answer is that they did indeed exist. There was pressure from African leaders on the Upper Senegal River, as well as cases brought before the Vatican by Africans.[28] However, it was British abolitionists who really drove the international campaign to end the practice.

Indigenous slavery

Like enslavement across the world, African slavery generally began with the powerful capturing men and women from weaker societies living around them. Frequently it was the result of conquest, and over time it became endemic. The earliest evidence is to be found on the Nile. Egyptians sailed southwards taking captives as they conquered new territories. These are depicted along the river. 'The first evidence was carved in stone in 2900 B.C.E. at the second cataract depicting a boat on the Nile packed with Nubian captives for enslavement in Egypt,' wrote Robert Collins.[29] A Nubian chief was shown bound to the prow of an Egyptian ship, being carried off to slavery with his followers.

The trade continued down the centuries, with Egyptians raiding for gold, slaves and ivory from Sudan and Ethiopia, carrying them down the Nile as commodities. 'Thereafter throughout the next five thousand years African slaves captured in war, raids, or purchased in the market were marched down the Nile, across the Sahara to the Mediterranean, or transported over the Red Sea and the Indian Ocean to Asia.'[30] Slaves were part of a complex, geographically extended trade long before Europeans penetrated the continent. The Ghanaian academic Akosua Adoma Perbi describes the antiquity of the institution in her region: 'From about the 10th Century A.D. gold from Ghana was exchanged for slaves, hides, ostrich feathers and other products from Western Sudan as well as cowries, perfumes, beads and horses from North Africa.'[31]

Men and women were held and exploited over the entire continent prior to European enslavement in the fifteenth century. Arabs and Berbers raided across the Sahara from North Africa, capturing people as they advanced deeper and deeper into the vast desert. The earliest markers put down by Berbers as they transited the Sahara date back more than 2,500 years.[32] From Ethiopia in the east to Mauritania in the west, men, women and children were taken captive. Abyssinian rulers enslaved the ethnic groups they conquered, using them in their palaces and farms and trading them with Arabia. At the time of the American Civil War in the 1860s, the Sokoto Caliphate in northern Nigeria and Niger had a slave population approximately the same as the number of people enslaved in the United States.[33] At the other end of the continent the Dutch imported Indonesians and Indians to work on their farms in the Cape, while the Batswana captured slaves from among the Khoisan.[34]

The 'tyranny of the Atlantic'

> The literature on slavery in Africa is still overwhelmingly dominated by material on the West Coast and the Atlantic slave trade. Even today, one can hear Africanists who should know better, referring to this as 'the' African slave trade.[35]

It is hardly surprising that African slavery is frequently reduced to the Trans-Atlantic trade. Images of ships laden to the gunnels with West African captives, packed so close to each other between decks that they had little space to breathe, are indelibly printed on European consciences, with good reason. Stories of their being dumped overboard if they died, or even to claim insurance, motivated the anti-slavery movement down the years. Nor can anyone turn away from the trauma their enslavement produced—stripping African peoples of their names, languages and heritage as they were taken into captivity. As Ngũgĩ wa Thiong'o wrote so memorably: 'Slaves, before they left the African shore, were branded with marks of their owners. Theirs, literally, was a baptism of fire.'[36] This enduring pain led to publications on slavery and investigations of the Middle Passage that fill university libraries. The subject has been central to concerns of the African American community.

This single focus has been described as the 'tyranny of the Atlantic'.[37] It has prevented a more careful, more inclusive perspective, which attempts to see African slavery in all its facets. 'At the heart of this historiographical tradition is a propensity to conceptualize the Atlantic as a "world" unto itself,' commented Richard Allen.[38]

> Studies of the African diaspora, for example, often ignore the fact that millions of enslaved men, women, and children were moved across the Indian Ocean as well as the Atlantic, and that this trade in African slaves to the Middle East and South Asia was of far greater antiquity than to the Americas.[39]

Practiced by Arab and Indian traders for centuries, the Indian Ocean trade was later joined by Europeans, who took slaves to their colonies. The Portuguese engaged in this practice by penetrating deep into what is today Tanzania, Mozambique and the Congo. The Mediterranean also saw enslavement from the earliest times, with

Greeks, Romans, Arabs and later the Ottomans occupying large parts of Africa. All practiced slavery on local peoples.

Finally, there was the enslavement of Europeans by Barbary corsairs—outposts of the Ottoman Empire in North Africa—who raided Italy, France and Spain. This aspect of African history is generally relegated to a completely different sphere of intellectual activity and not considered under the heading of African slavery at all. Yet they are clearly part of the narrative, since they were slaves upon the African continent. The corsairs travelled as far as the British Isles and even Iceland, accumulating over 1 million men and women during more than two centuries. Some were ransomed and others rescued, but the majority were not. Once captured, they lived and died in North Africa. The corsairs even fought the newly independent United States. These clashes led to an expeditionary force being sent to Tunisia and consequently to the establishment of the U.S. Navy. 'In 1794, in response to Algerian seizures of American ships, Congress authorized construction of the first 6 ships of the U.S. Navy,' wrote the State Department's official historian.[40] Hence the battle hymn of the US Marines:

> From the Halls of Montezuma
> To the shores of Tripoli;
> We fight our country's battles
> In the air, on land, and sea.

The African slave trade shaped relationships from Asia to the Americas.

Slavery abolished?

Ending slavery has been lengthy, and immensely costly, for those who lived in its chains. In 1807 the British Parliament passed the Abolition of the Slave Trade Act, ending the buying and selling of enslaved people within the British Empire, but it did not protect those already enslaved and traded between colonies. Slavery itself was finally made illegal by the Slavery Abolition Act of 1833, which banned the practice across the British Empire the following year. It seemed that London had put the worst excesses behind it. Yet when the British finally conquered the Sokoto Caliphate in 1903, they found they had some 2 million slaves on their hands. For other nations the practice was even more enduring. Slavery was only formally abolished in Saudi Arabia in 1962 and in Oman in 1970.[41] In parts of Africa it continues to the present. We need look no further than the reports of Human Rights Watch on the atrocities committed in Sudan during the long war that led to the independence of South Sudan in 2011.

> Human Rights Watch has long denounced slavery in Sudan in the context of the nineteen-year civil war. In this contemporary form of slavery government-backed and armed militia of the Baggara tribes raid to capture children and women who are then held in conditions of slavery in western Sudan and elsewhere. They are forced to work for free in homes and in fields, punished when they refuse, and abused physically and sometimes sexually. Raids are directed mostly at the civilian Dinka population of the southern region of Bahr El Ghazal.[42]

These attitudes, and the relations that they engender, have not been eroded by time. In 2023, Arab militia of the Rapid Support Forces attacked Africans from the Masalit ethnic group in El Geneina, capital of Sudan's West Darfur.[43]

> Gamar al-Deen was visiting a friend when gunmen poured into his neighbourhood on 27 April 2023. 'I came back to find they were all dead,' he says. 'My mother, my father, uncles, brothers, sisters. I wanted to die myself in that moment.' Deen, a teacher, lost a dozen members of his family that day. Several of his neighbours were killed too. At his friend's during the carnage, he saw a group of fighters strip a woman naked and then rape her in the street. 'They told us, "This area belongs to us, not you, you are slaves,"' he says.

It is hard to avoid the impression that international organisations are loath to confront the evidence of African slavery's contemporary aspect. This unwillingness may be—to put it another way—because 'Africanists have been anxious to dissociate slavery in Africa from its bad image in the Americas.'[44] From the African Union to the Arab League, there is a reluctance to openly discuss an issue that appears relegated to the past. The UNESCO Slave Route project initiated in 1999 refers extensively to the Trans-Atlantic, making limited references to other African slave routes.[45]

Defining slavery

Some regard the question of slavery through the lens of race. The suggestion is made that Europeans developed the industrial scale of the Trans-Atlantic trade at its most extreme because they were 'white' while their victims were 'black' and therefore considered inferior. No doubt racism played a part in these relationships; however, this problem was by no means restricted to Europeans. Berbers, who swept across the Sahara, regarded Africans in much the same way, as did many Arabs. This example was found in Morocco.

> Az-Zayani, a nineteenth century Moroccan chronicler, in his book *at-Turjuman al-Mu'rib*, said Sultan Isma'il gave the order to collect all black people. No black person was spared whether the person was slave or free black or *hartani*. In one year, 3,000 blacks were gathered from the area around Marrakech alone. There, the colour of the skin was reason enough for a person to be enslaved and enrolled in the army of the Sultan.[46]

Richard Pankhurst, among the most eminent Ethiopianists, summarised the issue when describing the plight of those seized along Ethiopia's border with Sudan:

> Many of the slaves thus captured were darker than average hue and sometimes of 'Negroid' appearance. Their distinct colour and features caused excessive pigmentation and non-Semitic appearance to be identified with servile status.[47]

Like peoples across the world, the strong preyed on the weak, the organised on the disorganised. People living on the periphery of societies were considered as legitimate targets for enslavement by the rich and powerful.

Academics have wrestled with the definition of slavery for years. Akosua Adoma Perbi outlines the problem eloquently:

> The Western conception of slavery can be summarised by these variables. First, the slave is a commodity; second, the slave is a

chattel; third, the slave is inheritable; fourth, his/her progeny inherits slave status, slavery is, therefore perpetual and hereditary; fifth the slave is property and sixth, the slave is kinless, marginalised and an outsider.[48]

She then points out that in Ghana not all aspects of this definition are applicable. The slave was not regarded as a chattel and was regarded as human. They were 'a person in a state of servitude guarded by rights.'[49]

Others have pointed out that violence was an integral part of plantations controlled by Europeans and Arabs but was less prevalent in other regimes, although slave systems were still characterised by brutal conditions of work, suicide and revolts.[50] It is argued that African slaves in the New World had a considerably harder time than those held in Africa itself. In the Americas, it is suggested, we find 'large gangs of slaves toiling in mines and on plantations, justified by the most naked forms of racism'.[51] Yet, when we examine the Sokoto Caliphate, it is clear that plantation culture and the use of gangs of slaves was certainly found on African soil, and their treatment was often no less brutal. At the same time, it is true that some slaves held in Africa might integrate into the local communities and earn their freedom or the freedom of their descendants. Some even won positions of leadership. While this certainly happened, it was by no means universal. African slavery might differ from American slavery, but it was—as Collins and Burns point out—'still slavery'.[52]

I do not intend to continue this definitional debate, important as it is. I would suggest that anyone enduring a transit similar to the 'Forty Days' Road' from Darfur to Egypt would hardly wish to quibble about such nuances. In total, the route traversed nearly 1,100 miles of almost waterless desert and required forty days' march to complete. The cruelty of their treatment and their death rates were comparable to those found on ships taking their human cargoes across the Atlantic or the Indian Ocean. Slaves generally 'knew their place', and if they did not, the lash soon reminded them of what it was. Slaves were not passive recipients of this cruelty and sometimes rose in revolt or found other ways of resisting their owners. But as a saying among the Akan of Ghana put it: 'A slave's life is in his master's hand.'[53]

I have used the term 'slavery' as defined by the Slavery Convention of 1926: 'Slavery is the status or condition of a person over whom any or all of the powers attaching to the right of ownership are exercised.'[54] Slave trading is defined by the same Convention:

> The slave trade includes all acts involved in the capture, acquisition or disposal of a person with intent to reduce him to slavery; all acts involved in the acquisition of a slave with a view to selling or exchanging him; all acts of disposal by sale or exchange of a slave acquired with a view to being sold or exchanged, and, in general, every act of trade or transport in slaves.

I have not included men and women who fall under what is termed 'modern slavery', which seems closer to indentured labour.[55] Some of the most poorly paid and harshly treated wage labourers endure conditions not very different from the enslaved. The lines between these forms of abuse are blurred and imprecise. No two systems were alike, and even within societies these practices change over time, but it should not prevent our studying servitude.

> Every slave system has had its own peculiarities with different rights and obligations, but classical slavery, European slavery, Islamic slavery, and African slavery are still systems of slavery. There is a common dimension that allows for comparison.[56]

I regard all those who have been enslaved in Africa as African slaves, irrespective of where they came from. This book is not, generally, an examination of their fate once they reached their destination. The lot of enslaved people, particularly in the Caribbean and Americas, has been extensively written about. I have made an exception for the Indian Ocean, where what happened to Africans once they arrived in Arabia, India or the Indian Ocean islands is explained, although only briefly.

The aim of this book is to provide an accessible, but by no means all-encompassing, introduction to this subject. There will, inevitably, be questions that are not explored. If errors creep in, I apologise; this is an enormous and complex subject. When I began discussing this project, I was astonished by how many well-informed friends and colleagues were unaware of the diversity of Africa slavery: that it extended well beyond the Trans-Atlantic trade with which they were so familiar, and which is taught in our classrooms. I hope the book responds to some of the quizzical looks I received when I first described how widespread and diverse African slavery really was, and still remains.

PART 1

THE TRANS-SAHARAN SLAVE TRADE

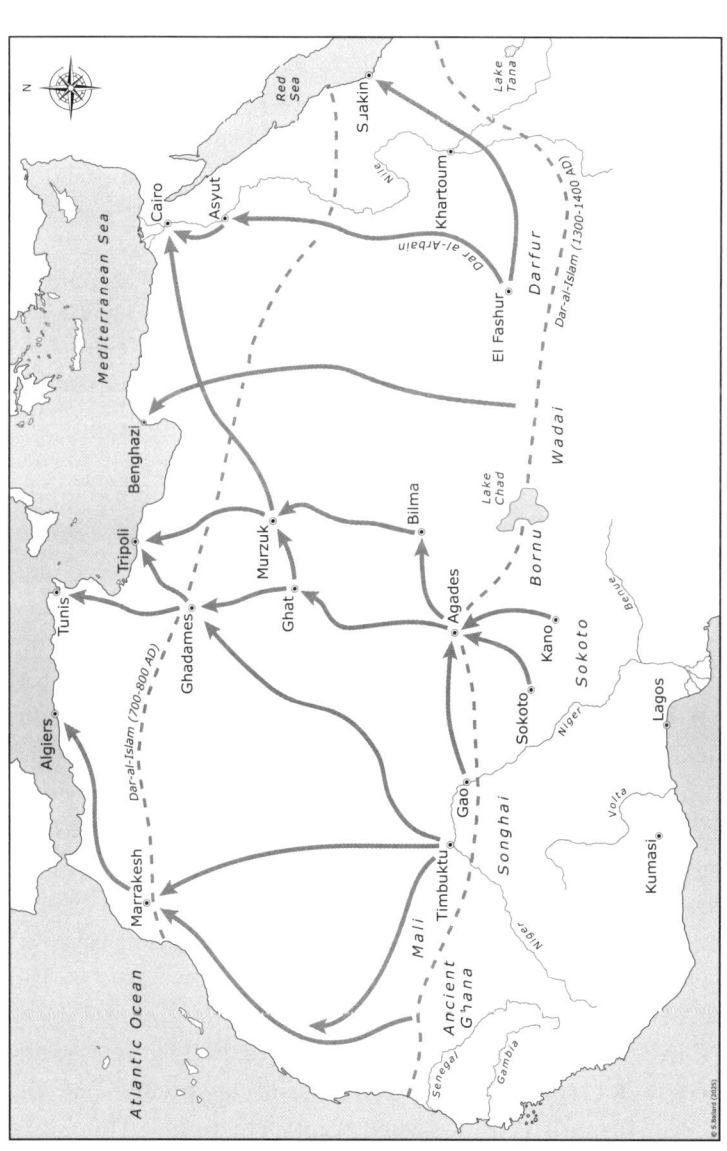

Map 1: Trans-Saharan slave routes and the expansion of Islam

The Dar-al-Islam shows the extent of Islamic control. The map is adapted from a variety of sources.

The enslavement of Africans down the Nile and across the Sahara is among the earliest authenticated forms of such servitude and has continued, almost without interruption, over the past 5,000 years, an event etched on the rocks of the Nile during the reign of the First Dynasty Pharaoh Djer.[1]

> The Nubian chief is bound to the prow of an Egyptian ship with his followers being carried off into slavery. During the millennia that followed slaves were sent down the Nile as goods in commercial transactions. The largest number of slaves, however, were captives seized during Pharaonic military expeditions south of Aswan into Nubia when Egypt was an imperial power during the Old, the Middle and the New Kingdoms that encompassed 31 dynasties and lasted from c.2900 to 332 BC.[2]

The practice was not restricted to Egypt. Down the centuries enslavement took place in societies bordering on the Sahara and across the Sahel, from Mauritania to Somalia, from Tunisia to Nigeria. Africans were also transported across adjacent seas, carried over the Mediterranean, the Red Sea, the Indian Ocean and—of course—the Atlantic.

The slave trade was shaped by many events over the millennia. The first was environmental: the gradual changes in the climate, which left areas of the Sahara that had once been green and productive a desert. A sharp fall in rainfall at the end of the last ice age occurred between 5,000 and 11,000 years ago. Over time the region dried out, transforming the lush landscape that had supported hippo, antelope and elephants into desert, scrub and sand dunes.[3] Agriculture fell away and travel from across this region became increasingly difficult. The second was the introduction of the camel, which provided a very effective means of transport over these vast, harsh spaces. This happened around 1680 BCE, when the species was introduced into Egypt to replace the horse as a beast of burden, although horses continued to be important as cavalry.[4] The camel was far more robust, and capable of carrying up to 150 kilograms over 100 kilometres a day.

The third intervention was human. North African slavery took place under the Greeks, Romans and Egyptians, but the events of the seventh century were transformational. The Arabs swept across North Africa, bringing with them the Islamic faith. Christian and pagan communities were forced to adopt Islam at the point of a sword. As the Arabs advanced there were 'repeated instances of enslavement by the Muslim armies.'[5] They advanced westwards until they held all of North Africa, before crossing the straits of Gibraltar into Spain and Portugal circa 711.[6] Their Iberian conquests connected Africa to the outside world in a way it had not been previously. From North Africa the Arabs also extended their influence southwards into the rest of Africa. Their conquests were by warriors, but their relationships were cemented by scholars, administrators, traders and merchants. Goods flowed across the Mediterranean and over the desert.[7] The Trans-Saharan trade would, in time, become as important a route for slaves as the Nile had been down the centuries. The Saharan routes also laid the groundwork for the Trans-Atlantic slave trade, which began with the arrival of the Portuguese off the West African coast in 1444.

1

ROUTES ACROSS THE SAHARA

The slave caravans used an intricate web of routes over the Sahara. Traders regularly transported gold, salt and people northwards. In the opposite direction they took manufactured goods and cloth. In some cases, there was no trade: raids were carried out and African slaves were transported in chains or in coffles—yoked together by the neck with leather thongs to prevent their escape.[1]

The Nile provided the earliest route, but many others traversed the Sahara. Most routes ran north to south while others ran east to west. Three major corridors crossed the barren terrain. One led from Timbuktu in Mali to Morocco, a second from Kano on the border of Lake Chad to Libya, and the third from Darfur and Ethiopia to Egypt. Many others criss-crossed the Sahara, making the desert accessible for commerce. For example, one of the most remote and most difficult ran from Wadai in what is now Chad to the Libyan port of Benghazi. This ancient route allowed slaves from the south to be brought up across the inhospitable wastes and exported to Egypt and later to the Ottoman Empire.[2] Many of the slaves were women, taken for domestic work or sexual services, and the trade continued along this route well into the 1920s. The British consul reported from Benghazi in March 1879 that:

> [T]his consulate is constantly besieged by runaway slaves, seeking my protection and intervention with the Turkish authorities to obtain their freedom ... Almost every Arab notable, without exception, residing in this town is a slave owner ... even the local government actually permits all its functionaries, to the utter disregard of [government regulations] to possess as many slaves as their circumstances will enable them to maintain.[3]

19

The conditions under which they travelled were appalling: sandstorms buried whole caravans. There were severe shortages of water and fluctuations in temperature. Some of the caravans were very substantial, with a report of annual caravans of 12,000 camels crossing the desert to Mali in the fourteenth century.[4] Nor did conditions improve over time. Even in relatively recent times, slaves making the Saharan crossing faced what has been described as 'an ordeal no less hideous than the so-called middle passage of the [Atlantic] ocean, with a mortality rate estimated by some to have been in the order of 20 per cent in the 19th-century caravans. Others put losses very much higher, exceeding survivals.'[5]

Over the ensuing centuries (600 CE–2000), 14 to 15 million sub-Saharan Africans would be transported to the Islamic world.[6]

The Nile valley was a source of African slaves over the centuries. They were brought from Nubia and Darfur in present-day Sudan, as well as Ethiopia. Greeks may first have encountered the Ethiopians when they accompanied Pharaoh Psammetichus II (594 BCE–588 BCE) on an expedition southward. An inscription records the presence of Greek mercenaries alongside the Egyptian forces.[7] The Greeks also crossed the Red Sea and Indian Ocean, reaching as far as the mouth of the Indus River as early as 510 BCE.[8] The routes they pioneered were followed by others, including Arabs, and intrepid sailors later travelled onwards to China. As the Arabs journeyed eastwards, they traded in the goods their clients valued. By the middle of the ninth century CE, African slaves had been brought to Chinese market by Arab traders.[9] This will be the subject of Part 2, 'The Indian Ocean and Beyond'.

For the Romans, African slaves were useful, but not essential; they had plenty among the Europeans whom they had defeated in their many wars. Captives taken in battles from Britain to Mesopotamia were enslaved.[10] Romans later replenished most of their human stock from markets in Asia Minor. Africa was, by comparison, relatively unimportant. It is estimated that around 11 per cent of North Africans were enslaved during the Roman period.[11] The Punic wars against Carthage (which centred on what is today Tunisia) between 264 BCE and 146 BCE saw Rome capture many of its enemies, some of whom were transported to Sicily to work on farms.

Rome also built forts deep inside the Egyptian territory it held, including one at the Kharga Oasis, on the notorious 'forty-day trade route', or *Darb el-Arbain*, so called because of the time it took to march slaves along the length of the road. The oasis lies deep in the desert, some 500 kilometres from Cairo and 200 kilometres due west of Luxor and the Nile Valley. A series of temples and fortifications were constructed in the second to fourth centuries CE in this barren and remote location, to protect this frontier of the Roman Empire.[12] The environment was so harsh and the enforcement so brutal that the death rate along the route was estimated to be as high as 30 per cent.[13] Over the centuries little changed. A German explorer and missionary, Theodor Krump, witnessed the Sudanese slave trade in 1702 in all its cruelty, commenting on the high rate of mortality and the suffering they endured on their journey to Egypt. 'Many of them, already in ill health as a result of this long and difficult journey, died. The Moors in these lands do not treat their slaves as human beings … they are bound and fettered together with heavy chains, like dogs.'[14]

Rome did not use its control of North Africa to attempt extensive Trans-Saharan trade.[15] However, it did send five expeditions across the Sahara, even finding 'the lake of the hippopotamus and rhinoceros' which has since been identified as Lake Chad.[16] The trade in exotic animals had been developed by the Carthaginians, with monkeys, lions and elephants being transported across the deserts, but the Romans extended the trade. Ever more exotic species of wild animals were brought for their circuses, which were so popular with the Roman crowds.[17]

Egyptian slavery

Egyptians used the Nile to travel deep into Africa, treating Nubia, to their south, as their natural hinterland. While the Mediterranean and the deserts guarded Egypt's other borders, the lands to the south held both promise and danger. The Egyptians viewed enslaving their southern neighbours as unremarkable. 'From the beginning of historic time, and undoubtedly before, there has been a trade in slaves throughout the Nile Valley spreading across the Red Sea and into the Middle East,' wrote Robert Collins.[18]

The Pharaohs, the Ptolemies, the Romans, the Arabs and the Turks in ancient and modern times all took slaves from the greater Nile Valley. In Pharaonic times most of the slaves came from Nubia or Ethiopia and were usually victims of war, as Verdi's opera Aida dramatically demonstrates with great gusto.[19]

Like other imperial powers, this relationship was accompanied by a confidence in Egypt's moral superiority and civilisation, although the relationship was complex, fluctuating over time, depending on the strength of the Pharaoh. The Egyptians regarded Nubians in much the same way as other great powers considered their neighbours: as a source of goods and as a potential threat. They traded with Nubia as well as clashing with them: slaves were by no means the only commodities the Egyptians sought. Ivory, animal skins, myrrh, incense, gold, aromatic woods and spices could all be obtained on these trade missions.[20] Egyptians had little interest in settling in Nubia.[21] They described the Nubians as 'Aetheopians'— or 'burnt faces'—who came from the 'miserable Kush', in their view a 'wretched' land, good only for gold, slaves and ivory.[22] Egyptians treated Nubians as an irresponsible and lazy nation, who indulged in sorcery. As a Pharaoh sternly instructed his southern viceroy in c. 1425 BCE: 'Don't be at all lenient with Nubia! Beware their people and their magicians!'[23]

Some of the earliest recorded slave raids are to be found inscribed on fragments of black basalt preserved in the Museum of Palermo. The 'Palermo stone' records the life of Pharaoh Sneferu, who reigned from around 2613 BCE to 2589 BCE. He led an expedition south, during which he is claimed to have captured thousands of slaves and livestock. The raid is recorded on the stone.

> [During the reign of] Sneferu ... The building of Tuataua ships of mer wood of a hundred capacity, and 60 royal boats of sixteen capacity. Raid in the Land of the Blacks (i.e. the Sūdān), and the bringing in of seven thousand prisoners, men and women, and twenty thousand cattle, sheep, and goats.[24]

Slaves performed many functions in Egyptian society, from porters along the Nile to soldiers defending the nation from its enemies. Some rose in rank, but the majority did not. Contrary to popular belief, slaves did not build the Pyramids—a task undertaken by Egyptian labourers who were 'treated with utmost respect and honor.'[25] Labourers constructing the Pyramids were skilled and supervised, not enslaved. Women slaves were particularly prized, to work in the home and to satisfy their masters in the bedroom. Nubians and Ethiopians fulfilled a range of roles: some were utilitarian, some for indulgence.

> Before the nineteenth century, slaves had been sought for centuries south of Aswan as domestic servants, concubines, and children for the households of Egypt. Many males were enrolled in Egyptian armies from the times of the Pharaohs to the twentieth century where they served as slave mercenaries ... There seems to have been a vigorous trade in female slaves from the Ethiopian Highlands who were highly prized and priced.[26]

These raids continued for millennia.[27] When Egypt's rulers were powerful, they pushed further down the Nile. When they were weak, they attempted to defend their southern border by constructing fortresses along the river. Just upstream of the first cataract was the frontier post of al-Qasr, 'the fortress, which was manned by a garrison and considered the gateway to Nubia.'[28] At the second cataract a further two fortresses were built. It was here that much trade took place, with goods bartered for slaves.[29]

Over the centuries Egyptian rulers relied on African slaves for their troops and imported them in large numbers. Yet even with the arrival of the Fatimid Caliphate in the tenth century CE, it has been hard to establish exactly where the subjugated men came from, although many appear to have been drawn from Ethiopia.

> Ethiopian slaves, who are so difficult to identify in medieval texts, were reputed for their warlike qualities as well as their loyalty— even before the advent of Islam. Of course, it would be difficult to affirm that many Fatimid black soldiers—freeborn or slaves— came from Bilād al-Ḥabaš (in Arabic sources, the word usually applied to the land and peoples of Ethiopia and 'at times to the adjoining areas'). Ancient Egyptian authors do not use the term Ḥabaš when they write about the Fatimid army. Yet they knew the Bilād al-Ḥabaš. Some of them were aware that the master of Egypt had diplomatic relations with the king of Ethiopia, and that the

Fatimid caliph allowed the patriarch of Alexandria to send a bishop who would become the head of the Ethiopian church.[30]

As late as the 1170s Egyptian infantry included African military slaves, sometimes in their tens of thousands.[31] It was only when the infantry was largely replaced by cavalry and a more modern military was recruited and provided with complexes housing mosques, barracks and palaces that slaves could be dispensed with.

2

THE ARAB CONQUEST AND ENSLAVEMENT

The Arab conquest of Egypt following the death of Muhammad in 632 transformed the country and the region. Islam was imposed on the Egyptians, much as it was on other North Africans. The relationship between the Islamic faith and slavery is the subject of much research and many books, but it is clear that slavery in Arabia pre-dated Islam and that the Prophet Muhammad both owned slaves and mentioned slavery repeatedly in his teachings. Although this is too complex an issue to be dealt with in detail, James Walvin provided a useful outline.

> [S]lavery was commonplace throughout Arabia well before the rise of Islam. But as Islam spread, between the eight and the fifteenth centuries, and especially into black Africa, it extended and confirmed the commonplace use of slavery and slave trading. At the apogee of Islamic influence, slaves were imported into Islamic societies from Africa, Europe, Central Asia and even India. At first, however there was no link between colour or ethnicity, even though large numbers of Islamic slaves were indeed black Africans. The crucial issue was the insistence that the enslaved should be non-Muslim, just as, later, Christian slave traders would not enslave fellow Christians.[1]

Islam—at least in theory—imposed restrictions on the relationship between master and slave. Arabs, and then their Berber converts, were required by their religion to treat slaves with a degree of respect and tolerance, although this was not always followed. Islam considered freeing a slave to be an act of piety, which God would reward, while master and slave could enter into a contract which would finally result in a slave's freedom. A woman taken as a concubine was to be given her freedom at the birth of her master's child. And the following injunction quoted, or was attributed to, the Prophet Muhammad:

> Fear God in the matter of your slaves. Feed them with what you eat and clothe them with what you wear and do not give them work beyond their capacity. Those whom you like, retain, and those whom you dislike, sell. Do not cause pain to God's creation. He caused you to own them and had He so wished He would have caused them to own you.[2]

Yet, like equally pious Christian injunctions, their application to the real world of slavery was frequently questionable.

By 646 Egypt had fallen and Arab armies were attacking neighbouring states, expanding their control along the Mediterranean, as well as down the Nile. There they encountered Nubians, who had converted to Christianity some two centuries earlier.[3] The Nubians responded robustly and continued hit-and-run attacks until the Arabs fell back on Egypt. In 652, accepting that war with the Nubians had not been a successful strategy, the new Muslim rulers proposed an alternative. They proposed and signed a treaty—the *Baqt*—to regularise relations between the Christian Nubians and the Islamic world.[4] It proved to be the most enduring treaty ever signed, lasting 600 years, with the Muslim world recognising the Nubians as sovereign. It did not, however, end the transportation of slaves northwards. Indeed, their transfer was part of the bargain: 'Each year you are to deliver 360 slaves which you will pay to the *imām* of the Muslims from the finest slaves of your country, in whom there is no defect. [They are to be] both male and female ... You are to deliver them to the *wali* of Aswan.'[5]

The Nile was by no means the only route by which Africans reached Egypt. The civilisation drew visitors and traders from across the Sahara. In addition to the journey along the Nile and the Forty-Day Route there was a third route which came to link Egypt to Sudanic Africa.[6] Their produce was much sought after and highly prized.

[Caravans] entered Egypt from the west and drew sultans, merchants, and pilgrims from a vast area of western Sudan stretching from ancient Mali to Bornu in what is now northeast Nigeria. These caravans, often richly laden with the gold of Takrur and slaves from a wide regional pool, wound through the Sahara to the Libyan oases and thence east through Awjila and Siwa oases, stopping at the Egyptian villages in the neighborhood of the Pyramids west of Cairo. Often they would join the Maghribi hajj caravans coming from Morocco, Algiers, Tunis, and Tripoli.[7]

Egyptian regimes changed over the centuries but enslavement endured. Rulers relied on slaves for their troops. The early Islamic conquerors of Egypt would only allow Arabs to provide troops for their garrisons, but the Abbasid Caliph al-Mutasim (r. 833–842) decided that the standing armies of Egypt would be recruited from other sources—mainly white slaves of Turkic origin, known as Mamluks, but also black Nubian slaves. This practice was gradually extended until one of his successors, Ahmad ibn Tulun (r. 868–884), had an army of 24,000 Turkic and 40,000 African slaves at his disposal.[8] He was followed by Khumarawayh (r. 884–896), who is said to have ridden in a procession, followed by 1,000 African guards:

> wearing black cloaks and black turbans, so that a watcher could fancy them to be a black sea spreading over the face of the earth, because of the blackness of their color and of their garments. With the glitter of their shields, of the chasing on their swords, and of the helmets under their turbans, they made a really splendid sight.[9]

The role of the African military slaves was complex, with some rulers relying on them as infantry, while others attempted to reduce their role. Saladin (r. 1169–1193) ended the use of African slave troops altogether. Some 50,000 of the slaves attempted to resist being dismissed, only to be massacred.

> Saladin sent troops to the Africans' lodgings known as al-Manṣūra [near Bab Zuwaila] and set fire to their possessions, [killing] children and women. When the news reached the Africans [in the city], they fled. Saladin attacked them with swords and closed their escape routes. After many of them had been killed, the Africans

asked for peace. They were given a positive answer and many of them left Miṣr for Giza.

Shams al-Dīn Tūrān Shāh, Saladin's oldest brother, crossed over to Giza with a group of [Saladin's] army and cut the Africans to pieces. There remained among them only a few fugitives.[10]

After 1173, Africans played no role in the Egyptian military until they were included in Ottoman forces in the sixteenth century.[11] The Mamluk Sultanate, which ruled Egypt from 1250 to 1517, had a marked preference for light-skinned slaves, even though the Mamluks themselves were former slaves, who had formed elite units within Arabic armies. They had little regard for the Africans who arrived in Cairo even though the city was a 'major trading hub' for slaves during this period. The captives were minutely examined before they were sold.[12] It was suggested that if there were doubts about their suitability it was advisable to wash them in potash, borax and vinegar, to remove any discolouration and reveal their health. A fifteenth-century Egyptian doctor described the Ethiopians who were brought to Cairo's slave markets as physically weak but with strong character, patient, intelligent and obedient, while their women were more docile than men but their children tended to be sly and thieving.[13]

In 1517 the Mamluks were ousted as rulers of Egypt by the Ottomans. Ahmed Pasha, who became the Ottoman governor in Egypt in 1523, ordered the governor of Upper Egypt, who had been raiding Nubian territories, to supply him with a thousand black slaves, whom he intended to train in the use of firearms. Black slaves were also taken from Cairo households and sent to the army.[14] African slaves were used in domestic roles in Egypt throughout the Ottoman period. Slavery continued all the way through Turco-Egyptian rule (1821–1881) and Anglo-Egyptian rule (1896–1956), despite British attempts to end the practice. Under the Viceroy of Egypt Muhammad Ali Pasha (r. 1805–1848), the slave raids became highly organised enterprises.[15] Muhammad Ali, who had experienced the loss of troops during his wars in Syria, Arabia, Greece and Crete, established a special camp at Aswan to receive the Africans captured during raids. Between 1822 and 1823 he took 30,000 African slaves for his armies.[16] Celebrations were held when the caravans arrived in Cairo.

> The arrival of the great Dar Fur caravan was ... a momentous occasion. Upon entering the frontier of Egypt, it was greeted by a representative of the governor of Upper Egypt ... who was trusted with the responsibility of registering taxable goods ... [L]eading merchants of the caravan were given coffee and presented with a *binis*, a long ceremonial gown which was worn over the caftan.[17]

The slaves and other products the merchants brought were then sent to markets in Daraw, Asyut and Cairo. Their prices depended on their age and gender as well as their ethnicity. Abyssinian boys fetched more than other Africans, white females—Circassians—ten times as much as Abyssinian women, and eunuchs two or three times as much as black adult males.[18]

Many thousands died from abuse and disease on the long march from Sudan to the southern frontier of Egypt, but this did not diminish the practice, and raids continued. Slaves would be traded at border towns for Maria Theresa dollars, Indian cotton, spices, perfumes and gold, with the profit usually sent on to India.[19] In 1843, Muhammad Ali sent 2,450 troops—many of them slaves—and 1,000 cavalry into Darfur. Despite the Africans resisting with great courage, their spears and arrows were no match for the Egyptian cannon and muskets. Captured together with their cattle, some 528 manacled slaves were examined to select the fittest to join Muhammad Ali's army, with the leader of the Egyptian forces, Ahmad Pasha Abu Widan, choosing the most beautiful women for his pleasure and giving the remainder to his troops.[20]

Slaves were also brought from Africa to fulfil the burgeoning demand for labour. When the American Civil War cut supplies of cotton from the American South in the 1860s, the demand for African slaves to increase the Egyptian output peaked. During the third quarter of the nineteenth century, Egypt is reported to have imported up to 5,000 slaves each year, totalling between 25,000 and 30,000 over the duration of the Civil War (1861–1864).[21] They were sent to villages on the Nile Delta.

Slavery has not ceased despite repeated attempts to bring it to an end and was still evident in the twenty-first century, as Jok Madut Jok, Sudanese Professor of Anthropology at Syracuse University, observed: 'The present slave-catching communities of Darfur and

Kordofan were part of the slave frontier in the nineteenth century. The same Arab groups currently engaged in slavery were slave raiders during both the Turkiyya [Turco-Egyptian Sudan from 1820 to 1885] and the Mahdiyya [Mahdist Sudan from 1885 to 1899].'[22]

Egyptians continued to refer to their African neighbours from Sudan colloquially as *abeed*, or slaves.[23] They were used in agriculture, but also in the home, as recorded in a nineteenth-century song.

> The Slaves must do the work in the house; if they are unwilling to work, they must be beaten with a whip or must be beaten with a stick. Then they begin to cry [and] be willing to work. Their language is difficult; people don't understand them. If they find a girl among them, who pleases us, then she doesn't need to do any housework. I make her my wife, so that we can sleep together in bed and 'eat the skin,' so that we will have children. Then she becomes pregnant and has a child. If it is a boy, then everything will be fine.[24]

Islam and the conquest of North Africa and Iberia

While Egypt continued this exploitative relationship with the South, two developments, already mentioned, took place which would re-shape Trans-Saharan relations. Around 300 BCE, camels spread west of the Nile and as far eastwards as Eritrea. They became common in Rome's African provinces, eventually replacing the horse as a means of transport, as the Sahara gradually dried. Before their arrival the horse and the chariot were the preferred means of transport, with paintings of chariots found in rock paintings across the Sahara from as early as the first millennium BCE.[25] For the Berbers, the camels were ideally suited to the terrain, giving them the means of subsisting in the desert, while enhancing their military capability and allowing Berbers to control the Trans-Saharan trade routes.[26]

The second was the arrival of Islam. Egypt had been captured by the Persians in 621 CE. The Prophet Muhammad died eleven years later and his successors waged wars against their Persian and Byzantine neighbours. An Arab army invaded Egypt and by 646 the whole country was in their hands. From there they continued their conquest along the North African coastline. Among the North

African communities whom they defeated and then converted to Islam were the Berbers. Initially the Arab conquerors took Berbers captive to help satisfy the demand for slaves in other lands under Islamic control.[27] They were sent to the marshes of Basra to help drain the swamps, until they became involved in the Zanj revolts of the eighth and ninth centuries. Others were put to different uses, including entertainment. An ideal singer was said to be a Berber woman who from the age of nine had spent three years in Medina, three in Mecca and then nine in Iraq.[28] But as the Berbers became integrated into Islam, it became forbidden to enslave them. Instead, from the eighth century, Berber traders ventured further and further southwards in search of new sources of supply.[29] Both Arabs and Berbers took to raiding across the Sahara, fighting and trading with the African communities in the Sahel. Africans were brought northwards from as far south as Lake Chad.

The Arab forces, by this time incorporating many Berber converts, reached the straits of Gibraltar and the Atlantic coast by 708. The whole of the North African coast was then under their control and they crossed into Spain, capturing large parts of the Iberian Peninsula. The conquering armies dealt with enslavement as an integral part of conquest.[30] The Arabs and Berbers traded slaves across North Africa and with what became the Umayyad Emirate of Córdoba that they established on the Iberian Peninsula.[31] European slaves from Iberia were taken in the opposite direction. Al-Istakhri, an Arab writing in the tenth century, wrote that: 'from the Maghrib there come black slaves (*khadam*) from the land of Sudan, and white slaves from al-Andalus and highly valued slave girls. An unskilled slave girl or man will fetch, according to her or his appearance, 1000 dinars or more.'[32]

White captives were particularly desirable.

> White Andalusi slaves and eunuchs (*ṣaqāliba*), captives from the Christian territories, were a precious export ware that was in high demand in the Islamic East, and there are many indications that the Umayyad regime [in North Africa] collaborated with the Berber slave-traders in this regard and participated in the slave boom of the early centuries. They also reexported black slaves previously bought from the North African slave-traders.[33]

The caliph in Baghdad is reported to have received 30,000 Christian slaves from Spain soon after the Muslim conquest, although this may have been an exaggeration.[34] In just one campaign against Barcelona in 985, some 70,000 were taken captive. So many Iberian slaves were put on the market that it became flooded and their price more than halved.[35] The Islamic conquests opened up a vast trade, which stretched from the Iberian Peninsula as far as China. A ninth-century Persian geographer, Ibn Khurradadhbi, described Jewish merchants taking Western slaves, both concubines and eunuchs, together with brocade, furs and swords, to trade in Egypt.[36]

Over the years the tables turned against the Muslim conquerors, or Moors. Christians began regaining territory on the Iberian Peninsula and it was the former rulers and their followers who were enslaved. This was to take eight centuries. In medieval Castile, slaves were generally the result of war, and by the late fourteenth century they were almost exclusively Muslim in origin.[37] Between the fall of Granada in 1492 and the final reconquest of Spain in 1610, some 3 million Muslims were driven out of the Iberian Peninsula or taken captive.[38] Those who fled found refuge in North Africa. Muslims who remained were regularly enslaved, sometimes for petty crimes such as begging, while Muslim women found guilty of adultery found themselves enslaved to the Crown and put to work as prostitutes in Crown-administered brothels.[39]

At the same time, it is important to acknowledge that the relationship was not uniformly conflictual. Spain signed treaties with North African rulers in 1767, 1782, 1784, 1786 and 1791 which saw trade increase and slaves freed.[40] Wars might be waged, but goods and populations continued to flow across the sea.

A great, churning circulation between the two shores of the Mediterranean included hundreds of thousands of men and women. Across that porous and much-navigated frontier the most active travellers were Spaniards, Italians, Maltese, Portuguese, Moroccans, Algerians, Tunisians, Tripolitans, and Turks ... The continuous flux of individuals who crossed the boundary between Christendom and Islam suggest that not everything involved confrontation between members of the two religions.[41]

3

TURNING TOWARDS THE SOUTH

Early Berber conquests of regions in the south-west of the Sahara took place before the arrival of Islam. In the seventh century BCE, the Berbers conquered peoples who had made their homes on the Tichitt-Walata escarpment, in what is today Mauritania.

> Those persons who were not killed or enslaved barely managed to eke out an existence, hidden in small groups in fortified little villages among the high rocks. The Libyco-Berber groups in the meantime were expanding farther and farther south, and there found, eventually, a rich field of gold and slaves to be exploited.[1]

Such raids provided both grain and slaves. The slaves were used to tend the flocks of the Berbers, to gather fuel and water and serve their master's domestic needs. Arab geographers referred to Africans as a 'primitive, savage and stateless people', who were fair game for slave raiders who came from organised and civilised states.[2] It was in an attempt to protect themselves from these raids that the Africans formed one of the first major West African states—Ancient Ghana.

Ancient Ghana, which lasted from c. 300 CE until c. 1200, was not geographically or ethnically related to the modern state of the same name. About four hundred miles north-west of contemporary Ghana, it was situated between the Sahara and the Senegal and Niger rivers, in an area that now comprises south-eastern Mauritania and part of Mali. It was part of the vast Sahel region stretching from the Atlantic to the Red Sea, between the desert and the lush tropical forest along the coast. This was a region of light rainfall in which farmers cultivated traditional, hardy grains prior to the arrival of

New World crops like maize, cassava, ground nuts and potatoes.[3] Cattle could be raised here, something that the tsetse fly of the forests made impossible. Towns and villages proliferated prior to European colonisation, and with them a series of kingdoms and empires rose and fell, shaping the lives of their people.

With the arrival of Islam, the Berber tribes were themselves first enslaved, but then transformed into slavers. They continued to capture peoples to their south while constructing a complex trade network. 'Between the end of the seventh century and the middle of the eighth they created a trading network that tapped the regions south of the Sahara, the Bilād al-Sūdān, as a new source for slaves.'[4]

The Berbers felt permitted to enslave anyone they conquered, as long as they were not Muslims, or 'people of the book'—Jews or Christians. It gave Arab and Berber forces license to continue raiding across the desert, returning with men and women.

> For over a thousand years after their acceptance of Islam they developed and controlled the desert transit routes of the slave trade and by their spread through the sub-Saharan Sahel steadily advanced the boundaries between *Dar el Islam* (the territory of peace, or the territory which submits to Islam) and the *Dar el Harb* (the territory of war or chaos), southwards, until the borders of the forests were reached in the thirteenth to fifteenth centuries AD.[5]

The Berbers came to control three vast confederations, centred on what is present-day Morocco. By the eighth century CE, their rule incorporated areas of the Sahara contiguous with Ancient Ghana, allowing an interchange of goods and ideas, including Islam.[6] Ancient Ghana, populated by Mande-speakers, came to act as intermediaries between the northern Arabs and Berbers who brought salt, which was exchanged for ivory, gold and slaves from the south. The people of Ghana attacked peoples around them, selling them on to merchants from the Maghrib.[7] Vast fortunes were made from this commerce. It is said that in the eleventh century a wealthy man in the Ghanaian town of Awdaghust, an oasis on the southern end of the Trans-Saharan route, might own as many as 1,000 slaves.[8] These were probably obtained from the south and laboured in the fields producing dates, henna and cereals, for which the area was known.

They also worked in metals and ceramics, with the techniques used suggesting they were southerners.[9]

Trade across the desert developed gradually. It is estimated that around 1,000 slaves a year were trafficked across the Sahara from 800 CE.[10] They were taken north from Ancient Ghana to Morocco, from Timbuktu to Algeria, from Lake Chad to Libya and, as we have seen, along the Nile from Sudan to Egypt. This slow—but steady—flow of people continued for a millennium, and in some ways continues to this day. (See Part 6, 'Slavery Today'.) It is impossible to be certain how many were forced to make the journey. Table 2 provides figures for the period between 650 CE and 1600, but not the earlier or later trades.[11]

Table 2: Trans-Saharan Slave Trade, 650 CE–1600

Period	Annual No. of Slaves	Estimated Total No. of Slaves
650–800	1,000	150,000
800–900	3,000	300,000
900–1100	8,700	1,740,000
1100–1400	5,500	1,650,000
1400–1500	4,300	430,000
1500–1600	5,500	550,000
Total		4,820,000

Ralph Austen, whose pioneering work on the statistics formed the basis for these estimates, attempted to arrive at some figures over a later period.

> In contrast to the European Atlantic slave trade, scholars do not have very precise statistics for the various Islamic enslavement systems in Africa. The best estimates are that between 800 and 1900 CE about 4 million people were driven across the Sahara. Another approximately 2 million came to Egypt by way of the Nile Valley from Ethiopia and Southern Sudan.[12]

It is probably no exaggeration to suggest that in excess of 6 million Africans were forced to make the journey in the 4,000 years prior to the beginning of the European slave trade with the arrival of the Portuguese off the coast of Senegal in 1445. However, there can be no certainty. As Ralph Ware points out, the 'true figure for pre-1600 might easily be double or two-thirds of Austen's estimates.'[13] The statistics also exclude those who died before, during or after making the journey. Some of the caravans experienced mortality rates of 20 per cent or more. Some put the figures even higher, estimating that 9 million slaves were taken across the Sahara with as many as 2 million perishing along the way, but this calculation appears to be an outlier.[14]

Crossing the Sahara was always extraordinarily difficult. It involved long marches, on poor food and little water. Slaves faced the threat of sexual abuse and caravans were constantly at risk of attacks. Water had to be rationed. Any mistake, or an empty well, could lead to death. The slave masters treated their victims as they pleased.

> Victims could be killed or left to face poverty and famine. They could be emasculated. They could be marched to death, with each point of transfer bringing unknown prospects for the slave. The legitimization of enslavement, therefore reinforced a tendency towards war and other forms of violence.[15]

It was not just the baking sun that killed. The desert could be bitterly cold, with night-time temperatures dipping below minus ten degrees Celsius and thick ice forming on drinking vessels. Sandstorms would also whip across the caravans, sometimes for hours on end. Was it any surprise that an English explorer found parts of the route littered with skeletons—both human and camel? Human remains were so thick on the ground that in some parts 'an explorer unacquainted with the track across the desert might almost without guide trace his way by their aid'.[16]

By the time they had reached their destinations, the slaves were emaciated and close to death. A caravan of 1,400 slaves reaching Murzuk, in southern Libya, in 1875 was described by one observer in graphic terms.

It was indeed a piteous spectacle. These poor oppressed beings were many of them so exhausted as to be scarcely able to walk; their legs and feet were much swelled [sic], and by their enormous size, formed a striking contrast with their emaciated bodies. They were all borne down with loads of firewood and even poor little children, worn to skeletons by fatigue and hardships, were obliged to bear their burden, while many of their inhuman masters rode camels, with the dreaded whip suspended from their wrists with which they, from time to time, enforced obedience from these wretched captives.[17]

For men and boys, the gruelling journey could be accompanied by the excruciating practice of castration. An elderly former slave in twentieth-century Morocco recalled witnessing these crude operations, many of which were fatal. 'Do you think I can forget that,' he said, recalling the castration of a fourteen-year-old boy. 'Even in my tomb I shall see once again the frightful spectacle of those tortured children.'[18] His anguish was appropriate: perhaps as many as nine out of ten boys who underwent castration are thought to have died during the procedure.[19]

Most of the captives crossing the desert were women, although eunuchs were also important. Ibn Battuta, the great Berber scholar and traveller, who journeyed across the Sahara (and then as far afield as China, India and the east coast of Africa) in the middle of the fourteenth century, came across one caravan of 600 female slaves.[20] This is unsurprising: women could be used in the household and the fields, as well as in the bedroom. Some female slaves were Berbers themselves, who might be traded onwards in the Muslim world. Like servants the world over, myths and prejudices became attached to their characters and abilities. While Berber women were renowned for their singing, housework and sexuality, African female slaves were highly regarded for being docile, robust and excellent wet-nurses, but also suitable to be trained as cooks.[21] Wealthy families would be composed of up to four wives and their children, slave concubines and their children, and slaves to carry out other duties, from grinding grain to water carrying and cooking. Male slaves would act as guards. They added to the prestige of the man who headed the household.[22] A few slaves rose to great prominence, finally taking power. The seventeenth-century Moroccan sultan Mawlay Ismail came to rule as a result of his leadership of a large black army, despite being the son of an enslaved African woman.[23] It is important not to exaggerate the significance of such examples.

4

GOLD, SALT AND SLAVES

The interconnection between the Arab and Berber kingdoms of the north and the black African states of the south bridged the Sahara and the Sahel. They also provided a tentative link between the westernmost and easternmost regions of Africa, particularly as Muslims were required to go on the hajj to Mecca at least once in their lives. Ancient Ghana was one of the most important Saharan kingdoms, but there were others, including Takur, Gao and Kanem-Borno, representing what has been described as a 'multi-ethnic, multi-coloured kaleidoscope' of southern Saharan societies which both traded and fought each other from the ninth to the twelfth century CE.[1] Cities sprang up, including Gao, Ghana, Walata and Zagha, all of which had populations in excess of 20,000.[2] They were complex urban settlements, walled towns—many on what are now deserted sites—between Lake Chad and the Atlantic.[3] As the climate of the region changed, however, the area became more arid. Towns were abandoned as populations moved further south, or retreated northwards towards the Mediterranean, leaving camel trains to continue the trade.

Slaves were traded across the Saharan networks, along with salt and gold, all of which were valuable commodities. The gold deposits of the area were vital to the wealth of these societies. Mines in the Sirba valley (south of the Niger River), the Bure goldfields (on the headwaters of the Niger) and Bambuk (on the headwaters of the Senegal River) were the source of the precious metal.[4] Is it any wonder that visitors to the Niger-Senegal region described it as the 'land of gold' and the king of Ghana was described as 'the wealthiest king on the face of the earth because of his treasures and stocks of gold extracted in olden times for his predecessors and himself'?[5] Most of the gold was mined by panning along the rivers, or in shallow excavations. Local farmers and their families would practise this during the dry season when farming was in abeyance. Along the Volta River, in the region's forests, deposits of ore were richer and mines were deeper, requiring permanent labourers and slaves.

These riches supported a series of empires—Ancient Ghana, Mali and Songhay. Slaves played an integral part in these civilisations. By the eleventh century the rulers of Ancient Ghana were reported to muster 200,000 troops, including 40,000 archers. They lived in splendour, residing in a multi-domed palace. Nor was the capital of Ghana the only majestic city. Sila, on the northern bank of the Senegal River, was described in the twelfth century as a 'metropolis, a meeting place and a good market.'[6] Its ruler, Takruri, lived in the town of Takrur, two days journey distant, on the south bank of the river. The twelfth-century geographer Al-Idrisi provided this description of his rule:

> He has slaves and soldiers, strength and firmness as well as widely known justice. His country is safe and calm ... The town of Takrur is larger than Sila, and has more trade. The people of al-Maghrib al-Aqsa [roughly modern-day Morocco] go there with wool, copper, and beads, and they export from there gold and slaves.[7]

However, over time, Berber trading with Ghana gave way to raids, contributing to Ghana's decline, as did changing trade routes and civil wars. As a contemporary scholar put it: 'The authority of the kings of Ghana was destroyed, their neighbours the Sosso subjugated the country and reduced its inhabitants to slavery.'[8] By 1235 Ancient Ghana's days were over, and what remained was incorporated into the Mali Empire, which flourished from the thirteenth to the sixteenth century.

The Empire of Mali, which lasted from c. 1230 to 1660, was centred on the city of Timbuktu, on the Niger River. Like its predecessor, Mali also traded gold with foreign merchants and employed slaves, as did its successor state, Songhay. The rulers of Mali became extraordinarily wealthy from the trade in gold. In Timbuktu they built schools and renowned universities, as well as modernising public buildings and mosques. These include the legendary Djinguereber Mosque, constructed in 1327, built in limestone and rendered with mud, which still stands today. A famous centre of learning, it remains one of three mosques that make up the University of Timbuktu and is a recognised UNESCO heritage site.[9] The architect was paid 200 kilograms of gold for its construction.

The mosque was built by Mansa Musa, renowned as the richest man in the world. Just how wealthy he—as well as the region—was can be judged by the journey the king made in 1324. Mansa Musa went on the hajj to Mecca, which took him across the Sahara on a journey of over 4,000 kilometres. He was not alone: his caravan is said to have consisted of 60,000 men, including 12,000 slaves.[10] It was reportedly like a city on the move. 'He rode on horseback preceded by 500 slaves, each carrying a staff of gold weighing 500 mithkal or about 6 pounds. In his baggage train of camels were 80 to 100 loads of gold each weighing 3 kantar or about 300 pounds.'[11]

So generous were the gifts that Mansa gave as alms during his time in Cairo that he caused the price of gold to plunge. He donated an estimated fifteen tonnes of gold that he had brought with him.[12] His fame spread across the world, with a Catalan atlas carrying an image of the king, holding a gold nugget in his right hand.[13] Stories of the great wealth of the region circulated widely, motivating European powers to send expeditions to explore the Western coasts of Africa in the hope of discovering the source of the gold.[14]

The Mali Empire was succeeded by the Songhay. Also situated on the Niger River, it extended from the Atlantic to well into what is present-day Nigeria.

> After a long evolution lasting nearly 800 years, the Songhay, who had settled on both banks of the middle Niger, established a powerful state in the sixteenth century and unified a large portion of the western Sudan, thus making possible the flowering of a brilliant civilization which had been in the making for centuries.[15]

Like their predecessor states, the Songhay used slaves on farms, as infantry and as servants around the home. The empire had a strict hierarchy, divided into nobility, freemen, members of guilds and slaves. Slave villages helped feed the court and the army.[16] These strengths did not, however, prevent the empire from being attacked and finally defeated by Moroccan invaders, who had arrived after a forced march of sixty days. Internal disputes and the Moroccan use of firearms overcame the Songhay's fierce resistance on 12 March 1591. It marked the end of an era. 'And so collapsed the last great Sahel empire whose rulers, absorbed in their domestic quarrels, had failed to recognize the extent of the Moroccan threat.'[17]

Sources of slaves

The supply of slaves was frequently the result of war or raids. Many of the states of the Sahel participated in these attacks. As the Muslim influence spread southwards, enslaving neighbouring ethnic groups became an increasingly common practice. Prisoners could be sold, a practice justified from an Islamic perspective, because they were considered chattels. Paul Lovejoy quotes a member of a Portuguese mission to the Senegal river in 1455–1456 reporting that a local king was raising revenue from slave raiding. Lovejoy comments that 'his report does indicate that the acquisition of slaves through wars and raids was common by the fifteenth century, which confirms evidence from elsewhere in the northern savanna, including Songhay, Mali, Borno and the Hausa states.'[18]

The raids extended from the headwaters of the Senegal River in the west to Lake Chad in the east. Those taken captive were enslaved and put to work in a range of roles. 'They could be soldiers, administrators, concubines, domestic slaves and agricultural workers. The participation of such African states as Ghana, Mali, Songhay, Kanem, Sennar and Adal in the slave trade occurred together with the extension of Islamic influences to sub-Saharan Africa.'[19] Many of those taken captive were sedentary farmers who were vulnerable to raids by better armed warriors from the desert on horseback or camel.[20]

Muslims were meant to be exempt from these practices. When Arabs came south and enslaved local Muslims, the rulers of these states felt entitled to complain to their northern neighbours. A letter from 1391–1392 by the king of Borno, Uthman ibn Idris, protested to the Mamluk regime in Egypt that raids were taking Muslims, including members of royal families, and selling them across the Sahara.

> The Arab tribes of Jodham and others have taken our free subjects, women and children and old men of our own family and other Muslims ... These Arabs have pillaged our land, the land of Bornu, and continue to do so. ... [They] are selling them to the slave-dealers of Egypt, Syria, and elsewhere, and keep some of them for themselves.[21]

The king demanded that the slaves should be asked if they were Muslims and, if they were, that they should be freed.

The relationship between North Africa and the Sahel changed fundamentally with the defeat of the Songhay Empire by the Arabs and Berbers (or Moroccans) in 1591–1592. It marked the end of the great ancient states of the western Sahel and the beginning of the early modern era.[22] Both the Berber armies and the Songhay used slave conscripts. As we have seen, slavery across the Sahara was not concluded by the Moroccan victory. Rather, the slave trade increased, since the Moroccans now controlled both ends of the route.[23]

Why was it necessary for the North Africans to continually replace their slave populations? Why did slaves not reproduce naturally? Others have asked why they did not apparently leave a more indelible mark on the societies of Morocco, Algeria and Tunisia, describing them as 'the missing descendants of such an enormous black diaspora.'[24] Some suggest that the children of slaves were simply merged into the wider community. Others point to the brevity of their lives, plagued by diseases (such as tuberculosis, from which they had no immunity) and the damp, cold conditions of the Levantine winters. This question has not been resolved, and can be extended across the Arab nations. As John Davis observed, 'Whatever the case, the fact remains that so long as the Arab World needed black slaves, it had to keep importing them, from across the Sahara, down the Nile Valley, or by sea from East Africa.'[25]

The sheer number and diversity of the societies in the region from which slaves could be drawn can be grasped from the description provided by Leo Africanus. Born in Granada in Spain, he described himself as an African and journeyed across the Sahara in 1513, recording his journey in a book: 'I my selfe saw fifteen kingdoms of the Negroes ... Their names therefore (beginning from the west, and so proceeding Eastward and Southward) [*sic*] are these following: Gualata, Ghinea, Melli, Tombuto, Gago, Guber, Agadez, Cano, Cafena, Zegzeg, Zanfara, Guangara, Borno, Gaogo, Nube.'[26]

The fifteen kingdoms were all along the Niger and—Leo Africanus recorded—all linked by routes to Egypt. Along the route he regularly encountered caravans with gold, skins, amber and slaves being taken northwards. This trade was to continue down the centuries and, in some areas, continues to this day. The North African enslavement followed patterns that had been started by Egyptians along the Nile. The Trans-Saharan routes which the Arabs and Berbers used continued to operate and flourish for generations. Over time, European raiding and trade, first by the Portuguese and then by the Dutch, British and French, would build upon, and radically transform, this slavery. However, the foundations had been established centuries earlier.

PART 2

THE INDIAN OCEAN AND BEYOND

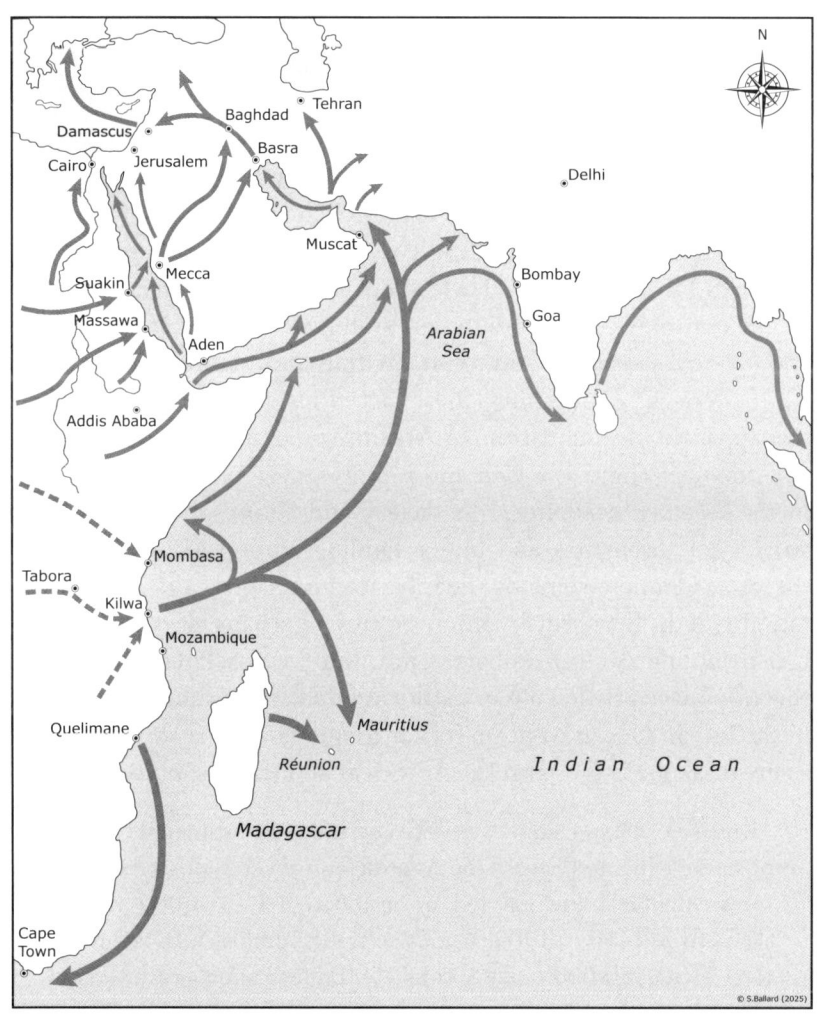

Map 2: Indian Ocean slave routes

The map is adapted from a variety of sources.

Whereas the Atlantic slave trade has been mapped out in relatively great detail in numerous studies, its Indian Ocean counterpart has remained largely uncharted territory and overlooked in Asian colonial historiography. Indeed, the sufferings of the slaves in Asia occurred mainly in silence, largely ignored by both contemporaries and modern historians.[1]

The question of slavery in the Indian Ocean has been, until recently, relatively little explored, receiving far less attention than the Trans-Atlantic trade. There is, for example, not yet an Indian Ocean equivalent of the vast database that has been developed to track journeys across the Atlantic on the SlaveVoyages website.[2] This omission has begun to be rectified, but there is much to do, and a range of reasons for the failure of scholarship.

'The eastward dimension of captivity and trading in Africans was neglected until the turn of the twenty-first century,' commented Shihan de Silva Jayasuriya. 'These silences may have been exacerbated by the complexities of indigenous systems of slavery and servitude and the experience of migrants within multicultural contexts.'[3] The 'silences' concerning these activities were exacerbated by the apparent disinclination of Muslim academics to engage with the subject. 'There is a rich and rapidly developing historiography in the Western academies on slavery and abolition in the Muslim world. Yet discussion and understanding among Muslims outside these academies remains deeply impoverished and shockingly uninformed,' Bernard Freamon argues.[4] Perhaps slavery has been too troubling or too embarrassing, but local scholars have until recently played little role in exploring this area. Human trafficking in the Indian Ocean went on for far longer, and its scale was at least as great, as the trade with the Americas and the Caribbean.

There is a striking similarity between the total estimated number of slaves exported across the Atlantic and those sent to Asia. The trans-Atlantic trade carried an estimated 11,313,000 million slaves from 1450 to 1900. The Asian trade numbered an estimated total of 12,580,000 from 800 to 1900. The important difference between the Trans-Atlantic and the Asian slave trade, however, is the time span in which the exploitation of slaves took place. The eleven million slaves of the Trans-Atlantic trade were exported to the Americas in only four hundred years, and intensity that had dramatic effects on the African societies engaged in the trade. The twelve and a half million slaves exported to Asia during eleven centuries obviously did not have the same traumatic impact experienced on the western African coast in just four centuries of the Trans-Atlantic trade.[5]

Even the Asian figure of 12,580,000 is something of an under-estimate, since the trade started well before 800 CE and continued beyond 1900. Despite the huge numbers involved, there is little evidence of an active African diaspora, as Edward Alpers pointed out:

> The African presence in the Indian Ocean world represents one of the most neglected aspects of the global diaspora of African peoples. Yet very significant numbers of people of African descent today inhabit virtually all the countries of the western Indian Ocean littoral … African voices have been actively silenced in this diaspora both by the cultural contexts of their host societies and by the way in which the scholarly production of knowledge has reflected such cultural domination.[6]

Arabs made their way down the East African seaboard centuries before the Portuguese sailed into the Indian Ocean in 1498. From the eight century, they settled, traded and intermarried.[7] The Arabs helped found ports, including Lamu, Malindi, Mombasa and Zanzibar. By the time the Europeans sailed into these seas, Arabs had established an extensive network of routes, bringing goods and Islam to the region. Merchants also used their control over the region to obtain slaves whom they went on to sell in Arabia, Persia, India and beyond. Evidence of trade is to be found all down the east coast of Africa from the late first millennium CE. 'Exports from Africa included ivory, gold and slaves in exchange for beads, cloth, ointments, perfumes, oils, syrups, and decorated bowls from the Middle East, Indian subcontinent and Far East.'[8] Although there was some indication of Africans being taken as slaves across the Indian Ocean in earlier times, the trade began in earnest in the eighth and ninth centuries CE, although evidence is fragmentary at best.

Even after the Europeans sailed into the region in the sixteenth century, the Omanis asserted themselves until they came to play a dominant role. Their hold over Zanzibar allowed the Omani Sultanate to serve as a hub across the ocean and a base from which to control the East African coast, and then the interior. With Indians administering their operations and controlling Omani finances, while Baluchi mercenaries undertook much of their fighting, the Omanis came to control the enslavement in a considerable proportion of the region.[9] By the early nineteenth century, Oman extended its hegemony over much of the African coast: from Cape Delgado, in what is today Tanzania, to the northern Kenyan port of Lamu.[10]

Africans were trafficked across the seas for many reasons and by many nations. The Chinese treated them as objects of fascination. Indian rulers deployed thousands as troops. African women became objects of pleasure in the harems of Arabia, while eunuchs became trusted servants around the home.[11] Britain transported slaves from the Gold Coast (now Ghana) and Angola via St Helena all the way to Sumatra.[12] The French depended on Africans for their sugar plantations in Réunion, while the Dutch sent them to farms in the Cape. The Portuguese shipped vast numbers round the Cape and onwards to Brazil and even the United States. The picture is complex, diverse and without a simple narrative.

Trade across the Indian Ocean was—until the invention of steam—dominated by geography and wind patterns. The north-east monsoon blew from November to February from a north-easterly direction, taking sailing vessels from India towards the African coast, as far as Zanzibar. It allowed dhows to travel from the Arabian Peninsula to the African coast in anywhere from twenty to forty days.[13] This was followed from April to September by a reversal, when the monsoon blew from the south-west, taking boats from Africa towards the Indian subcontinent. Navigating these routes was no easy task, but the winds made the extensive trade possible.

5

SLAVERY BEFORE THE ARRIVAL
OF THE EUROPEANS

The first sailors to navigate the region may have been Egyptian, visiting the Horn of Africa, possibly as early as 5000 BCE.[1] Their voyages were followed by the Greeks, who are believed to have reached the coast of India. Were they involved in slavery as well as travel? We do not know. The Romans also developed a keen interest in the region. In 1 BCE, Emperor Augustus ordered a detailed survey of lands beyond his realm, with expeditions to Ethiopia and Yemen and reports of trade across the Persian Gulf. Roman vessels travelled to India each year for commerce.[2] Roman colonies were established in India, notably at Arikamedu in Coromandel, now a UNESCO World Heritage Site.[3]

> Excavations at the site have uncovered substantial evidence of a Roman trading settlement including amphorae, lamps, glassware, coins, beads made of stone, glass and gold, and gems. Based on these finds it appears the settlement engaged in considerable trade with the Roman and later Byzantine world during an extensive period from the 2nd century BCE to the 8th century CE.[4]

India was not just a recipient of goods but also sent quantities of luxury goods to Rome, including spices, perfumes, textiles and ivory, as well as fortune tellers, and elephants with their mahouts.[5] Roman beads have been found as far south as the Rufiji Delta in Tanzania, indicating just how extensive the trade networks were in this period.[6]

China, Indonesia and Japan

It is impossible to consider the Indian Ocean in isolation. Over many centuries it was integrated into a system of trade that linked nations from the coast of East Africa all the way to southern China via the Silk Route. Many participated in these chains of commercial relationships over thousands of kilometres. The route stretched from Europe's richest slave market in Dublin, where Viking raiders sold their captives, all the way to Shandong, in eastern China.[7] Jewish traders took slaves among the goods they traded on a vast network that stretched from western Europe to Africa, Arabia, India and China in the ninth and tenth centuries.[8]

> They journey from west to east, from east to west, travelling by land and by sea. From the west they export eunuchs, young girls and boys, brocade, beaver pelts, marten and other furs and also swords … They returned from China with musk, aloe wood, camphor, cinnamon and other eastern produces.[9]

Arab traders also ventured westwards along the Red Sea and the African coast, before returning eastwards, carrying goods and slaves as far as China. The Chinese had an ancient and well-established system of slavery, going back to at least the Ch'in Dynasty in the third century BCE.[10] A manuscript found in the city of Dunhuang (or Tun-huang) on the Silk Road in north-western China contained a poem said to have been dreamed by a young bridegroom:

> Chinese slaves to take charge of treasury and barn,
> Foreign slaves to take care of my cattle and sheep,
> Strong-legged slaves to run by saddle and stirrup when I ride,
> Powerful slaves to till the fields with might and main,
> Handsome slaves to play the harp and hand the wine,
> Slim-waisted slaves to sing me songs, and dance,
> Dwarfs to hold the candle by my dining-couch.[11]

By the time of the Tang dynasty (618 to 907 CE), Africans could have been among the slaves serving their Chinese masters.[12] Arab merchants brought them as they traded between East Africa and Canton (Guangzhou as it is now known), until the city was sacked in 878 by a rebel army.[13] Slaves served as crew for the Arab traders. In

724, an African girl was sent to China as part of a tribute consisting of luxurious and rare merchandise.[14]

Zhu Yu (c. 1075–after 1119), a scholar of the Song Dynasty, wrote:

> The wealthy in Guang[zhou] maintain numerous foreign slaves … the people of Guangzhou call them 'wildmen' (yeren). As for the color of these slaves, it is black as ink. Their lips are red and their teeth are white. Their hair is curly (quan) as well as ochre-coloured. They are both male and female, and they inhabit various mountains across the sea.[15]

African slaves were also traded with Indonesia, a commerce that pre-dated the arrival of Islam. Javanese tax records categorised Africans as 'sub-status people, either slaves or bonded servants.'[16] However, owning them was considered a privilege. Most were owned by the king, or his near relatives. They served as part of the ritual in a wedding ceremony.

> Two white umbrellas flanked them
> As they walked the short way together before coming to a halt.
> The umbrella-carriers were dark-skinned girls, one a pujut [from the Andaman islands] and the other an African;
> They were like two planets accompanying the moon.[17]

From the sixteenth century, African slaves also became a status symbol in Japan, and Japanese were said to have travelled to Nagasaki to see Africans in 1547.[18]

The Chinese began exploring the Indian Ocean and the African coastline. Zheng He (1371–1433) famously undertook seven expeditions, including visiting the East African coast. The most extensive voyages included up to 300 vessels and 27,000 men in ships of four decks— among the largest wooden ships ever constructed. The aim of the journeys was to display the wealth and power of the Ming Emperor Yongle (r. 1402–1424) to the world. The fleet was sent to foreign lands, 'proclaiming the edicts of the Son of Heaven and giving gifts to their rulers and chieftains. Those who did not submit were pacified by force.'[19] Zheng He carried precious goods, such as silk and porcelain to trade and was seeking exotic animals, like giraffe, in return for the imperial court.[20] There is no indication that he traded in slaves.[21] Rather, the voyage suggests the scale of the trade across the regions and Chinese influence.[22] The imperial fleets were discontinued, but commerce did not evaporate, with porcelain from China found from Sudan to the ruins of Great Zimbabwe.[23] Nor did the trade in people.

> Until the foundation of the People's Republic of China in 1949 China was the largest and most comprehensive market for the exchange of human beings in the world. In many parts of China, notably the south, nearly every peasant household was directly or indirectly affected by the sale of people.[24]

India

Just as in China, Africans were not the first people to be enslaved in India. Slavery on the subcontinent dates back to the Mauryan period (322 BCE–184 BCE).[25] The majority of these slaves were Indians. Africans who were trafficked to the subcontinent arrived later, brought by Arab traders: 'Arabs were undoubtedly masters of the Indian Ocean from the 6th century AD till the advent of the Portuguese in India. During this period, they were the chief promoters of the enslavement of Africans into India.'[26]

However, how and when the first African slaves (known locally as *Habashis*, *Cafre* or Sidis) arrived on the Indian subcontinent is far from clear. As Ann Pescatello pointed out: 'Our knowledge of the numbers, status and functions of *Habashis* prior to the arrival of the Portuguese in South Asia is severely circumscribed and necessarily gleaned from scattered court and travel records.'[27] One of the earliest accounts of an African slave transported to India concerned an Ethiopian, Jamal ud-Din Yaqut, who rose to become Master of the Royal Stables in Delhi in 1236.[28] By the fourteenth century there was a growing trade in African slaves, as the government in Delhi gained control of both of India's coastlines and 'could control and take advantage of the maritime networks that engaged in slave trading with Africa.'[29]

Even when enslavement was rife, African merchants, sailors, entertainers and missionaries—both Muslim and Christian—also made the journey.[30] Many who travelled to India were freemen and freewomen. There was an exchange of expertise and craftsmen.

Mark Horton argues that there was what he calls a 'hidden trade' in everything from cloth to beads. 'Indian artisans may have moved to East Africa, [and] Africans may have moved, as well, around the Indian Ocean, not as slaves but as genuine artisanal communities.'[31] In 1520 a Portuguese priest wrote of Ethiopian priests clothed in fine white Indian cloaks, while the priest himself was given Indian cloth by the emperor.[32] Indian goods were much sought after in Africa and came to be traded for gold and ivory, as well as slaves from the Ethiopian highlands. As a Portuguese official observed in 1516, Arabs 'make raids on horseback, in the course of which they capture large numbers of Abyssinians [i.e. Ethiopians] whom they sell to the people of Asia.'[33]

The most illustrious African visitor to India of this period was Ibn Battuta (1304–1369), a Berber born in Tangiers. He came across African slaves so frequently during his travels through India that he hardly considered their presence remarkable. Ibn Battuta's achievements were quite extraordinary: he is possibly the greatest explorer of all time. He made journeys that would have been arduous in the twenty-first century, let alone the fourteenth, visiting many parts of southern Europe, Arabia, Central Asia, China and South and South-East Asia, as well as large areas of Saharan Africa and Africa's east coast. His three great journeys are calculated to have totalled around 117,000 kilometres—far surpassing the famed travels of Marco Polo, at 24,000 kilometres. Before dying in Marrakesh in his mid-sixties, Ibn Battuta dictated the most important travelogue of this period: *A Gift to Those Who Contemplate the Wonders of Cities and the Marvels of Travelling*, commonly known as *The Rihla*.

It was during his second journey that Ibn Battuta made his way across the Indian subcontinent, the Maldives, Sri Lanka and China, before returning to North Africa. During his time in India, he came across *Habashis* (as the African slaves were known) distributed throughout the subcontinent, from northern India to Ceylon. They were employed primarily as guards or men-at-arms on land or at sea.[34] In July 1342, for example, he was south-east of Delhi, in the town of Allapur in Uttar Pradesh:

> The governor of Alabur [Allapur] was the Abyssinian Badr, a slave of the sultan's, a man whose bravery passed into a proverb. He was

continually making raids on the infidels alone and single handed, killing and taking captive, so that his fame spread far and wide and the infidels went in fear of him. He was tall and corpulent, and used to eat a whole sheep at a meal, and I was told that after eating he would drink about a pound and a half of ghee, following the custom of the Abyssinians in their own country.[35]

Ibn Battuta encountered African slaves in the southern Indian city called Qandahar (today the village of Ghandar on the mouth of the Dhandar river in Gujarat), where he describes meeting Ibrahim, the owner of six ships.

> We embarked on a ship belonging to the Ibrahim ... called *al-Jagir*. On this ship we put seventy of the horses of the sultan's present ... [Ibrahim] sent his son with us on a ship called *al-Uqayri*, which resembles a galley, but is rather broader; it has sixty oars and is covered with a roof during battle in order to protect the rowers from arrows and stones. I myself went on board *al-Jagir*, which had a complement of fifty rowers and fifty Abyssinian men-at-arms. These latter are the guarantors of safety on the Indian Ocean; let there be but one of them on a ship and it will be avoided by the Indian pirates and idolaters.[36]

Ibn Battuta then travelled to Colombo in Ceylon (Sri Lanka), where he again found the ruler guarded by 'about five hundred Abyssinians.'[37] When Ibn Battuta arrived in the Indian port of Calicut he saw a fleet of huge Chinese junks, each with four decks carrying up to 1,000 troops on board. The ships were highly sophisticated, with sailors having their wives and slave-girls living in their cabins, which were complete with latrines. Security was—once more—provided by Africans. 'The owner's factor [or agent] on board ship is like a great amir. When he goes on shore he is preceded by archers and Abyssinians with javelins, swords, drums, bugles and trumpets.'[38]

The majority of African slaves served their Indian masters as troops. A minority rose in the ranks and went on to become powerful in their own right, since there was a practice of releasing them from servitude on the death of their master. African women also went on to become the wives of Muslim monarchs.[39] Rukh-ud-din Barbak, who ruled in Bengal (r. 1459–1474), may have bought as many as

8,000 Ethiopians serving in his army. His son, Yusuf, had even larger numbers, with some 20,000 Ethiopians fighting for the sultanate.[40] Some of these slaves rose to prominence, serving their lords, but sometimes toppling them and taking power for themselves.

> The *habashi* [Ethiopians] played a crucial role in the politics of the Bahmanid, Adilshahi, and Nizamshahi sultanates that ruled much of south India between the fourteenth and the seventeenth centuries ... In fifteenth-century Bengal a corps of 8,000 *habashi* slave commanders actively supported their own candidates from the royal family. From 1486 to 1493 four *habashi* generals even occupied the throne and ruled as king.[41]

The presence of the Ethiopian slaves continued to be felt long after Ibn Battuta's exploration was over. Quite how their numbers fluctuated is impossible to say, but there are reports of Ethiopians clashing repeatedly with the Portuguese after Goa had fallen to the Europeans in 1510. The Ethiopians are described as 'quite deeply entrenched' and are said to have resisted the Portuguese fiercely.[42]

Malik Ambar: From Ethiopian slave to Indian leader

The role of Ethiopian slaves in the armed forces of Indian rulers was exemplified by the most famous African slave to serve an Indian master: Malik Ambar (1548–1626). He was to play a leading role in the complex political life of the Deccan, in central India, leading armies against the encroaching Mughal Empire. Ambar was frequently portrayed in Indian portraiture as tall, powerful and clearly African, despite his gorgeous Indian robes.[43] An Oromo, Ethiopia's largest ethnic group, Ambar was born in the eastern Ethiopian town of Harar.[44] In this period Arab raiding parties were penetrating deep into Ethiopia. Ambar was taken to Arabia and then to Baghdad, where he converted to Islam. This should have made his enslavement forbidden, but in the fifteenth century a Moroccan jurist, examining the case of another Ethiopian slave who had been converted, ruled that since his servile condition arose from his previous beliefs, it remained legal.[45]

In 1571 Malik Ambar's master sold him in India to Chengiz Khan, who had been an Ethiopian slave himself, but had risen to become prime minister of the sultan of Ahmednagar in the north-western Deccan. Ambar had entered the complex world of Indian military slavery. African slaves played a pivotal role in the conflicts of Indian states of this period. Not only were they excellent, if expendable, warriors, but they also stood outside of the kinship circle. They were intended to enhance the stability of the state, without representing the kind of challenge that a family member might pose. As a saying from the eleventh century put it: 'One obedient slave is better than three hundred sons; for the latter desire their father's death, the former his master's glory.'[46] However, as Ambar's life showed, this was not always the case.

Like all such slaves, Malik Ambar had no possibility of returning to Africa and had to make the best of his circumstances. However, he was by no means badly treated. On Chengiz Khan's death in 1574–75, his widow gave Ambar his freedom, as was customary. He left Ahmednagar, married and went to serve the neighbouring sultan of Bijapur, who put him in charge of a contingent of troops, bestowing on him the term 'Malik', meaning the leader of a community. Ambar returned to Ahmednagar in 1595, accompanied by 150 cavalry.[47] At the time the city was under attack from the Mughal emperor, Akbar, who captured the city's fort in August 1600. However, the Mughals had not extended their control over the surrounding territory. Fighting the Mughals from the countryside, Malik Ambar's cavalry gradually grew, until he had 7,000 troops under his command. Using guerrilla warfare, he kept the Mughals at bay.

'Royal slaves often controlled independent constellations of power within the court and helped to centralise control in the hands of the ruler,' observed Shihan de Silva Jayasuriya.[48] This is exactly what Ambar did. He decided to promote the twenty-one-year-old son of the former ruler, ensuring that Murtaza Nizam Shah II was installed as the new sultan. To cement their relationship, Malik Ambar took the precaution of marrying his own daughter to the future sultan. From being a lowly slave, Ambar now had links to a royal family. His fortune, and with it the fortune of his puppet sultan, continued to grow. In 1610, Malik's forces were able to capture Ahmednagar Fort from the Mughal army. At this moment, however, Ambar's fate encountered an unexpected obstacle. His daughter became engaged in a furious row with the sultan's first wife, a fair-skinned Persian, who described Ambar's daughter as a 'mere slave-girl'. With Ambar's daughter being a darker-skinned woman, there were obvious racial overtones to their quarrel. The conflict between the two women outraged Ambar, who soon had his revenge. He arranged for the sultan and his Persian wife to be poisoned, placing on the throne the sultan's five-year-old son.[49] Ambar ruled not as chief minister, but as regent. He not only strengthened his hold on the sultanate but also enhanced its power, going on to build the infrastructure of the state. He constructed a series of intricate networks of aqueducts, canals and reservoirs, known as the *Neher*, with which he supplied the needs of Ahmednagar. It was a system so well designed that it survives to this day.

Malik Ambar took charge of the defence of Ahmednagar with the help of tens of thousands of Indian and African troops. They confronted the Mughal forces of Emperor Jahangir (r. 1605–27), defeating them at the battle of Bhatvadi by a combination of night raids and attacks on their rear. Ambar even resorted to opening Bhatvadi Lake, flooding the plain and turning it into a mirc. The battle culminated in a final cavalry charge in which the Mughal forces were utterly routed. 'Ambar systematically wore down his opponents—so much so that many Mughal soldiers came to his side, whom he wisely welcomed with open arms.'[50] For two decades, the Mughal Empire had failed to destroy Ambar, and Emperor Jahangir was reduced to issuing a series of insults against his adversary, describing him as 'Ambar, the black faced,' or 'the crafty one.'[51]

It was old age that finally defeated Ambar, who died in 1626. In his official memoir the Emperor Jahangir reversed his assessment of his opponent, declaring that although a slave, Ambar was nonetheless:

> an able man. In warfare, in command, in sound judgement, and in administration he had no rival or equal ... He maintained his exalted position to the end of his life and closed his career in honour. History records no other instance of an Abyssinian slave arriving at such eminence.[52]

The defence of the Deccan did not long survive Malik's demise. In 1633 his son was forced to hand Ahmednagar over to the Mughals, as Prince Aurangzeb led the imperial armies in capturing it for his father, Emperor Shah Jahan. Despite this, no one doubts Malik

Ambar's achievements. Brought to India in servitude, Ambar ended his life a kingmaker, respected even by his enemies. Nor was he alone: in the period 1486–1493, no fewer than four Ethiopian slaves rose from military commanders to occupying Indian thrones and ruling as kings.[53]

Current African communities in the Indian subcontinent

After this illustrious period the power of the African military slaves went into decline. The Mughals did not use military slaves in their armies. Africans continued to be brought to India as slaves by Europeans. By 1790, the Dutch, British, French, Danes and Portuguese were reported to have trafficked 74,000 slaves to India.[54] The Africans, or Sidis, as they were known, were mostly male and had to marry local women. They were gradually absorbed into the local populations. Over time their communities, which had once been so significant, faded from memory, although they did not vanish.[55] The Sidis ruled two Indian states: Janjira, in today's Maharashtra, from 1618, and Sachin, in modern-day Gujarat, from 1791.[56] Both were absorbed into India at independence in 1947. Janjira was a base for African traders and for free African migrants, with a democratic system of electing Sidi leaders. As late as 1851, the traveller Richard Burton commented on the strong African character of the people of the Sind.[57] How many slaves there were on the Indian subcontinent is impossible to say. Estimates range from 6–8 million (the 1840 World Anti-Slavery Convention figure) to 16 million (by Sir Bartle Frere, whose figure included all the British protectorates and princely states).[58]

Perhaps 100,000 Indians continue to identify themselves as Sidis to this day, living in Gujarat, Karnataka and other states—a tiny fraction of India's 1.2 billion people.[59] Elderly Sidis continued to speak Kiswahili into the twentieth century, while the musical instruments and drumming characteristic of Swahili culture can still be found in India.[60] A further 150,000 Sidis live in neighbouring Pakistan, where they face discrimination and racism.[61] Many live in a Karachi slum notorious for its gangs, drugs and violence. Yaqoob Qambrani, president of the Pakistan Sheedi Ittehad, a community group representing Sidis in the country, complained that many opportunities are closed to them because of discrimination in education and work. He believed this stemmed from Pakistan's 'deep-rooted culture of blaming and shaming "black-face"', which portrayed Sidis as 'the evils, thieves and unwanted'. 'When anyone from our community boards a public transport bus, everyone else tries to keep distance. We are not blind to … how others look and treat us,' Qambrani declared.[62]

Iran and Iraq

There have been few studies of the slave trade by scholars from the Iran and Iraq region. Writing about African communities in Iran, Joseph Harris found no published material in English or French, and reported that the Iranians whom he consulted likewise knew of no articles on the subject in Arabic or Persian.[63] Nonetheless, Harris did discover isolated references to African slave communities and the towns and villages that they built. Some communities still exist near the port of Bandar Abbas who appear to be descendants of African slaves who worked on date plantations. There is clear evidence of African slaves being transported to and sold in Iran.[64] For example, there are references to an Iranian slave trader owning as many as 12,000 Africans as early as 936, while other reports spoke of hundreds of black and white eunuchs who served in the royal harem in the eighteenth century.[65] This continued well into the nineteenth century, with the women stereotyped: Georgians and Circassians were considered 'beautiful' while Ethiopian women were thought of as intelligent and honest.[66] Together the slaves were responsible for educating royal children and teaching them good manners. It is estimated that during the nineteenth century some 115,000 enslaved East Africans disembarked at Iranian ports.[67]

Africans who were captured in, and transported from, the Horn of Africa fulfilled a variety of tasks for their Iranian masters. The majority of men were 'iron-workers, carpenters, weavers, basket and rope makers, gardeners, body-guards or domestic servants; women served as wives or concubines in harems or domestic servants; and the smallest group were castrated boys intended for service as their owners' personal servants, household managers or security guards.'[68] Their treatment during the voyage from their homeland could be utterly ruthless. Africans found to have smallpox were thrown overboard as they were being transported.[69] Others bore the scars of brutal lashings.

In recent years there has been some interest in the question among Iranian scholars, who suggest that the increased importation of Africans to Iran related to their use as troops in the eighteenth and nineteenth centuries.[70] According to one estimate, some 114,000 slaves were taken from East Africa in the nineteenth century alone.[71] Several treaties were signed between Britain and Iran designed to end the trade, but apparently with little effect.[72]

Slaves began being transported to Iraq from the seventh century, just prior to the arrival of Islam. Exactly where the slaves came from and precisely when they arrived is hotly contested. Some authors suggest that they were Ethiopian, while others disagree. Perhaps the most that can be concluded is that they were captured, bought or otherwise obtained from East Africa.[73] These 'Ethiopians' were enslaved in a variety of ways. Some were taken in Arab raiding parties penetrating the Horn of Africa. Others were captured by Ethiopian rulers and traded with Arabs after long and difficult journeys, during which many of them died.[74] This will be explored in detail in Part 3 on internal African slavery. Some men were taken captive to bolster the Iraqi army of the time, serving the Abbasid Caliphate (750–1258).[75]

The Africans in Iraq received little attention from Arab chroniclers, who only referred to them in passing. There is one exception: the slave revolt that began in Basra in 695 and rocked the regime.[76] African troops numbered in their thousands, but far larger numbers were employed in the arduous task of draining the marshes and salt flats south of Baghdad in the delta of the Tigris and Euphrates.[77] The slaves, known as Zanj, spoke little Arabic and laboured in huge work gangs ranging from 500 to 5,000 members.[78] Their brutal treatment led to revolts by the East African slaves from 869, who were joined by local peasant farmers and black troops from the caliph's army sent to crush them. Led by an Iraqi, Ali bin Muhammad, as many as 300,000 slaves are said to have participated in the resistance. The rebels captured several important cities, controlling territory near the mouth of the Tigris River for fourteen years. It was not until 883 that the rebels were finally defeated by an army sent by the Abbasid Caliphate from Baghdad.[79]

Following the uprising the Africans were considered unreliable and their enslavement declined markedly in the region, only to re-emerge in the eighteenth century, some 900 years later. Then slavery resumed in substantial numbers, coinciding with an upturn in trade and the growth of manufacturing.[80] Africans had been imported to serve as pearl divers in the previous years, and routes used for their transportation from East Africa were developed as demand for soldiers, farm labourers, canal builders and dock hands grew. The supply of slaves rose from 500 to 600 a year in the mid-eighteenth century to between 2,000 and 3,000 per annum in the mid-nineteenth century. It then fell away as British anti-slavery patrols interrupted the trade.

Arabia

The history of slavery in Saudi Arabia is possibly even more poorly researched than elsewhere in the Muslim world. Links across the Red Sea can be traced back to 1000 BCE.[81] When the Ethiopian state was powerful it exercised suzerainty over parts of Arabia; when it was weak this declined or fell away, so that the Ethiopian state shrank back to control the highlands of the Horn of Africa. One of the important elements in this relationship was slavery, a trade which has continued for millennia. Reliable evidence is hard to find and frequently distorted or obfuscated.[82] This has not been assisted by attempts by the Saudi royal family to impose restrictions on, and a centralisation of, documents held by the official archives. The restrictions are designed to produce a sanctioned historical record that does not run counter to the official narrative.[83]

Writing a history of Arabian slavery has therefore proved difficult. Benjamin Reilly pieced together evidence from a variety of sources. He found the narrative of Nasir-i Khusraw, a Persian traveller in the tenth century CE, who came across some 30,000 Zanzibari and Ethiopian slaves working in Al-Hasa Oasis of eastern Arabia, tilling the fields and orchards of their owner.[84] Reilly consulted the evidence of seventy-nine Europeans to uncover the pattern of slave labour in the nineteenth and twentieth centuries. He described African villagers living in the wadis of western Arabia. Some were slaves, others the freed descendants of slaves. The distinction between the two appears to have been minor, since freed slaves took on the status of clients, and were expected to perform much the same role as slaves for their masters, while working on their plots.[85] There was no shortage of demand. Paul Lovejoy suggests that the overall number of slaves imported into Arabia over the Red Sea every year rose to the tens of thousands in the nineteenth century.[86] Others put the number of African slaves absorbed by Arabia at between 150,000 and 805,000 in the nineteenth century alone.[87]

Trapped in agriculture, harvesting dates, the Africans' experience was a bitter one. Charles Doughty, who was forced to spend several months in the historic oasis of Khaybar in 1876 and 1877, argued that 'the negroes are poor in the abundance of their palm valleys', which were owned by Bedouin landlords, who arrived each year 'at midsummer ... to gather their part of the date harvest.'[88] The slaves—either 'Galla' (Oromo) from Ethiopia or from Sudan— were allowed to grow their own crops in the shade of the dates, but had to supplement their own harvests with food purchased from the Bedouin. Not all would have been used in agriculture: some were employed in domestic service in towns like Mecca. The British officer T. E. Lawrence came across them in 1916 in the village of Wadi Safra. Many Africans 'had come to Arabia as children on pilgrimage with their "fathers"—a trick to avoid seizure at sea by the abolitionist British—and [were] then sold in Jedda or Mecca by their supposed parent.'[89] Most slaves living in Mecca were African.[90] The 'Nubians' were said to be given the hardest tasks, including building and quarrying. Others, imported from Sudan, were given general tasks, but also on building sites, in the home and in trade. Some were freed, since emancipation was particularly meritorious under Islam. The Arabian demand for slaves was only curtailed thanks to the most vigorous efforts of Britain, which deployed the Royal Navy in the Red Sea precisely to halt this insatiable market for slaves.

> From Morocco in the west, to the heartland of Arabia (present-day Saudi Arabia) in the east, British naval officers and consular officials regularly tried to stop the persistent Arab demand for black slaves ... Indeed it survived for more than a millennium, into the twentieth century, and may have engulfed more Africans than the number swallowed by the Atlantic slave ships.[91]

Oman

Of all the Arab states, Oman made possibly the greatest impact on the history of African slavery. Without access to minerals or industry, and with little agriculture beyond date plantations, Oman relied on trade and slavery, which became the cornerstone of its existence. 'Slavery was an old institution in Southern Arabia—older than the Islamic religion—and by the late eighteenth century it was a pervasive one as well. Slaves were "very numerous," and a "great mart for slaves" flourished in Muscat. One imam reputedly owned 700 male slaves.'[92]

Omanis had been trading and settling along the East African coast since the first century CE, interacting with local Swahili rulers and joining them in trade. Swahilis had sent slaves to Arabia from as early as the tenth century.[93] Female concubines were much prized, particularly those Ethiopians with lighter skin colour and Caucasian features. The slaves were often well treated and some were freed by their masters.

Several factors encouraged the development of the Omani slave trade. The first was the role of Indian merchants who came to reside in the sultanate and dominated trade in coffee and pearls, while acting as bankers to the sultan.[94] Their financial skills helped develop and maintain trade and enslavement across what became a very large empire. The second were the Baluchi mercenaries, who played a pivotal role in the Omani security system, serving as the crack troops in the sultanate's many wars. 'For the Arabs of Oman these Baluchi corps, real mercenary troops, constituted their military power, the *shawkah,* an indispensable tool in the conquest and maintaining of power.'[95] They were a formidable force. European travellers in Arabia described the Baluchi warriors as, 'naked to the waist and armed with a knife and a double-handed sword, with fierce glares and of threatening presence.'[96] There was also a limited role for other actors in the Indian Ocean, prior to the arrival of the Europeans: the Swahili coastal elite, who acted as brokers between the Omanis and the trading networks that existed in eastern and central Africa.[97]

The arrival of the Portuguese challenged the Omani hold on the region. In 1507, Portugal managed to capture Muscat, Oman's main port, but not the interior, and the Omanis expelled them in 1650. This opened the way for a complex and conflictual relationship between the Arabs and the Portuguese, but also between the Omanis and other powers, including the British. Oman's victory resulted in Portugal losing control of the ports of East Africa in 1698.[98] The Omanis dominated the Swahili coast, putting garrisons into Kilwa, Zanzibar, Pemba, Mombasa and Pate.[99] The reign of Oman's most powerful ruler, Said bin Sultan (r. 1804–1856), coincided with a vast expansion of the clove trade in Zanzibar and the accompanying slave trade that was required to harvest the crop. It was so lucrative that the sultan finally decided to relocate his capital from Muscat to Zanzibar.[100] This will be explored below.

6

EUROPEANS IN THE INDIAN OCEAN

After rounding the Cape of Good Hope, the Portuguese sailed up the East African coast in 1498. There Vasco da Gama and his crew found, to their surprise, a series of rich, well-developed port cities. These included ports on the islands of Mozambique, Kilwa in present-day Tanzania, and Mogadishu in today's Somalia. Between these were towns in Zanzibar (in Tanzania), Malindi, Mombasa and Shanga (all in Kenya). These were flourishing, mainly Swahili cities, which celebrated the Islamic faith. They were connected to the outside world by the Arab traders, as well as the African interior. By 1500, Swahili merchants were already active enslavers, exporting as many as 2,000 to 4,000 African slaves from Madagascar to the Lamu islands and then onwards to the Persian Gulf and Arabia.[1] The trade did not diminish: by the mid-seventeenth century the Swahili traders were moving an estimated 2,000 to 3,000 slaves a year from Madagascar to Arabia.[2]

Portuguese travellers described the beauty of Kilwa. It was a town 'with many fair houses of stone and mortar, very well arranged streets … with doors of wood, well carved with excellent joinery.'[3] Zanzibar, too, was beautiful, and the islands' rulers had grown rich on trade. In 1512, a Portuguese sailor wrote: 'The kings of these isles live in great luxury; they are clad in very fine silk and cotton garments, which they purchase at Mombaca [Mombasa] from Cambaya [an Indian state in modern Gujarat] merchants.'[4] As an archipelago 25 to 50 kilometres from the mainland, Zanzibar was ideally situated to exploit the African interior. The main island, Unguja, approximately 85 kilometres long and 30 kilometres wide, was a manageable base from which to operate. The slave trade continued to flourish. By the seventeenth century, between 3,000 and 6,000 Africans were being seized and transported by Swahili, Comorian and Arab merchants annually.[5]

Having rounded Africa, Vasco da Gama and his entourage were greeted at the Indian port of Calicut with surprise and disbelief. 'May the devil take you! What brought you here?' a Tunisian merchant exclaimed on seeing them.[6] The Portuguese, followed by the Dutch, French and English, would dramatically alter the operation of the Indian Ocean slave trade. However, as Richard Allen argues, slaving nations built on earlier systems, just as they had on the Atlantic coast of Africa.

> Although the details of how these men, women and children were enslaved and transported often remain hidden from our view, it is clear that Europeans in the Indian Ocean, like their counterparts in the Atlantic, tapped into already existing slave trading networks to secure their cargoes. Such was the case in Madagascar and along the eastern African coast, where Swahili merchants were involved in slave-trading networks that linked northwestern Madagascar, the Comoros, and the Swahili Coast with the Red Sea and the Persian Gulf long before French and Omani traders began to make increasing demands on these networks during the second half of the eighteenth century.[7]

Indeed, when the Portuguese captured the port of Malacca on the Malay Peninsula in 1511, they found a well-established indigenous slave culture, with Malaccan merchants recorded as having 3,000 slaves.[8]

Europeans brought with them new vessels to facilitate enslavement. While the Arabs, Indians and others had transacted slaves in bondage for many centuries, they did so with relatively simple ships. The dhows were excellent craft, but their hulls were constructed of planks held together by coconut rope. European vessels were generally larger, hardier and armed with more cannon. They could carry heavier cargo (including people) over greater distances. The Europeans, having already circumnavigated most of Africa, also did not regard themselves as limited to one ocean. Slavery was transformed into what has been termed a 'pan-Indian Ocean network.'[9] Men and women would also be sought from far beyond Africa, although Africans continued to make up the majority of the human cargoes in the western Indian Ocean.[10] Slaves were also brought from as far afield as 'the islands of the Far East, the Asian steppes, Nepal, Bengal, the Malabar Coast and the shores of Baluchistan to the cosmopolitan centres of the Middle East and the centres of commercial production in East Africa.'[11]

The Portuguese regarded East Africa as a source of slaves for their lucrative colony, Brazil. What had once been a trade that was mainly (but not exclusively) across the Indian Ocean was now transacted all the way from the South China Sea to the Atlantic. The Europeans were responsible for increasing the demand for slaves on sugar, clove and nutmeg plantations in the Indian Ocean, as well as in Brazil.[12] This led to rising numbers of slaves being exported. However, the Europeans were not alone: they exported approximately the same number of Africans between 1500 and 1873 as the Arab, Muslim and Swahili traders who sent their human cargoes to Arabia, Persia and India.

Table 3: Transoceanic Slave Exports from Eastern Africa, 1500–1873[13]

Period	Arab, Muslim and Swahili Slave Exports	European Slave Exports	Total Slave Exports	% Total Slave Exports by Europeans
1500–1600	100,000	12,500– 25,000	112,500– 125,000	11.1–20.0
1600–1700	100,000	33,000– 65,000	133,000– 165,000	24.8–39.4
1700–1800	400,000	237,000– 433,000	637,000– 833,000	37.2–52.0
1801–1873	337,000	473,000– 633,000	810,000– 1,000,000	57.4–66.3
Total (No.) or Average (%)	937,000	755,500– 1,156,000	1,692,500– 2,123,000	44.6–54.5

From the first the Portuguese were in competition with others wishing to exploit what was believed to be the rich trade with East Africa. Although Swahili traders had been operating along the coast for centuries, they had a limited interest in developing colonies that encompassed large areas of the interior. They regarded the hinterland as a source of slaves and ivory, but little else. Unlike Asian powers, they relied on trade and not on taxes on land, or local produce, for their revenues.[14] Other imperial powers were also in evidence. The Ottoman Empire was a force in the north, but their influence did not extend much beyond the Red Sea and the Horn of Africa. The Persian Safavid Empire (1501–1736) and the Mughals in India (1526–1857) were powerful but saw themselves as essentially land-based powers, regarding maritime strength with disdain—the sphere of mere traders. This attitude was encapsulated in a saying attributed to one of the Muslim rulers of Gujarat: 'War by sea are merchants' affairs, and of no concern to the prestige of kings.'[15]

The Portuguese were the first to purchase and transport slaves between the settlements they established across the Indian Ocean region, where their territory was termed the *Estado da India*.[16] This led to a complex web of interactions to provide labour and assistance wherever it was required. Several hundred Mozambican captives were taken annually into Portugal's Indian and East Asian possessions from the early sixteenth century until the 1830s. Asian slaves were sent in the opposite direction, with Chinese slaves being brought from Macau to Goa and, occasionally, to distant Mozambique. Men were used as household servants, artisans and craftsmen, building fortifications and working in the factories and ships that transported the lucrative spices to Europe.[17] Women became concubines or prostitutes, while also working in the homes of their masters.

The Portuguese regularly used violence in attempts to establish a monopoly of trade in the Indian Ocean. In some ways they had few options: the products that they had brought from Europe to trade for spices, silks and other Asian goods held few attractions for their Asian customers, who turned them down.[18] Instead, the Portuguese used a combination of force and inter-Asian trade to obtain the goods they desired.

The Portuguese also understood the complementarity of trade in textiles, precious metals, ivory, and spices. Indian fabrics from Gujarat and the Coromandel coast enabled them to acquire gold and ivory from Sofala (in Mozambique), with which it was possible to buy spices in India and Southeast Asia (slightly later, gold and silver came from the Americas).[19]

The Portuguese strategy was, at first, successful and they were able to double or even treble their investments in voyages by shipping spices to European markets.[20] However, in time, their monopoly was undermined as some Arabs found ways of evading Portuguese ships, while others turned to land routes to transport commodities to markets in the Middle East and beyond. Competition drove down profits. The seas around the Cape were treacherous and the journey was lengthy. Portugal often lost ships, men and commodities. Their dream of dominating the region was soon over. In the end the Portuguese lost most of their strategic possessions to the Omanis.

> By the middle of the seventeenth century, the official Portuguese position in the Indian Ocean was in tatters. Most of its major forts—Melaka, Cochin, Colombo, Hurmuz—had been lost. On the East African coast the *Estado da India* retained toe holds only in Mozambique, and Mombasa until the 1690s.[21]

This 'toe hold' was not perhaps as insignificant as the term might suggest. Mozambique was a huge territory that was developed to serve the settlers and the motherland. Neither it nor Angola on the west coast could be described as insubstantial. Holding Mozambique allowed Portuguese settlers to establish plantations granted to them by the Crown, and to continue to hunt for slaves. The Zambezi valley proved a major route into the interior for settlers.

As the Omani presence in the Indian Ocean grew, the influence of Lusophone Africa declined. Over time the Omanis expanded their control all along the East African coast until they had a 'network of ports, held together more by shared commercial interests than a state structure.'[22] The Portuguese had constructed a small trading post near Zanzibar harbour in the 1570s, with a major stronghold in Mombasa: Fort Jesus. In 1649, the Omani forces felt confident enough to attack the Portuguese in Zanzibar, destroying the settlement. The Omanis brought with them Baluchi mercenaries who settled in Zanzibar's coastal villages and around the fort, providing the sultan with protection and security.[23] This was followed by the Omani conquest of Fort Jesus in 1698, after which the Portuguese withdrew from Zanzibar altogether.

Omani trade with East Africa flourished. In the 1820s, an Omani, Saleh bin Haramil al-Abray, began experimenting with clove plantations, only to become the largest producer on the islands of Zanzibar. Exports rose from 280,000 pounds in the 1840s to almost 5 million pounds in the 1850s.[24] So lucrative was the trade that Sultan Sayyid Said bin Sultan al-Busaidi (r. 1804–1856), Oman's most illustrious, but ruthless, ruler, transferred his capital to Zanzibar.[25] The sultan brought Baluchi troops with him to Stone Town and was accompanied by Indians who had previously been part of a vigorous mercantile community in Muscat.[26] The Indians settled on the island and along the east coast, forming a 4,000-strong community by the early nineteenth century.

> There they worked as traders, bankers and customs collectors, having won the Omani rulers' confidence quite some time ago. Said convinced them to accompany him to East Africa, encouraging them to settle and spread their commerce to the coastal and interior regions of East Africa and broaden their roles in the East African economy.[27]

Indians helped finance and staff the Omani administration. While the Arabs made a fortune from trade and their clove plantations, the Indian community oiled the wheels of commerce.[28] The sultan's income from customs grew fivefold from 1807 to 1862.[29] The expansion was underwritten by members of the Indian community, who extended loans in Zanzibar and along the East African coast. Sir Bartle Frere, the British governor of Bombay who visited Zanzibar in 1873, remarked that 'Throughout the Zanzibar coastline ... all banking and mortgage business passes through Indian hands. Hardly a single loan can be negotiated, a mortgage effected, or a bill cashed without Indian agency.'[30]

Indians also became substantial plantation owners, utilising slaves to grow the valuable cloves. Slavery was outlawed across the British Empire in 1833, yet the practice continued. In 1860–1861, Colonel

Christopher Palmer Rigby, British consul on Zanzibar, recorded emancipating 8,000 slaves owned by Indians, although, as British subjects, their enslavement had been illegal for three decades.[31]

The foreign powers were far from united. European disputes and wars were extended to the Indian Ocean. Europeans competed and then clashed with each other for trade and influence. It was the French who, from the seventeenth century, exploited slaves in large numbers. The islands of Réunion and Mauritius, making up the Mascarene archipelago, were discovered by the Portuguese in the sixteenth century. The Dutch were the first colonisers, introducing 300 Malagasy slaves in the 1640s.[32] They were followed, in 1715, by the French. Britain took the archipelago for a brief period (1810 –1815) during the Napoleonic Wars, but otherwise it remained French until independence in 1968. From 1720, Reunion and Mauritius became plantation settlements, developing an insatiable appetite for slaves to tend and harvest sugar, coffee, cloves, indigo and spices. By 1807–1808, the slave populations on the islands totalled almost 133,000.[33] The incessant demand for slaves can be explained by the high mortality rates: the slave population declined by 1.2 per cent a year, felled by a range of diseases from smallpox to beriberi, cholera, intestinal parasites and fevers.[34] Many did not even make it to the plantations, with death rates on the voyages to the islands estimated at between 20 and 30 per cent.[35] To feed the almost insatiable demand for slaves for the plantations, they were imported from an extraordinary range of sources.

Slave censuses and contemporary accounts of Mauritian life reveal the truly global extent of the catchment area that supplied European Indian Ocean establishments with chattel labor. Slaves from Madagascar, Mozambique, and the Swahili Coast, the most important sources of bondmen and -women in the Indian Ocean, came from a large number of ethnocultural populations. At least thirteen such groups on Madagascar furnished slaves to the Mascarenes, while those of Mozambican and East African origin were drawn from fourteen populations that can be identified with certainty, some of which were located as far away as modern Malawi and eastern Zambia. Slaves from West Africa (described as Bambaras, Guineans, and Wolofs), the Comoros, and Ethiopia also reached the islands, as did bondmen and -women from the Persian

Gulf (Arabs, Persians), the Indian subcontinent (Bengalis, Goans, Lascars, Malabars, Orissans, Telegus), Malaya, the Indonesian archipelago (Balinese, Javanese, Makassarese, Niasans, Sumatrans, Timorese), and even China.[36]

While the French ranged far and wide for slaves, they concentrated above all on Madagascar. Merina rulers became enormously wealthy from enslavement until the 1820s, when a treaty between Britain and the Merina Kingdom, which was ruled by an indigenous Malagasy family, curtailed the trade.[37] The status of the slaves was transmitted down the generations, since, unless both parents were from a superior group, their offspring were relegated to a lower group and enslaved. Ending this status proved very difficult indeed.[38] The Royal Navy patrolled the Madagascan coastline to try to ensure that the ban on the slave trade was enforced. The plantation owners shifted their search to Mozambique to acquire the labour they needed.

The seventeenth century also saw the arrival of the Dutch in the Indian Ocean. They set about sourcing slave labour from across the region.

> The Dutch Indian Ocean slave system drew captive labor from three interlocking and overlapping circuits of subregions: the westernmost, African circuits of East Africa, Madagascar, and the Mascarene Islands (Mauritius and Réunion); the middle, South Asian circuit of the Indian subcontinent (Malabar, Coromandel, and the Bengal/Arakan coast); and the easternmost, Southeast Asian circuit of Malaysia, Indonesia, New Guinea (Irian Jaya), and the southern Philippines.[39]

The Dutch East India Company's various outposts recorded 66,350 slaves in 1687–1688,[40] with the Cape of Good Hope receiving a substantial number. Throughout the seventeenth century, Africa remained a 'relatively insignificant' source of slaves for the Dutch, with the authorities preferring to look to their Indian or Asian colonies for labour.[41]

About a quarter of the slaves imported into the Cape came from Africa (first from western and central Africa, and then mostly from Mozambique), while approximately the same numbers came from

Madagascar and the remainder from Indonesia and India.[42] During the entire period of slave importation (1652–1808), some 63,000 men and women were brought to the Cape.[43] Other estimates put the figure higher, at 80,000.[44] The imported slaves were put to use by the Dutch East India Company. A larger number were owned by the private farms that sprang up.[45] White farmers, most of whom were Dutch, also enslaved local people. Raids were conducted against the indigenous Khoikhoi from as early as the 1730s.[46] As in other parts of the Company's sprawling empire, slaves at the Cape used various forms of resistance. Some at the Constantia wine farm ran away; others went on the run as a group, raiding farms and attempting to steal cattle from the Khoikhoi.[47]

The British also began slaving in the region in the seventeenth century, transporting human cargoes from East Africa and Madagascar to Sumatra, Bombay or Madras. However, the numbers involved were relatively minor. Slaves were taken annually in the hundreds, possibly thousands, but nowhere near the numbers Britain transported across the Atlantic.[48] Britain came to exercise control over the Indian Ocean, as they gradually extended their domination of India, and occupied the Cape in 1795, ending the Dutch East India Company's role in the region.[49] Although the British relinquished the colony to the Dutch in 1802, they reannexed it in 1806 after the start of the Napoleonic Wars to counter potential French influence. Over the next few years, as pressure for abolition grew in London, measures were taken to emancipate the South African slaves. Importation of slaves ceased in 1808 after the British Slave Trade Act came into force, but it was only in 1834 that the emancipation of the Cape slaves was finally enacted. The slow pace of freedom led to two slave revolts: in 1808 in Malmesbury and in 1825 in the Bokkeveld. Both were rapidly suppressed.[50]

Meanwhile, the independent white farmers had come to depend on slavery, or slave-like systems of labour. When these practices were abolished, the Dutch (later Afrikaner) farmers were furious and protested to the authorities. After 1836, many left the Western Cape altogether, trekking deep into the interior of southern Africa. The farmers extended slavery to the African peoples they came across, when this proved possible. It is estimated that almost 14,000 African slaves were taken in raids between 1731 and 1869.[51] Slavery ceased in those parts of southern Africa that Britain held. Beyond British control, the practice continued for several decades, leading London to sign an agreement in 1852 to recognise the independence of the Afrikaners' republics in return for their assurance that enslavement would end.[52]

7

OMANI HEGEMONY

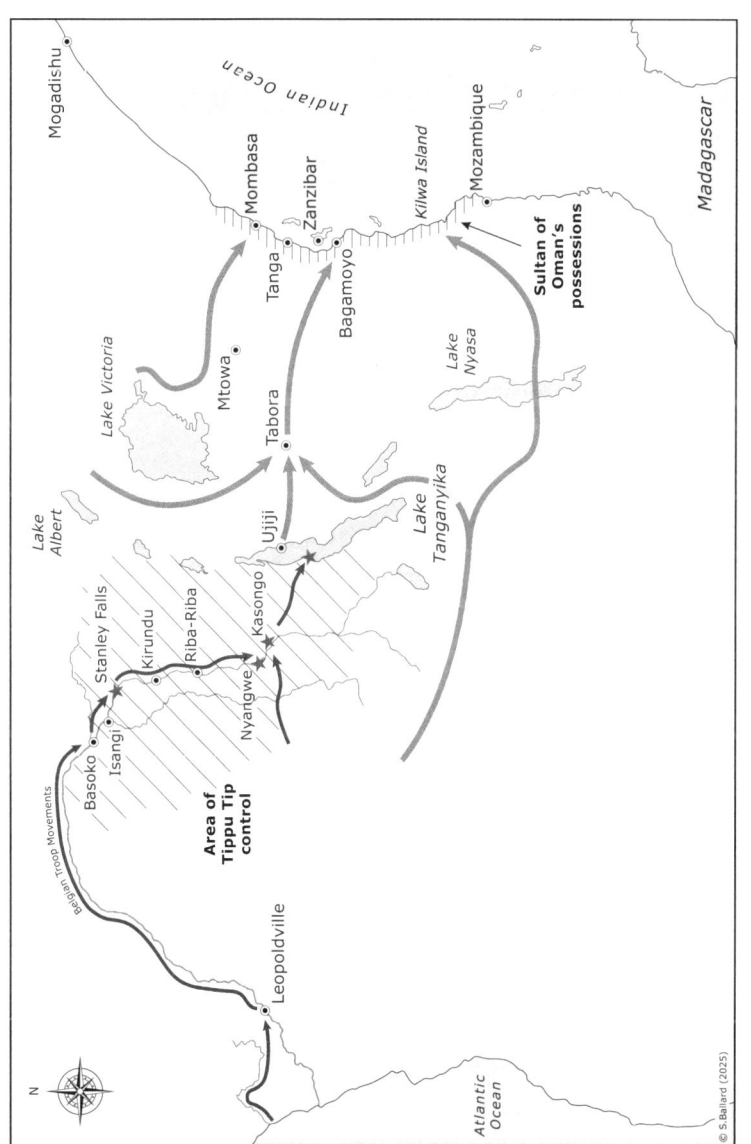

Map 3: Belgian–Omani War of 1892–94 and Arab slave routes

The map shows clashes between forces sent by King Leopold of Belgium and those of Tippu Tip, loyal to the Sultan of Oman. The map is adapted from a variety of sources.

The growing Omani presence in the Indian Ocean was at the expense of the Portuguese. By 1649 the Omani forces felt confident enough to challenge the Portuguese, attacking them in Zanzibar and destroying their settlement. The Omanis brought with them Baluchi mercenaries who did much of the fighting and then settled in Zanzibar's coastal villages and around the fort. They also provided the sultan with protection and security.[1] The Portuguese withdrew from Zanzibar altogether following the Omani capture of Fort Jesus in 1698.

Omani trade flourished, and with the development of the clove industry the demand for slaves on Zanzibar rocketed. Clove plantations were enormously labour-intensive and the slave population of the islands rose from about 15,000 prior to the clove plantations to more than 100,000 by the 1830s. The work was hard and disease was rife, leading to a soaring mortality rate of 15 to 20 per cent per annum. The labour force needed to be continually replaced, with 9,000 to 12,000 slaves being imported every year. As the human cargoes reached Zanzibar, the dead were tossed overboard. The sick and weak were left to die on the beach so that taxes did not have to be paid.[2] The survivors were oiled and attractively clothed to be sold in the islands' slave markets. A British Royal Naval commander, Philip Colomb, witnessed the sale of some 300 slaves in 1868 by approximately twenty auctioneers. Some were fit and healthy, but one auctioneer's slaves attracted the captain's attention.

> His 'lot' appeared to be lately imported; they were all young boys and girls, some of them mere babies; and it was amongst them that the terribly painful part of the slave system was to be seen. I mean the miserable state, apparently of starvation, in which so many of these poor wretches are sometimes landed. The sight is simply horrible, and no amount of sophistry or sentiment will reconcile us to such a condition of things. Skeletons, with a diseased skin drawn tight over them, eyeballs left hideously prominent by the falling away of the surrounding flesh, chests shrunk and bent, joints unnaturally swelled and horribly knotty by contrast with the wretched limbs between them, voices dry and hard, and 'distantly near' like those of a nightmare—these are the characteristics which mark too many of the negroes when imported.[3]

Into the African interior

As described above, the rulers of Oman dominated the east coast before the arrival of the Europeans. In the 1770s, an Omani governor was appointed to the port of Kilwa, and gradually their power extended into the African hinterland. 'As each part of the coast came under Omani rule, some form of accommodation was sought with the pre-existing ruling factions to facilitate commercial exploitation with the minimum of administrative expenditure or organisation.'[4]

Arab and Swahili slavers and traders gradually penetrated deeper and deeper into the African interior. Omani plantations were extended along the coast controlled by the sultan from Zanzibar. Their estates produced rice, maize, millet, beans, sorghum, coconuts and sesame, with the Omanis and their Baluchi troops establishing hundreds of farms by the late nineteenth century.[5] Sultan Said—himself one of the largest clove producers—set about developing the pre-existing systems of African enslavement on a colossal scale. This expansion was driven not only by the utility of slaves in the plantations, but because of their role as domestic servants, porters and artisans, as well as courtesans to satisfy the pleasure of their masters, and for export. Other slaves became trusted armed guards, who accompanied the caravans as they penetrated the African interior.[6] The sultan's raiders, working with coastal Swahilis and supportive African tribes, pushed inland using a combination of trade, slave raiding and political control. The slave trade was dominated by the Omanis, but they were not without allies. The Baluchis were rewarded with land, allowing the sultan to control whole regions of the African interior.[7]

> During the 19th century, the growth in the volume of trade managed by the Indian mercantile communities, with the consent of the Arabs and the military protection of the Baluchi mercenaries, inevitably led to a gradual but progressive weakening of the African populations ... Entire squadrons of Baluchi soldiers settled in the interior of the African continent at Tabora and at Kigoma, on Lake Tanganyika ... Other Baluchis joined the caravans which traded with the interior, travelling as far as the Congo.[8]

Many of the slaves had been captured by one African chief at war with another, and then sold to the Arabs.[9] Omanis, armed with rifles, would lead the raids on villages, searching for slaves. Their caravans would cover hundreds of kilometres, working for a year or two, before returning to the coast. Temporary stations would be established along the way to support their operations, as they pillaged and looted the homesteads that they found.

> The means used varied little. Violence occupied the first place. Isolated in the hostile milieu of the great equatorial forest, tackling peoples who had been without contact with the exterior and whom they regarded as savages, these bands acted mercilessly to seize men and goods. Using such methods, the expeditions swiftly exhausted the resources they were exploiting.[10]

The Omanis' penetration of the interior in search of slaves was extraordinary, as they travelled further and further into central Africa. By the 1850s they had traversed the entire continent, reaching the Angolan coast at the port of Benguela, where they sold ivory and slaves.[11] The missionary and explorer David Livingstone met Arabs from Zanzibar in what is today Namibia's Caprivi strip.[12] The impact on African communities was devastating. They fled to the hills, seeking sanctuary in caves, or else built platform villages on lakes in an attempt to escape the predations of the slavers.[13]

Oman developed Kilwa as their premier slave port. By the 1840s, between 10,000 and 12,000 people were being exported through it every year.[14] Omani settlers, with the aid of Swahilis from the coast and local tribes, established informal colonies in the interior from which to operate.

> The first Arab merchants reached the commercial centre at Tabora, halfway between the coast and Lake Tanganyika, in the 1830s, and thereafter the Muslim presence in the interior grew at a phenomenal rate. Muslims, including Arabs, Swahili, and converts among the Nyamwezi and Yao, dominated a vast network of trade routes that stretched beyond the lake country to the basin of the Congo River by the 1870s.[15]

By the mid-nineteenth century, as the slave trade was diminishing in the Atlantic, the number of slaves being captured by Oman was reaching its peak. Ismael Montana estimates that 'between 1859 and 1872, the Arab slave raiders procured and furnished Zanzibar with nearly 20,000 slaves annually. While up to half of the enslaved were put to work on the commercial agricultural plantations, the rest were destined to other parts of the Swahili coast, Arabia, or the Persian Gulf.'[16]

The American journalist Henry Morton Stanley, who travelled extensively in the region in this period, came across Arab slavers living in considerable style in their settlements, their homes boasting Persian carpets, fine copperware and luxurious bedding.[17] Arab slavery and the settlements that the Arabs established have had a long-lasting impact on the region. The descendants of these Omani raiders are still to be found in East Africa, from Rwanda and Burundi to Kenya and Tanzania (including Zanzibar). Many maintain ties with their former homeland, which they visit regularly, while continuing to wear traditional Omani clothing and marrying within their communities, even if most can no longer speak Arabic.[18]

The Africans whom they captured were marched hundreds of kilometres to the East African coast, enduring the harshest of conditions. The British consul in Zanzibar, Edward Seward, in 1866 witnessed a caravan of over 300 slaves who had been purchased for cotton cloth.[19] Fed on boiled sorghum and water once a day, they were forced to march for nine hours before camping. They walked in line, with men tied together with forked sticks and women and children with their hands bound. On the way they witnessed children killed by blows from clubs, men stabbed and strangled, and the route stank of rotting corpses of those who had made the journey before them.

David Livingstone travelled with the Arab and Swahili slavers for four years and was horrified by what he witnessed. He recorded a massacre in 1871 in the important slaving centre of Nyangwe. Livingstone saw Arabs firing on villagers following an argument, leaving hundreds dead. 'All told some 400 or 500 individuals died, with others being captured by the Arabs to be made slaves. In addition, the Arabs crossed the river and began attacking and setting fire to many of the villages on the left bank. Livingstone counted 17 villages in flames.'[20] In the 16 July entry of his 1871 Field Diary, Livingstone writes that 'the murderous assault on the market people was Hell without the fire and brimstone … It filled me with unspeakable horror.'[21] On 26 July 1872, a lengthy letter by Livingstone was published in the *New York Herald* and subsequently re-published in London's *Daily Telegraph*.[22] It described conditions and had a powerful effect on both sides of the Atlantic, helping the British Anti-Slavery Society's campaign against the trade. In August 1872, the government's programme for Parliament contained the promise that the British authorities would take 'steps intended to prepare the way for dealing more effectually with the slave trade on the east coast of Africa.'[23]

Oman confronts Belgium

The Omanis controlled areas along the East African coast, as well as deep in Africa's interior, at a time when an event was to take place that would transform the history of the continent: the 'scramble for Africa'. This was the name given to the events unleashed by the Conference of Berlin of 1884–1885. Held by the German chancellor, Otto von Bismarck, at the request of King Leopold of Belgium, it laid the foundations for dividing Africa between the competing European powers.[24] The Conference also laid the foundations for what became known as the 'Congo Free State'— the personal property of the Belgian king. Leopold had become obsessed with the notion of expanding his influence after reading an account of Congo in *The Times* by a British explorer, Lieutenant Cameron. Cameron described it as a land of 'unspeakable riches' just awaiting 'an enterprising capitalist.'[25] The Conference gave the king permission to take a vast area of central Africa. Leopold argued that his mission was to stamp out Arab slavery practiced by the likes of Tippu Tip in the heart of the continent. To this end, the king held the Brussels Anti-Slavery Conference of 1889–1890. Many were taken in by Leopold's promises. Sir Bartle Frere, Britain's high commissioner for southern Africa, had remarked that the king had explained his aims and that 'his designs are the most philanthropic and are amongst the few schemes of the kind … free from any selfish commercial or political object.'[26]

The reality was quite the opposite. Far from providing Leopold with 'unspeakable riches', the Congo Free State proved to be a costly burden. To turn the project around, the most unspeakable cruelty was employed to harvest its rubber and ivory, with local people pressed into service.

> In the process all manner of hideous acts were committed. Rubber quotas were assigned, and if the output was too low, villages would be burned and Africans shot. Others were flogged or mutilated—the chopping off of hands was by no means uncommon. Women were kidnapped and held as hostages. In a true reign of terror, vast stretches of land were de-populated by murder and by the flight of terrified natives. Massacres were not rare.[27]

Photographs of adults and children without hands began appearing in the press and provoked international condemnation. In 1908, the Belgian government took over the administration of Congo—paying off the king's debts. It was a grotesque example of the abuse that colonialism could initiate. However, as the Belgians penetrated deeper and deeper into the Congo, they inevitably came up against the other expanding power: Oman.

The sultan of Oman held territory west of Lake Tanganyika and east of the Belgian Congo Free State through the slavers who operated out of Zanzibar or from the coast that he controlled.[28] This resulted in intense competition between the Arabs and the Belgians for land, slaves and ivory, and led to a war in 1892–93 that the Belgians eventually won.[29] The Arabs were led by Tippu Tip (c. 1837–1905)—whose real name was Hamad bin Muhammad al-Murjabi. One of the wealthiest and most powerful men in the region, Tippu Tip was born in Zanzibar, of mixed Omani and Swahili heritage. Tall, at 6'2", he was generally immaculately dressed. Zanzibar controlled the African hinterland through local agents, including Tippu Tip. A trader in ivory, which he marked with his initials, HM, Tippu Tip is best known as a slaver. Some of his agents were Swahilis from the coast, but far more were *ngwana*, or freemen—a term that was later used for Africans from the interior.[30] He recognised the authority of the Sultanate of Zanzibar, which exercised influence (even if it did not govern) a vast area of central Africa.[31] As the British explorer Richard Burton remarked: 'When the flute is played in Zanzibar, they dance in Ujiji'—a town on the shores of Lake Tanganyika, a thousand kilometres west of the island.

Tippu Tip was immensely shrewd, co-operating with European traders, explorers and missionaries when it suited him, but never losing sight of the wealth he might extract from the relationship. From 1860, Tippu Tip led caravans deeper and deeper into the interior of Africa. Trading in ivory and slaves, he made a fortune, with some of his expeditions lasting for as long as twelve years.[32] By 1895, he had reportedly acquired 'seven "shambas" (plantations) and 10,000 slaves.'[33]

Tippu Tip became master of Manyema, a region of central Africa north-east of Lake Tanganyika. From Manyema, Tippu Tip organised annual caravans taking slaves and ivory to the sea. 'As they filed past,' wrote the missionary Alfred Swann in 1882,

> we noticed that many were chained together at the neck. Others had their necks fastened into the forks of poles about six feet long, the ends of which were supported by the men who preceded them. The women, who were as numerous as the men, carried babies on their backs in addition to a tusk of ivory or other burdens on their heads.[34]

The march to the sea involved a journey over weeks or months that left men and women in a terrible condition, as witnessed by Swann.

> Feet and shoulders were a mass of open sores, made more painful by swarms of flies which followed the marked and lived on the flowing blood. They presented a moving picture of utter misery, and one could not help wondering how any of them survived the long tramp from the upper Congo, at least 1,000 miles distant.[35]

Tippu Tip's aims were primarily commercial, but his control over the region meant he had to exercise political influence as well.

> [W]hen he commenced operating in the forests of Manyema, among mainly stateless and politically unstable peoples, he was forced to exercise a kind of suzerainty, with a Swahili-Arab bureaucracy and with slave armies, so as to procure ivory. The centre of Manyema, around Tippu Tip's headquarters at Kasongo, was well-ordered and productive, but the ivory frontier, which reached well to the west of the Lomami river and down the Lualaba towards the future Stanley Falls, was lawless and violent.[36]

Tippu Tip's westwards expansion was bound to come into conflict with the Belgian King Leopold's private enterprise, the Congo Independent State, which was moving eastwards. In 1886, Tippu Tip accepted the king's offer of the governorship of the Stanley Falls area, for £30 a month, provided that he did not continue his enslaving on the king's territory. It was a condition Tippu Tip had little intention of accepting.[37] Leopold was in a relatively precarious position. The king had expended large sums on the Congo, with little to show for his investments. He kept pressing eastwards, attempting to ensure that the trade in ivory was routed via his Congolese state, and not via Zanzibar. In 1891 Leopold decided to send a large and well-armed expedition under the governor of the region, Guillaume van Kerckhoven, to seize all the ivory he could find.[38] Tippu Tip was at the time on an extended visit to Zanzibar, but he heard of growing Arab resentment at these seizures. Van Kerckhoven was utterly ruthless, but the spark that ignited the war was an expedition south of the Stanley Falls, into the heart of the Arab territory, by Arthur Hodister, a Belgian commercial agent. Hodister had been described by Tippu Tip as 'a great friend of mine', but his arrival in the area after the killings inflicted by van Kerckhoven proved to be the last straw. Hodister and three of his European colleagues were reported to have been tortured, butchered and eaten by local people in May 1892.[39]

The killings sparked off what is sometimes called a war, but it is perhaps better described as a series of brutal engagements, over a large area of central Africa. The fighting, from 1892 to 1893, pitted the interests of the Belgian king against the sultan of Zanzibar, although both were acting through intermediaries and far from the scene. Tippu Tip himself remained hundreds of miles from the conflict in Zanzibar. However, his son, Sefu, led an army that was reportedly 10,000 strong, working in an alliance with other Arab-Swahilis in the region. The Belgians had fewer troops, but they had modern weapons, including machine guns, and trained African soldiers. The troops were drawn from across Africa, including Hausas, Ethiopians, Somalis, Egyptians and several hundred Xhosa from South Africa.[40] By April 1893, they had put the Arabs to flight. The campaign was a triumph for King Leopold, who managed to extend the Congo Free State all the way to Lake Tanganyika.[41] Tippu

Tip's home at the walled stronghold of Kasongo was captured, depriving the trader of a luxurious two-story house built around a courtyard.[42] The final battle took place on 20 October 1893, just west of Lake Tanganyika. Sefu was among the fatalities.[43] Tippu Tip had lost not only his son, but a fortune in ivory and 20,000 muskets. He also lost his influence over central Africa, while retaining his possessions in Zanzibar, where he died in 1905, still a wealthy man.

8

THE PORTUGUESE AND THE BRITISH

Although the Omanis had forced the Portuguese out of Zanzibar, Lisbon continued to exploit their colony in Mozambique, which was, by the eighteenth century, the only Indian Ocean territory outside of Goa remaining under Portuguese control. The Portuguese pushed deep into the interior, using the Zambezi River, which is navigable for its first 300 miles, and penetrated as far as Malawi. The authorities established crown estates in the Lower Zambezi, known as *prazos da corao*, or *prazos* for short.[1] These estates were run by Europeans, Indians or people of mixed race who held a privileged position over the others on the estate, whether they were free Africans or slaves. Established through conquest, they were powerful institutions.

> The basis of the prazero's power was his large achikunda, or slave army, which he acquired through slave raids, purchase, and the indigenous practice of voluntary enslavement. It was not uncommon for such powerful early prazeros as Antonio Lobo da Silva to own 4,000 to 5,000 slaves, and one prazero was reputed to have 15,000 slaves.[2]

The *prazeros* acted as intermediaries, acquiring slaves by raiding and trading and then selling them on for export,[3] sometimes in competition with the indigenous peoples, particularly the Yao.[4] Exports of slaves rose dramatically during the Napoleonic Wars as demand for sugar turned Portugal's other colony, Brazil, into one of the world's largest producers. Although Portugal had banned slavery in 1836, its governor in Mozambique paid little heed.[5] Even if he had wished to stop the enslavement his administration was powerless to do so, with just a few hundred troops at his disposal, compared with up to 10,000 soldiers working for the private slave armies of the Arab and African agents who engaged in the capture and escorting of the slave caravans to the coast.[6]

Many were exported via Delagoa Bay. There was an 'intense and growing' demand for slaves in the French Réunion and Mauritian islands, as well as Brazil.[7] Attempts to halt the international trade, together with an incessant demand for cheap labour on plantations, led to a paradoxical rise in enslavement. The Treaty of Paris of 1815, which gave France five years to end its slave trade, and Brazil's agreement to halt the trade in return for British recognition of Brazilian independence in 1826 had the same impact: as the prospect of a shortage of slave labour approached, the numbers of slaves transported across the Indian and Atlantic oceans from Delagoa Bay rose.[8]

The profits from the human trade were enormous, calculated as up to 1,000 per cent, with a similar margin made taking captives onwards to Brazil.[9] Portuguese, French and Brazilian merchants are estimated to have transported 126,000 Africans from Mozambique Island to the Brazilian port of Santos between 1664 and 1859.[10] Even this was only a fraction of the African slaves transported via the Cape and onwards to other parts of Brazil and the Caribbean, with some being taken as far as the American city of Charleston. Overall, some 293,000 slaves were taken from Mozambique across the Atlantic over almost two centuries.[11] It was only in the 1860s, after opposition to slavery in Brazil by the imperial government (followed by slavery's formal abolition in Brazil in 1888), that the trade from Mozambique once more turned to the French plantations of Reunion and Mauritius. Indians played a similar role in Mozambique to the one they undertook in Zanzibar. Gujarati merchants facilitated the slave trade from Mozambique Island and arranged the transportation of some 3,540 to India between 1770 and 1834.[12] Indian-manufactured cloth, and later firearms, were traded for ivory and slaves. The trade gave British Indians access to great wealth. By 1861, around three quarters of all immovable property on the islands of Zanzibar and Pemba were owned by or mortgaged to the Indian community.[13]

Developments in South Africa in the nineteenth century also shaped the trade. The attacks known as the *Mfecane* (or *Dificane*) by the Zulu on neighbouring African peoples from the late eighteenth to the mid-nineteenth century not only devastated their neighbours but opened the way to slavery. The offensives resulted in the killing of over a million people, leaving the countryside strewn with their bones and displacing even larger numbers across southern Africa.[14] Under Shaka kaSenzangakhona (r. 1816–1828), the Zulu also took part in the Portuguese slavery in Delagoa Bay. Although the Zulu did not originate the trade, the numbers of Africans displaced by and fleeing the Zulu army were an important component in increasing the supply of slaves. As Linell Chewins and Peter Delius conclude, the Portuguese were responsible for encouraging and participating in attacks, but Zulu regiments 'raided into the Bay area, creating prisoners for sale. In the 1820s, during Shaka's rule, there is strong evidence that Zulu regiments participated.'[15] The military tactics they used were copied by others to conquer new lands.

> These regiments moved north, destroying every established state they encountered and enslaving people in the Zambezi valley, the Rhodesian plateau, and parts of Tanzania. Between the combined impact of the *dificane* and the slave raiders from the coast, many captives were seized. War-lord-ism [*sic*] had become the dominant feature of the East African interior from Tanzania to South Africa.[16]

As we saw earlier, by no means all enslavement in southern Africa involved the Zulu. For example, there is evidence that the Bakwena enslaved the Bakgalagadi in the nineteenth century, in what is today Botswana. Both were Bantu peoples, but this subjugation was not on the scale or lasting impact of the *Mfecane*.[17] These instances of enslavement took place in addition to the slavery practiced by the Dutch, Portuguese and British in the region.

Britain

The Indian Ocean market in slaves was transformed—albeit slowly—by the British decision to abolish the trade in 1807, following an impassioned ten-hour debate in the House of Commons. Ending slavery in the British colonies and on the seas that London controlled took considerably longer. Slavery was finally made illegal in 1833 by extending the 1807 legislation to make the purchase or ownership of slaves unlawful across the British Empire. There was a strong humanitarian impetus to ensure that Britain stamped out the practice around the globe.[18] Although the British had long established their dominance in the Indian Ocean as a means of ensuring their control over their Indian empire, bringing slavery to an end proved to be extremely difficult and lengthy and absorbed many resources. It has been calculated that nearly 2 per cent of British national income was spent on suppressing the slave trade in the Atlantic alone, every year for sixty years.[19]

Britain's Royal Navy, acting out of Cape Town and Mauritius, began anti-slavery patrols early in the nineteenth century. Twenty-seven slave ships were captured off the Cape from 1808 to 1816, while Mauritius was 'even busier', with forty-eight vessels seized from 1811 to 1825.[20] Britain signed treaties with various Arab sheikhs in 1820 and 1836, but these appear to have had limited success. It was not until 1847 that the British managed to persuade the sultan of Zanzibar to ban the export of slaves beyond his dominions in East Africa, making the slave trade to Arabia and the Persian Gulf illegal.[21] However, the Royal Navy's efforts were rather half-hearted, with just a single, ancient vessel anchored off Zanzibar. David Livingstone published his observations of the continuing scale and cruelty of Arab slavery in 1858. The book became a bestseller, rousing British public opinion, which demanded more robust action. In the same year, the Royal Navy despatched HMS *Lyra* to the East African coast with specific orders to enforce the anti-slavery treaties. This was followed by HMS *London* in 1873 and then HMS *Sidon*. But Britain was not sending the finest of its fleet: HMS *Sidon* was described as 'an old tub, that any dhow on the coast could beat.'[22] It was all too easy for a dhow to simply be beached and for its crew and passengers to disappear into the interior. In the mid-nineteenth century, despite the efforts of the navy, some 10,000 Africans were still exported each year across the Indian Ocean.

The Indian Ocean and Atlantic patrols were costly in terms of lives and expenditure, and not popular with most senior officers. George Groschen, First Lord of the Admiralty, complained bitterly to the prime minister in 1871:

The fact is, half our expenditure is not for war service in the strict sense but for keeping the policing of the seas, of protecting commerce during times of peace, and for carrying out our views as to protecting those barbarous and backwards races against kidnapping and various forms of outrage. Philanthropy costs money.[23]

Nevertheless, the Royal Navy continued to sustain an Indian Ocean Squadron until the late 1880s. 'The Royal Navy's role in the suppression of the transoceanic slave trades represents a remarkable episode of sustained humanitarian activity,' Huw Lewis-Jones observed, 'involving patient diplomacy and problematic wrangling over treaty arrangements, dangerous and exacting naval operations, and intense political debate at home questioning the cost and purpose of the patrols.'[24]

Despite these efforts, the trade continued. As late as 1872, Rear Admiral Cumming, the Royal Navy's commander of the Zanzibar station, calculated that no fewer than 15,129 slaves passed through the island's customs house between 1 May and 31 December.[25] It was not until the navy threatened to blockade and bombard Zanzibar in 1873 that the sultan of Oman was finally persuaded to act against slavery. On 5 June in that year, the sultan agreed to ban the export of slaves from one part of his dominion to another, close all slave markets, and liberate and protect all enslaved peoples.[26] Even then, patrols at sea were only partly successful, and it was only after land-based patrols were instituted that most trade was substantially reduced.[27]

Ending a practice that had persisted for over 2,000 years in the Indian Ocean was never going to be easy. The Royal Navy was still boarding dhows and discovering slaves as late as 1922.[28] Freed slaves formed a community in cosmopolitan Aden, where they were given some of the lowliest of tasks. The descendants of the slaves, known as Sidis, were categorised as 'outcaste groups', along with other groups who were looked down upon: the Akhdam and the Jabarti.[29] Slavery was only formally abolished in Saudi Arabia in 1962 and in Oman in 1970.[30] Its impact is still evident in the discrimination practised in both states. The U.S. State Department's report on human rights in Saudi Arabia in 2022 found: 'Descendants of former slaves in the country, who have African lineage, faced discrimination in both employment and society.'[31] Similarly, the State Department reported that Oman has many female migrant workers from as far afield as Zimbabwe, the Philippines and Ethiopia who still have no legal protection.[32] Omani law criminalises slavery and trafficking, but domestic workers are excluded from the legislation. Instead, they are covered by a 2004 ministerial decision, which the State Department says 'does not provide effective rights protections or adequate complaint mechanisms for this population.' Enslavement has cast a long shadow across all those states that have benefitted from it.

PART 3

INDIGENOUS SLAVERY

The previous chapters have already shown how systems of enslavement existed long before European colonialism. Slave societies were prevalent across the African continent. In West Africa alone, they were found down the centuries and only later linked to the demand from European powers. As Martin Klein explains:

> These slaving states had a number of features in common. All made war regularly; Oyo and Dahomey sent their armies into the field every dry season. Others relied heavily on raiding into neighbouring areas. Most had forces of warriors recruited from slaves. Asante depended largely on tribute from the three to five million people it ruled, many of whom owed a certain number of slaves every year.[1]

Paul Lovejoy goes further. He writes that:

> It is now generally understood how widespread slavery was in Africa before the colonial era. In many areas slaves constituted a majority of the population, at least by the end of the nineteenth century. Furthermore, even before that time, slave raiding and kidnapping contributed to insecurity and instability almost everywhere.[2]

This part looks at two examples of indigenous African slavery: Ethiopia in the east and the Sokoto Caliphate in the west. Both were extensive and used very substantial numbers of slaves, who were employed at home as well as being exported abroad by their rulers. However, it is important to remember that other African slave societies flourished as the nineteenth century drew to a close but before the expansion of colonialism left almost the whole of the continent in European hands. Slave-dependent societies produced vast wealth and power for the ruling elites.

> The result was magnificent cities and brilliant courts. Kano and Sinsani became bustling commercial centres. Abeche in Wadai became the largest city in North Central Africa. The court of the Mangbetu king in north-eastern Zaire was quite literally brilliant, shining with burnished copper and dazzling the visitor in the king's presence. This court, as many others, was sustained in this period by the labor of slaves.[3]

9

ETHIOPIAN SLAVERY

The Ethiopian Kingdom (later an empire), like many other African states, used slaves from the earliest times. The practice was linked to conflicts which have afflicted the people of the Horn of Africa down the centuries. Richard Pankhurst, among the most eminent of historians of Ethiopia, offered this summary:

> Warfare, which in the Ethiopian region dates back to the dawn of history, led to the capture of slaves of many ethnic groups. A significant proportion of the men, women and children thus seized were taken, however, from the less powerful communities of the periphery of the state, notably from what is now the borderlands of the Sudan, from peoples who, being in many cases culturally distinct, were regarded as morally easier to enslave than other inhabitants of the area.[1]

Pankhurst went on to highlight the racial component of enslavement: many of the slaves captured were of a darker complexion than their Semitic conquerors and had what was regarded as a more 'Negroid' appearance. The process of 'othering' the slave in Ethiopia was part of the justification for their treatment, as it was in communities around the globe. The complexion and beauty of women from the Horn made them particularly attractive for traders, since they could be sold at a premium. While human cargoes taken across the Atlantic were predominantly male, most of those in the Indian Ocean trade were said to be women.[2]

Descriptions of servitude can sound remarkably impersonal. So, before discussing the details of Ethiopian (or Abyssinian) slavery, it may be helpful to consider the plight of just one group of child captives from Ethiopia's largest ethnic group: the Oromo. Their story was unearthed by a friend and colleague, Dr Sandra Shell, who found their detailed records in an unlikely source: a South African archive. Her book, *Children of Hope*, describes how Oromo children, being transported to Arabia, were freed by a British naval vessel on patrol off the Horn to fight slavery in the 1880s. Sixty-four boys and girls were taken to the South African mission station of Lovedale in Grahamstown, where they were well cared for and educated.[3] What is so remarkable is that the missionaries not only took individual statements from each child, but photographed each of them, so that we can see them and know their stories. This record revealed just how they came to be enslaved, and what their experiences were from capture to freedom.

The years 1888 and 1889 were ones of intense hardship for the Oromo people. They had been hit by severe drought, followed by a terrible outbreak of rinderpest, a disease which wiped out many of their cattle. Famine was widespread and in these dire circumstances some families, unable to feed their children, sold them or gave them away so that they might survive. In addition, the newly crowned emperor, Menelik II, engaged in slave raids among the Oromo. So extensive were his raids that Harold Marcus described Menelik as Ethiopia's 'greatest slave entrepreneur'.[4] The emperor indirectly benefitted from the trade, receiving the bulk of the proceeds, plus a tax on each slave brought into his own Shoa region and for every slave sold there.

Frequently the slave gangs that captured the children were locals, although most of the children (71 per cent) did not recognise their captors. The remainder were mostly their kin, neighbours or people they knew. Nearly a quarter said they were taken by 'Abyssinians', although it is not clear what they meant by this term. Their captors were mostly men, although a handful of women also seized them. Violence was used in capturing about half of the boys and about a third of the girls. They were then sent on arduous marches to their final destinations. Most of the boys would have remained in Ethiopia, but around a half of the girls were destined for export, since Oromo women were regarded as particularly lovely and commanded a high price in the export markets of Arabia.

The distances that the children were forced to travel were astonishing, since some were as young as seven. Over the two months that their captors made them walk, most traversed 2,000 kilometres. Some went far further, with one boy said to have trudged over 6,000 kilometres. So difficult were the journeys that they often attempted to escape, only to be re-captured, beaten and chained. Every child experienced some form of abuse after they were enslaved. One of the boys spoke of being held captive under a bed, bound and gagged.

Many were traded in the slave market at Aussa, in the Afar region. The local sultan was described by being as 'one of the greatest slave catchers' by Commander Charles Gissing of Britain's Royal Navy, who finally freed the children. From Aussa they were marched to the coast and put on board dhows at the port of Rahayta (in the far south of modern Eritrea, bordering on Djibouti), before setting sail for Jeddah and the slave markets of Arabia. There the children would have been sold once more, had it not been for Commander Gissing of HMS *Osprey*. He disabled the slave vessel by opening fire on their sails, overpowered their captors and freed the cowering, frightened children who had been packed into the holds.[5]

The children were taken to Aden and cared for, but they did not thrive. The Muslims were given into the care of local families, but the Christians among them were sent off to South Africa. Years later, the Ethiopian government granted them the opportunity to return, but most chose to remain in South Africa for the rest of their lives. They made the best of their circumstances, married and had families. Among their progeny was one who became an eminent intellectual and political activist: Neville Alexander. Dr Alexander's political activity in the National Liberation Front led him to be imprisoned on Robben Island from 1963 to 1974, where he served time with Nelson Mandela. His grandmother, Bisho Jarsa, had been amongst the Oromo children taken to the South African mission station. In her old age she stopped communicating in any language that Neville, her grandson, could understand, instead speaking in Afaan Oromo. 'Don't worry,' his mother reassured him, 'She's speaking to God.'

Early slavery

Although slavery has been part of Ethiopian history from earliest times, tracing its origins is difficult for two reasons. Firstly, there is a reluctance among Ethiopian scholars to tackle the subject.

> Slavery remains one of the blind spots in the historiography of the Horn of Africa and Ethiopia in particular. This is peculiar in light of the fact that in the territories of the Horn slavery left a significant impact on the sociocultural fabric, and that the ports along the Horn of Africa coast fed the slave trade to the Arab, Ottoman and Indian Ocean worlds for many centuries.[6]

This minimisation of the history of enslavement was exacerbated by a second problem: the paucity of clear evidence, particularly in the earliest periods.

Egyptian slavery was examined in Part 1, 'The Trans-Saharan Slave Trade', outlining the use of Ethiopians as infantry as well as labourers in homes and farms. We know they were brought up the Nile, but were they from Sudan or Ethiopia? The answer seems to be that they came from both. Although Egyptians did raid southwards over the centuries, most of the enslavement was done by others. The men and women they received were generally transported up the great river as part of trade with neighbouring states. Enslavement was not inimical to diplomacy. Indeed, during Egypt's Fatimid Caliphate (c. 909–1171 CE) relations with Ethiopia were good, with the patriarch of Alexandria sending a bishop to become the head of the Ethiopian Church.[7] Rulers might have cordial ties and be involved in diplomatic exchanges, but this did not prevent them from engaging in the entrapment and transportation of their subjects, or their neighbours.

The Nile was just one route for slaves. A second, probably more important route was via caravans that took their human traffic to the coast and then onwards by boat. As early as the first millennium BCE, colonies of foreign merchants, Greek, Egyptian, Arab and perhaps even Indian, established themselves along the Red Sea to participate in this trade.[8] The Eritrean port of Adulis was a hub for transporting these slaves from the first century CE.[9] Over time, Ethiopia (or Abyssinia as it was known) fluctuated in power. When it was strong, its rulers extended their control to the shore and beyond. Ethiopia's Aksumite kings invaded southern Arabia twice, most notably in the middle of the sixth century, when the Aksumites fought local rulers who had attacked their communities.[10] The Ethiopians are said to have sent a force of 120,000 men in a giant armada of seventy ships to conquer Yemen in 525 CE.[11] This gave Ethiopia control over the Bab el-Mandeb, the straits at the mouth of the Red Sea. It was one of the most significant trading routes in the medieval world, and remains so to this day, connecting the Red Sea to the Indian Ocean. Through Adulis, another ancient Eritrean port, the Ethopians sent goods ranging from gold and ivory to exotic animals and slaves to India, Arabia, down the east coast of Africa, and via Egypt to the Middle East and Rome.

However, the prosperity of Aksum did not last. In 541–542, a virulent outbreak of bubonic plague swept across the Mediterranean, before reaching the Horn of Africa with devastating consequences. By the middle of the sixth century economic decline was apparent. Grand buildings were falling into disrepair and the great quarries that serviced the city were abandoned.[12] Aksumite troops, particularly slaves, who had fought in Arabia decided to remain there, refusing to return. The Ethiopian king attempted to subdue them, but the troops he sent also defected to join the former slaves.[13] Their descendants formed an identifiable community that exists in Arabia, known as the Akhdam, or colloquially the '*Mukhallafat Abraha*' ('Abraha's leftovers'). They were forced into conditions of serfdom and forbidden from engaging in social rituals with Arab families, including eating and intermarriage. The Akhdam were required to live in modest buildings, or properties enclosed by a fence, and relegated to the most menial jobs like garbage collection.[14]

Over time, Ethiopia's hold over Arabia was lost. Its control of the Horn in general was eroded and took many hundreds of years to re-establish. By the reign of Emperor Lalibela (r. c. 1181–1221), Ethiopia had recovered and renewed its trade links with both Egypt and Aden, although it no longer held parts of Yemen. The commerce in slaves was controlled by Muslims along the coast of the Horn, with Arabs taking most of the profits. Slaves were taken by dhow up the Red Sea to satisfy the Egyptian demand for Ethiopians, who were used as soldiers. As Harold Marcus explains: 'In return, Cairene and

Alexandrian merchants shipped textiles and finished goods to the port of Mitsawa [in present-day Eritrea], by then Ethiopia's most important emporium.'[15] Over the succeeding centuries, the trade fluctuated with the fortunes of Ethiopia's emperors.

During the fourteenth century, imperial rule was on the rise, and with it the nation's economy. Ivory and slaves were being captured and transported from southern and central Ethiopia to the coast, to be exported to the Middle East. A Yemeni scholar, Muhammad Jazim, published a collection of rare administrative documents from late-thirteenth-century Yemen that survived in a private library in Sana'a.[16] They provided an insight into the slave trade from Ethiopia to Yemen, including prices and taxes paid for different categories of slaves. Slaves were listed as 'products' and arranged by prices and quality.

> The good eunuch is expensive up to a hundred *wiqīya* [a common weight measure] in coins, and that is precious. … The eunuch of medium quality is for 50 or 60 *wiqīya*. The regular eunuch is for 40 *wiqīya*. The uncastrated slaves: the good slave is the pure Ethiopian slave boy … as long as he is flawless. His price in Ethiopia is 20 *wiqīya*, and the one of medium quality 15 or 14, and the one of lesser quality 12, 11 or 10. As for female slaves: the good slave girl of excellent quality is for 20 *wiqīya*, and of medium quality for 15 or 16, and of lesser quality for 12 or 10.[17]

Archaeological discoveries on the Dahlak islands in the Red Sea point to this desolate archipelago as having been an important staging post for slaves between Ethiopia and the Arab world, with an estimated 3,000 to 4,000 slaves having been held here each year.[18] Between the eleventh and the thirteenth centuries, the route was controlled by the self-styled sultans of the Dahlak archipelago.[19]

The trade from Ethiopia followed three distinct routes to the ports of Massawa (Mitsawa), Zeila, or Berbera in present-day Somaliland.[20] One went from Sudan to Massawa along a route north of Lake Tana. The second linked the south with Shoa, the historic kingdom of the Ethiopian highlands centred on present-day Addis Ababa, and then continued to the two Red Sea ports. The last brought the human and other cargoes from the southern provinces through Shoa to the ocean. Over time these routes were adapted and modified. By the seventeenth century, a caravan network had developed linking the Sudanese Kingdom of Fazughli with the Ethiopian Empire. Sudanese slaves and gold were paid for with Ethiopian coffee.[21]

Thus far enslavement has been portrayed as a trade controlled by Ethiopian rulers, but this was not the only way in which men and women were taken into servitude. In 1529, Ahmad ibn Ibrahim al-Ghazi (commonly known as Ahmad 'Gragn' or 'left-handed') invaded Ethiopia from Harar with an army mostly consisting of Somalis. He regarded this as a jihad against a Christian state by his Islamic warriors. Many were nomads, but they were armed with flintlock rifles, the first time Ethiopian troops had faced such weaponry. At the battle of Shimbra Kure the Ethiopian forces were defeated, opening the way for Imam Ahmad to expand his hold over Ethiopian territory. During some of his campaigns Ahmad Gragn is said to have taken large numbers of slaves, and such quantities of other loot that they became an encumbrance, slowing down his jihad. At the battle of Miyazya in 1531, so much booty was seized that Ahmad Gragn turned on his supporters, asking why they had taken it.[22] When they replied that they wanted to return home with their treasures he told them: 'Throw away your possessions. None of you may travel except with his mule, and with whatever slaves he had before ... If any of you disobeys me, I will cut off his head.'[23]

Ahmad Gragn was finally routed at the battle of Wayna Daga in 1543 when the Ethiopians, strengthened by Portuguese troops, defeated the Muslim jihadists. The memory of the invasion and the atrocities that were committed lives on, with Ethiopian children being told of the destruction wrought by Ahmad Gragn on churches, towns and monasteries down the centuries. His jihad is also remembered for the many thousands of slaves—Christians and Muslims—that he took captive.[24] They were exported to a range of destinations in Egypt and Arabia, as well as Persia and India.

Slave exports rose rapidly in the sixteenth century and kept rising throughout the seventeenth and eighteenth. A Portuguese Jesuit, Antonio Fernandez, who visited the region at the end of the sixteenth century, described the enslavement of men and women in the Kingdom of Janjero, which was independent until 1894 when it was conquered by Menelik II. The priest explained how some of the kingdom's slaves were traded for clothes and silk from India, China or the Arabian Peninsula, as well as being diplomatic gifts to other states in Ethiopia and abroad:

> Whenever the King wants to buy some foreign cloth from the merchants and they agree that 3 or 10 or 30 slaves shall be given for it, all he does is to give orders to his servants who go into the houses and take the sons and daughters of the people living in the country and deliver them to the merchants. He does the same when he wants to make a present of one or more slaves, male or female, to one of the Emperor's servants, or another King, or a neighbouring prince; he orders that the handsomest sons or daughters of any of his subjects should be taken, so long as they do not belong to a family which he had said was exempt, and he delivers them as prisoners to anyone he pleases.[25]

A Scottish traveller, James Bruce, who visited Ethiopia in 1770 described the brisk slave caravans embarking from Massawa to Arabia and India, with Ethiopian women in particular demand in Cairo, Istanbul and India.[26] By the nineteenth century, Ethiopia had recovered from one of its periodic declines and its trade was growing. Slaves were very much part of the economy and Harold Marcus provides a graphic description of their role in society.

> Middle Easterners long had bought Ethiopian slaves for their armies, their fields, their homes, and their beds. The *habasha* slaves, as they were generically classified, were not usually from Abyssinia but from southern and western Ethiopia, whose societies could not protect themselves from the raiders' firearms. Religious law did not permit Christians to participate in the trade, but they could buy, own, and use slaves; and rulers such as Sahle Sellassie could tax transactions as the slaves were marketed or as the traffic passed through Shewa and its dependencies. Since Christians could not be involved, Muslims dominated the slave trade, often going farther and farther afield to find supplies.
>
> Slaves were often provided by Oromo and Sidamno rulers who raided their neighbours or who enslaved their own people for even minor crimes. The merchant villages adjacent to the major markets of southwestern Ethiopia were invariably full of slaves, which the upper classes exchanged for the imported goods they

coveted. The slaves were walked to the large distribution markets, such as Basso in Gojam, where they were sold on site. In some cases, Christian rulers established an isolated slave market some distance away from a larger, general commercial center. [27]

Slave caravans departed from the southern regions of Ethiopia three times a year (depending on the harvest), and the king and his high officials oversaw their passage through Shewa to the sea, increasing his revenues from taxes and duties, as well as gifts from the merchants. Many of the slaves were women, who had been sold to be used in harems. 'After many generations of intermarriage with Ethiopian slave-girls, a large segment of the population of Hijaz, Yemen, Southern Arabia and the Persian Gulf possessed Ethiopian blood, and Ethiopian customs somewhat influenced the mannerisms of these areas.' [28] In the seventeenth century, Ethiopian rulers sent missions as far as Persia and Constantinople to act as agents to enhance the trade. Some were former slaves, and Ethiopians were to be found across the Middle East, some rising in government service, theological studies and trade.

10

ETHIOPIA IN THE MODERN ERA

The nineteenth century saw two of the nation's most powerful emperors ascend the throne: Yohannes IV (r. 1871–1889) and Menelik II (r. 1889–1913). Yohannes, from the northern region of Tigray, and Menelik, from the central highlands of Shewa, managed to end the chaotic era of the princes, during which rivals engaged in bitter contests for power, reducing the strength of the central state. Yohannes and Menelik also saw off Islamic challenges from the Ottomans and Sudan's Mahdi, while Menelik defeated the Italian invasion at the famous battle of Adwa (1 March 1896). Their reigns were as complex as the challenges they faced. The details are beyond the scope of this book, but the outcome is not. Ethiopia went from being a mainly Christian highland kingdom to an immensely enlarged multi-ethnic, religiously diverse state in which lived in excess of eighty ethnic groups. Under Menelik the capital was moved to Addis Ababa, and he ruled over a mighty kingdom whose extension coincided with the European 'scramble for Africa' of the 1880s. Mebratu Kelecha summed up the resulting expansion: 'By the end of his reign, Ethiopia's territory had tripled and grown to include the Oromo territories, parts of modern-day Somalia, and various southern territories, including the regions of Sidama, Wolayta, Kaffa, and Gedeo.'[1]

While Yohannes was on the imperial throne, Menelik was already powerful. He was the king of Shewa and used his power to extend his influence southwards, forcing local elites—including the ruler of the Gibe region of Jima—to submit in return for autonomy.[2] Jima made extensive use of slaves on large farms taken from the traditional cultivators. The rulers who accepted Menelik's sovereignty were required to pay an annual toll, including slaves. Menelik, wary of his relationship with Yohannes, bought weapons from the French enclave of Obok (present-day Djibouti) to supplement the armaments he had previously been sent by the Italians to win his favour.[3] He used slaves—as well as gold, ivory, musk and coffee—to obtain the weapons that his forces required before his ascension to the throne in 1889. During this period, Ethiopia was under pressure from European powers, including Britain, to end enslavement, but with limited results.

However, expansion and slavery went hand in hand.[4] The western areas of Benishangul and Gumuz, bordering on Sudan, had been forced to pay tributes in slaves, ivory and gold down the centuries, with the enslavement of the Gumuz dating from the thirteenth century.[5] Like many ethnic groups along the Sudanese border, they were referred to by derogatory terms: *Shankilla* in Ethiopia and *Abdi* in Sudan, both meaning slave.[6] Under Menelik these practices continued, but Ethiopia's western border regions were subject to enslavement not just from Addis Ababa, but also from Sudan. Forts and residences of slave traders, constructed in the mid-nineteenth century, have been discovered in the Benishangul region of north-western Ethiopia, suggesting that slaves were captured and transported to Sudan in the nineteenth century.[7]

Menelik demanded slaves as labour in his imperial palace and on his farms. Gold, ivory, coffee, hides and musk as well as slaves provided the foreign exchange the emperor required to purchase the modern weapons that he used to defeat the Italians at the battle of Adwa in 1896.[8] To obtain growing numbers of slaves he intensified slave raiding. Sheikh Abd al-Rahman Khojele, the ruler of the town of Asosa (capital of Benishangul), raided the Mao people to the west of the urban area. In subsequent fighting many Mao (and others) were taken captive, leading large numbers to flee into Sudan for protection by the British, who had taken control of the country.[9] Sheikh Abd al-Rahman Khojele was not the only local leader to engage in these activities, with the Amhara-Agaw slave raiding into the Gumuz country in the period 1900–1935. Most rich and notable families in Ethiopia owned slaves. By contrast, the British created a settlement for liberated slaves in Sudan at Wadi Halfa. The Slavery Repression Department, complete with 110 staff and a network of posts along the Ethiopian border, worked to free the enslaved populations.[10]

Yet Menelik's achievements were extraordinary. Not only did he see off the Italian invasion; he also reformed his nation, building schools and roads, and linking Ethiopia to the sea via a railway to Djibouti. However, in one area he failed to make real progress. Despite international pressure, slavery remained a feature of Ethiopian society. Menelik's predecessors, Tewodros II and Yohannes IV, had outlawed slave trading, and Menelik himself closed several slave markets, but the practice was not eradicated. In 1913, having suffered from repeated strokes and declining health, he died. Menelik was to be followed by his nominated successor, Lij Iyasu. However, Iyasu was too young to be crowned, so the empire was ruled by a regent. The young prince angered many traditionalists by cavorting in night spots in Addis Ababa and getting too close to the Muslim population, arousing concerns among the clergy and the Ethiopian nobility. Then, fatally, he was tempted to take Ethiopia into the First World War on the German side.[11] The nobles and the church hierarchy, egged on by the French, British and Italians, overthrew Lij Iyasu. Ras Tafari was appointed crown prince, before being crowned Emperor Haile Selassie in 1930.

Haile Selassie made efforts to halt the enslavement of his people, without eradicating it. As early as 1918 he had issued an edict banning the slave trade as a step towards its ultimate abolition.[12] However, the law remained a dead letter.[13] Resistance from the Orthodox Church, which saw slavery as 'an integral aspect of Ethiopian life', meant that the emperor was reluctant to push through a rapid programme to end enslavement.[14] A joint British and Ethiopian commission, sent to delimit where Ethiopia's borders lay, reported back to London that vast areas of the country remained desolate because of slave raiding, with 'overgrown native fields, burnt houses and ruined shrines,' with convoys of slaves being marched openly along roads.[15] The British Foreign Office was loath to publish the reports, since they wished to avoid coming under pressure from the influential Anti-Slavery Society—and public opinion—to try to halt the slave raids. Haile Selassie attempted to persuade southern landlords of the advantages of turning slaves into tenants to increase agricultural production. He issued yet another edict in 1923, once again outlawing the slave trade.[16] While the emperor legislated and spoke out against the practice, his own family continued to benefit from it. Some 600 slaves were sent to Haile Selassie's wife as late as 1927.[17] This was a question the emperor found exceptionally difficult to tackle, and slavery continued along the Kenyan and Sudanese borders even after his coronation in November 1930.[18] An American, Boake Carter, who travelled across Ethiopia in this period provided a colourful description of a slave raid:

> The [cattle] herders are often women. The slave hunter waits, tense and muscle-bounded. When the herd passes, he leaps, a panther-like leap of great power. A cloth descends over the luckless girl's head. In a trice powerful arms encircle her. Off to the thicket she is carried ... And the life of slavery for that girl has begun![19]

The emperor was forced to admit in his autobiography that: 'this slavey problem is recognized in the hearts of men as something that is not preordained by nature in terms of master and slave but had yet remained firmly established by custom.'[20] As late as 1935, there were reports that enslavement was still rife in areas like Benishangul.[21]

With the Italians threatening to invade his country once again, Haile Selassie finally attempted to take firm measures to halt the trade in slaves, which was being investigated by the League of Nations. The emperor took the worst-affected areas under direct rule, but it was a case of too little too late. 'While these moves were successful in staving off a League of Nations mandate, they failed to prevent the Italian military invasion of Ethiopia, which accomplished what Emperor Haile Selassie I and his predecessors had failed to accomplish: the end of slavery and the slave trade in Ethiopia.'[22] Even as war with Italy loomed, slaves were photographed carrying funds raised by the Ethiopian aristocracy for the military to the imperial palace.[23]

In May 1936, Haile Selassie fled from the country in the face of Italian aggression. The new rulers exploited the emperor's apparent tolerance for slavery. Enslavement proved to be an excellent propaganda tool for Mussolini in his attempts to legitimise his invasion of Ethiopia with the international community. The Italians made much of their 'civilising' mission. They forcefully eradicated the practice, executing some of the most notorious slavers.[24] The Italian authorities issued proclamations 'declaring that all slaves were free, and reported that they had established villages for freed slaves and were employing those who wished to leave their masters.'[25] Postcards showing Italian troops cutting the shackles of grateful slaves were printed to underline the point. Historians estimate that there were between 300,000 and 500,000 slaves in Ethiopia in 1935, with the Italians claiming to have freed 400,000 in one province alone.[26] The Italian claim was propaganda, part of its war effort, but it underlined the scale of the problem.[27]

The experience of slavery

Richard Pankhurst published a detailed study of how slaves fared after being taken into captivity.[28] Several European observers of men and women in captivity remarked on how well they appeared to be dealing with and accepting their condition. A British traveller, C. T. Beke, describing the slave route from the Ethiopian highlands to the port of Massawa in 1844, observed:

> The slaves go along without the least restraint, singing and chatting, and apparently perfectly happy. They are generally treated with attention, stopping frequently on the road to rest and feed. They are mostly well dressed … The girls, almost without exception, have necklaces of beads. In fact, it is not to [sic] the interest of the owners to treat them otherwise than well; for as more than one merchant has said to me at Yejubbi, when asking for medicine for them, 'they are our property (kabt, literally cattle), and we cannot afford to lose them.'[29]

The British envoy to Shoa, Captain W. C. Harris, wrote in 1844 about a slave caravan bound for the coast at the Gulf of Aden:

> Although the majority of the slaves … were of tender years, and many of them extremely pretty, they did not excite that interest which might have been anticipated. Children were accustomed to such harsh treatment in their own country, they had very readily adapted themselves to the will of their new masters, whose obvious interest it was to keep them fat and in good spirits. With few exceptions, all were merry and light-hearted.[30]

A very different perspective was provided by the testimonies from the enslaved themselves. This was the experience of a young Oromo, called Aga. 'I left my country with many Gallas [slaves]. Many of us left the country, and we were very frightened ... Whenever we ate, our stomach burnt with fire, for we were full of longing we could not sit and we could not sleep. The sand burnt our feet.'[31] Another Oromo, Akafede Dallee, who was also taken captive, said: 'There are many Gallas who can do nothing but grieve at the separation from their fathers and mothers.' He urged Aga to: 'Bear courageously the fact you may not see your father and mother again.'[32]

An Oromo slave called Hika, captured in the 1860s, took the name Onesimus, and was sent to Sweden by Protestant missionaries, where he was subsequently ordained a priest. He eloquently summed up the plight of the slaves in his reminiscences.

> I could hardly eat or drink because of my sorrow, particularly when I thought about my mother ... I had been in the hands of eight different owners. Particularly in the beginning I was very bitter as I longed very much for my mother. I cried so much that I had sores under my eyes, and when I tried to brush away my tears they burnt like fire.[33]

The experience of slavery remains deeply ingrained. The Gumuz suffered slavery until the second half of the twentieth century, well into the reign of Emperor Haile Selassie and possibly even longer.[34] The Amhara were not alone in this practice. John Young recalls Gumuz explaining to him that 'Oromos were taking slaves until 1993 and that students had to carry weapons to school to defend themselves', to prevent the children from being captured and enslaved.[35] Gumuz elders continue to relate the deprivation they suffered well beyond this, describing the confiscation of their property, their eviction from their lands and their enslavement. They are by no means the only ethnic group with these memories. Ethiopians alive today recall the slaves they knew in their childhoods.[36] Parents would ask for a fair-skinned Oromo slave and a darker-skinned slave from the border region with Sudan when they were asked for their daughter's hand in marriage. Slaves were regularly beaten in public to show a master's ability to rule. Abductions and shackling were normal, and if babies cried when their mothers were seized, they were killed.

On 5 November 2021, during the war launched by Ethiopia and Eritrea against Tigray, an alliance was formed between the Tigray People's Liberation Front and eight other ethnic groups.[37] In a live feed from the National Press Club in Washington, where the alliance was signed, the Oromo representative complained bitterly: 'I have been treated like a slave all of my life.'[38] The wounds of enslavement in Ethiopia run deep and have not been expunged.

11

THE SOKOTO CALIPHATE

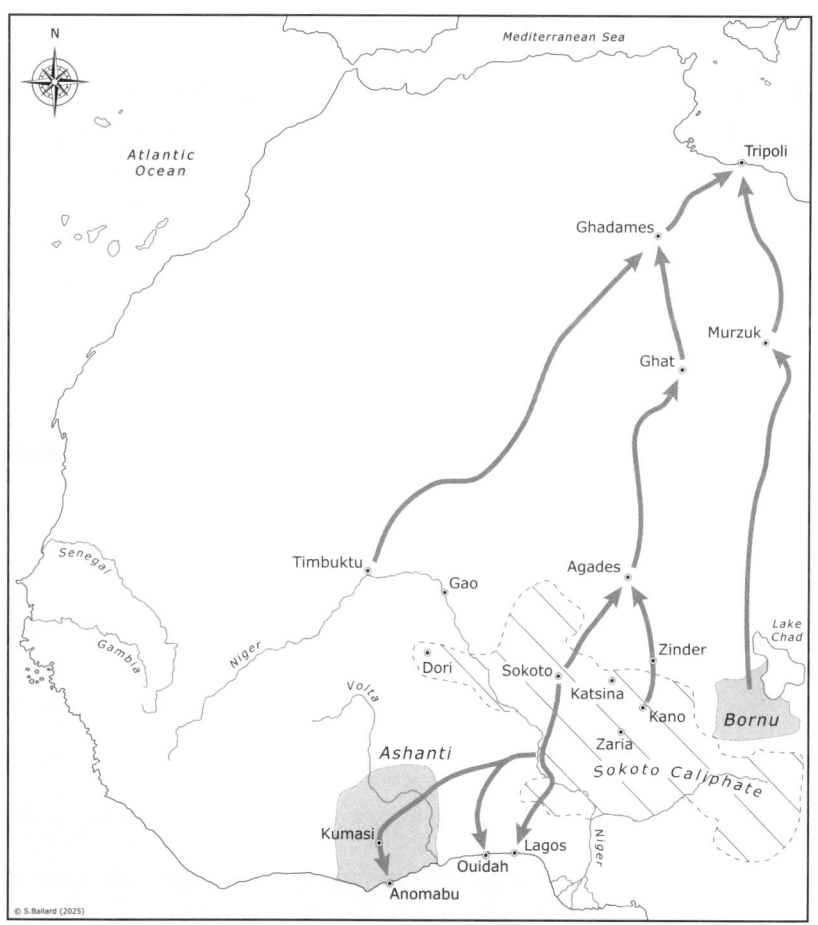

Map 4: Sokoto Caliphate slave routes

The map shows the extent of Sokoto, Borno and Ashanti control. The map is adapted from a variety of sources.

Stretching across northern Nigeria and Niger, the Sokoto Caliphate was a state based on enslavement.[1] In the middle of the nineteenth century, it extended more than 1,500 kilometres, from the mountains of Mandara, in present-day Cameroon, to the city of Dori, in what is now Burkina Faso. The caliphate was one of several slave empires that were created by West African jihads in the eighteenth and nineteenth centuries.[2] The Sokoto Empire lasted for a century and was only finally extinguished when Britain conquered it in 1903, and proceeded to free its slaves. Outside of Nigeria, the Caliphate is not generally recognised or understood, although regional domination and enslavement were at the heart of its existence.

> As the history of the Sokoto Caliphate demonstrates, slavery was a byproduct of jihad and an ideology of subordination that subsequently was subjected to reform and ultimately suppression under European colonialism. Slavery was a long-established institution in the Central Sudan before the establishment of the Sokoto Caliphate after 1804. Under the Caliphate, however, slavery became even more prevalent, to the extent that it can been argued that slavery was the backbone of this economy and society … The Sokoto Caliphate was the largest independent state in sub-Saharan Africa in the nineteenth century, comprising some thirty emirates, in addition to the twin capital districts of Sokoto and Gwandu … It is even possible that there were as many slaves in the Sokoto Caliphate in the middle of the nineteenth century as in the United States at the outbreak of the Civil War in 1860, when there were 4 million slaves in the United States. Certainly, the Caliphate was one of the largest slave societies in modern history, with probably more than there were in Brazil or in all the colonies of the Caribbean at the time, either in the eighteenth or nineteenth centuries, certainly in excess of 2 million and perhaps more than 4.5 million.[3]

If the Sokoto Caliphate's reliance on plantation slavery is indeed comparable in scale to the enslavement in the United States at the time of their civil war, it is certainly far less widely discussed or acknowledged. Some books by respected academics which provide excellent summaries of the slave trade in general make no mention of the Sokoto Caliphate.[4]

The Fulani and the rise of Usman dan Fodio

The origins of the Fulani are unclear. Writing in the 1960s, Hugh Johnston described the Fulani as 'one of Africa's greatest enigmas.'[5] He concluded that: 'The most widely accepted theory is that the Fulani came originally from the Middle East or North Africa and gradually worked their way round the bulge of the continent to the region of Senegambia.'[6] This is supported by work suggesting that they arrived in the area of Niger and the Lake Chad basin from Senegal and Mali in the 1460s.[7] The Fulani regard themselves as a distinct people, with their own language (Fulfulde). Their genetic make-up indicates that they have links with North Africa and Europe,[8] or else with East African peoples like the Somalis and the Beja.[9] Either way, they saw themselves as distinct from the local people they encountered, particularly if they did not embrace the Islamic faith. Across the Sahel the Fulani developed a tradition of spreading religion by the sword in the pre-colonial era. This included the establishment of religious rule in Fouta Djallon, Central Guinea, in 1725, followed by another in Futa Toro along the Senegal river in 1776.[10]

By the eighteenth century, the Fulani were well established in what is sometimes described as 'Hausaland'—that portion of northern Nigeria, Niger and neighbouring states between the confluence of the Niger and Benue rivers.[11] Their arrival brought considerable prosperity, facilitating trade across the Sahara. The mainly pastoral Fulani bought and sold goods with the mainly sedentary Hausa, exchanging dairy products for grain and other goods. At the same time, there was only limited intermarriage between the two groups. The Fulani had little respect for their neighbours, some of whom had not embraced Islam. An indication of how the Fulani regarded non-Muslims and pagans can be found in the writings of a German explorer, Ulrich Seetzen. In 1808, he wrote that when he visited the town of Ader, between Sokoto and Agadez, he found the Fulani on good terms with the Tuareg. However, he said that those whom the Fulani regarded as 'blacks' and who did not follow Islam were held in very low regard. The 'blacks' were said to 'adore fetishes, consume fermented drinks, eat "everything"—including the flesh of "dogs, wolves, foxes and snakes."'[12]

It is against this background that Usman dan Fodio rose from being a Fulani scholar and preacher to become a respected religious leader. He emerged from a devout Islamic family who launched the jihad that founded the Sokoto Caliphate in 1804. The Sokoto jihad was spearheaded by men who wanted a return to a pure form of Islam based on their understanding of seventh-century Arabian cultural and religious practices.[13] Usman dan Fodio insisted that the enslavement of freeborn Muslims was forbidden. Indeed, to escape slavery, many rallied to his cause.[14] At the same time, Usman took it upon himself to decide who was a true Muslim and who was not. He had little respect for his neighbours, considering that there was no true Islam in 'Bilad al-Sudan'—the land of the blacks.[15] Usman did not deny that some black Africans considered themselves Muslim, but declared that 'the status of a land is that of its ruler,' and that they were therefore legitimate targets to attack.[16] Indeed, he went further, arguing that there was no part of the land of the blacks that was part of the land of Islam: 'I have read in the writings of a certain scholar [a statement] which reports that there are absolutely no lands of Islam in the lands of the blacks.'[17] Black Africans could therefore be legitimately enslaved. The jihadists also believed that they had an absolute right to impose their religious beliefs on anyone—Fulani or Hausa—who followed traditional, ancestral beliefs. Usman ruled that the enslavement of non-Muslims was both right and proper.[18]

This was one factor in the rise of the Caliphate. The other factors were social—particularly the corruption and nepotism practiced by traditional rulers of Hausaland.

> [Usman dan Fodio] criticised the traditional dynasties for claiming the right to rule by heredity and force rather than through consultation. They used arbitrary punishments rather than holding trials under the strict rules of procedure and evidence demanded by Islamic law. They imposed unauthorized taxes, such as *kudin gari* and *kudin salla*, a tax on Islamic festival days. They took women without permission and kept up to a thousand wives. They ignored the needs of the poor and unfortunate in society while they lived luxuriously and demanded presents known as *gaisuwa*, or 'greetings.' Even those who conveyed subjects before the ruler demanded bribes for so doing. Their slaves abused anyone who

ventured near royal plantations, while their animals grazed at will on other people's farms. Muslims were drafted into their armies to support states that Usman Dan Fodio declared were non-Muslim. Their judges ruled in favour of those who could offer the largest bribes. They punished anyone who disrespected them, and they bestowed grandiose titles which have no basis in the strict and simple administration preferred by Islam.[19]

Travellers and merchants were particularly badly affected by the predatory behaviour of the traditional rulers, with their animals seized, taxes extracted and goods taken as random. One of Usman's first demands of Sultan Bawa of Gobir was to lighten the taxes on his people and only to levy taxes that were approved by Islam.[20]

Usman dan Fodio had been preaching in the city of Gobir, with the approval of the city's Hausa leadership. However, when Yunfa, a former student of dan Fodio, became the sultan of Gobir, he restricted Usman's activities, eventually forcing him into exile. Many of his followers went to join Usman, who began to gather supporters from other regions. Believing he was threatened by his former teacher, in February 1804, Sultan Yunfa declared war on Usman, who was left with little choice but to respond. Usman was urged on by his third son, Muhammad Bello. Bello had become impatient with his father and wrote to him in 1804 threatening to wage war against Yunfa himself if Usman did not launch his jihad.[21] His father promptly obliged.

Elected 'Commander of the Faithful' by his followers, Usman dan Fodio initiated his jihad. In a series of fierce battles, he succeeded in taking Gobir in 1808 and establishing the Caliphate the following year.[22] This did not end his wars, and a series of other Hausa states, including Katsina, Kano, Zazzau, Adamawa and Bauchi, fell to the jihad. Hausa chiefs were driven out and supplanted by Fulani emirs.[23] It was Bello who chose the village of Sokoto as the capital of the Caliphate, laying it out on high ground and surrounding it with a wall.[24] Usman dan Fodio decided it was time to withdraw from public life, concentrating on spiritual and religious matters, while leaving the running of the state to others. Bello went on to play a central role in the Caliphate, formally succeeding his father in 1817 and ruling Sokoto until his death in 1837.

Sokoto grew to become an impressive city, surrounded by a series of walled fortresses, known as 'ribats' or 'rabats'. They were designed to guard its frontiers but also to encompass markets, administrative buildings, schools and mosques. The *ribats* that were developed under Bello were part of a programme to settle previously pastoral Fulani communities. 'Bello ... intended the ribats he established to serve as military settlements, as centres of craft production, as drivers of the caliphate economy, as locations to settle and pacify the Fulani people in order to foster their incorporation into Hausa society, and as centres of Islamization.'[25]

Ribats were central to the economic and political life of the Caliphate, encouraging the establishment of plantation agriculture and the trade that accompanied this, as well as fostering Sokoto's expansion.[26] The Caliphate came to encompass thirty-three emirates that owed their allegiance to the sultan of Sokoto, although they exercised considerable autonomy and independence from the centre. This decentralised administration had advantages, but it also meant that over the years there was constant competition and conflict between the emirates. The Caliphate's wars against their neighbours shaped the region's history.

12

PLANTATIONS AND SLAVERY

The plantations were the foundation of Sokoto's economic life and its wealth. The Caliphate distributed land holdings to individuals and families, who in turn developed their estates to grow a wide variety of crops.[1] The largest holdings went to the Fulani elite. They cultivated cotton, indigo, millet and sorghum, as well as irrigated crops such as rice, tobacco, onions, sugar cane and wheat. Their plantations produced kola and shea nuts. To care for and harvest these, Sokoto relied on vast numbers of slaves. They were essential for every aspect of the Caliphate's economic life, as well as serving in domestic households as servants or concubines. 'Slavery was a long-established institution in the Central Sudan before the establishment of the Sokoto Caliphate after 1804. Under the Caliphate, however, slavery became even more prevalent, to the extent that it can be argued that slavery was the backbone of this economy and society.'[2]

Slaves were also used across the economy, including in the production and dyeing of cloth, leather and iron work and soap production.[3] The scale of the industry was substantial. At the end of the nineteenth century in the Kano area alone there were some 50,000 dyers working in 15,000 dye-pits.[4] The slaves were organised into gangs, overseen by slave masters, and lived in compounds away from their owners. Merchants invested in their slaves and their cost was low since there was a plentiful supply of defeated opponents.

> Caliphate military campaigns fed a steady stream of war captives into the economy, and this ready supply of slaves accounts for the relative stability of slave prices during the whole [nineteenth] century, with real prices perhaps even declining in the last third. The

aristocracy retained many of these captives, but a well-developed commercial sector also transferred them to central markets.[5]

Cowry shells were a useful store of value but slaves were the preferred currency, easily tradeable for choice goods, including horses, weapons and expensive cloth. They were accepted by local and foreign merchants, including Arabs and Tuareg, and oiled their exchanges.[6] The trade in slaves allowed Sokoto to import goods from Europe and North Africa. Cottons and calico came from Lancashire, beads from Venice, needles, mirrors and paper from Nuremberg, sword-blades from Solingen, silk from Lyon and Trieste and red fezzes from Leghorn.[7]

The conditions of enslavement appear redolent of those of the American South, but Paul Lovejoy argues that this comparison is misleading. He suggests that the market for slaves was weaker in Africa, that race was not a significant issue, that slaves were used in a narrower range of functions and that emancipation was much more difficult in the United States.[8] The final point is certainly true: slaves who were born into an African slave community could be given favourable treatment. They might be given land to work on by their masters and could then pay for their freedom.[9] However, if they missed a payment, they forfeited the sums they had already paid. At times their masters gave the slaves their freedom as an act of Islamic piety, although they frequently remained dependants of their masters. Concubines who gave birth to the child of a freeman were themselves freed, with the birth of the child said to have 'broken the shackles' of slavery.[10] Relatives would sometimes venture into military camps to trace their newly captured relatives and might— if fortunate—be able to pay for their freedom. Although Usman dan Fodio had opposed ransoming captives, he had approved of paying ransoms for his own soldiers if taken by the enemy. Over time the system became embedded, and ransoms were paid in instalments for the return of high-profile captives.[11]

Foreign visitors seldom witnessed slaves being overworked and saw young women working on farms who were dressed in neat white aprons, decorated with strings of glass beads.[12]

> [T]he overall principles of treating slaves fairly, holding them to be members of the family, and promising manumission as

an appropriate reward for good work and behaviour had real advantages for slave-owners. For instance, allowing favored slaves to marry and form families helped increase the master's slave population, while also providing the master with a means of disciplining slaves, since a slave's dependent could be sold if that slave proved troublesome.[13]

Slaves could also rise to positions of power. For example, in 1819, a slave known as Barka became an influential, titled official in Kano.[14] Over thirty years he served two emirs, advising them on warfare, statecraft and politics. He had several wives and children and enjoyed expensive robes, owned many horses and oversaw tax collection.

Others painted a very different picture: of slaves who were harshly treated, poorly fed and poorly clothed. If they misbehaved, they could be savagely beaten with a whip made from hippopotamus hide and shackled to prevent their escape.[15] Men as well as women were sometimes tied to trees to receive the beatings. Slave owners could also banish slaves who misbehaved to state-operated prisons for punishment or reform. On their arrival their offence and punishment would be explained by the master.

> Thereafter, the erring slave was admitted into the facility through a succession of two doors, being severely beaten in the process. The conditions at Gidan Ma'ajin Watari were terrible, as an early colonial record indicated. 'A small doorway 2ft. 6 in. by 18 in. gives access into it; the interior is divided by a thick mud wall (with a smaller hole in it) into two compartments, each 17 ft. by 7 ft. and 11 ft. high. This was pierced with holes at its base, through which the legs of those sentenced to death were thrust up to the thigh, and they were left to be trodden on by the mass of other prisoners until they died of thirst and starvation. The place is entirely airtight and unventilated, except for one small doorway or rather hole through which you creep. The total space inside is 2,618 cu. ft., and at the time we took Kano (1903) 135 human beings were confined here each night, being let out to cook their food, etc., in a small adjoining area. Recently as many as 200 had been interned at one time. As the superficial ground area was only 238 square feet, there was not, of course, even standing room. Victims were crushed to death every night—their corpses were hauled out each morning.'[16]

Torture by prison guards or fellow inmates was routine. It was ultimately the master who decided the length of a slave's imprisonment.

To satisfy Sokoto's many needs, the Caliphate required 10,000 additional slaves a year, and sometimes more.[17] Both Usman and his son Bello insisted that no freeborn Muslim should be enslaved, yet the practice continued despite their edicts. The leader of Borno, with whom Sokoto was at war, was scornful of their declarations, accusing the Caliphate's leadership of hypocrisy for continuing to enslave Muslims. 'Tell us therefore why you are fighting us and enslaving our free people,' Shehu Muhammad al-Kanemi demanded of Bello.[18]

Sokoto attacked its neighbouring societies, which fell into two categories. One consisted of smaller, stateless tribes who were largely pagan. They were viewed as idolatrous heathens, whom the Caliphate considered could be enslaved with impunity.[19] Sokoto's magnificent cavalry, clad in armour, proved to be an irresistible force. They swept southwards, overwhelming their enemies. 'The horsemen invaded the forest region to capture people who could not effectively resist—often they belonged to stateless societies.'[20]

The second category were states hostile to Sokoto, against whom war was waged. These included Abuja, Borno, Ibadan, Maradi, Tessawa and Zinder, and these conflicts required far larger mobilisations. They too produced slaves, since if they were vanquished, even if they were Muslim, it was argued that they had not been good practitioners of the faith.[21] Those taken captive in conflict were considered part of the booty of war and were the main payment for the Caliphate's troops.[22] States in the southeast of the Caliphate produced the largest number of slaves, with many coming from Bauchi and Adamawa.[23] Mohammed Bashir Salau argues that after the initial phase of the jihad, most slaves that Sokoto obtained were non-Hausas and non-Muslims who were captured primarily from within the Caliphate and its bordering regions.[24] These included the Mbum, Gbaya and Duru. Adamawa raided communities up to 200 or even 500 kilometres from the emirate's capital to capture the men and women it required.[25]

13

SLAVE TRADING AND THE END OF THE CALIPHATE

Slaves taken by Sokoto were often traded internally, but many were exported. Some were taken on the caravan routes that had criss-crossed the Sahara for centuries, as discussed in Chapter 1. The Trans-Saharan trade used routes developed over the centuries. Abd al-Rahman Aga, an ambassador to the Nordic states from Tripoli, explained in 1772 how this operated.

> The prisoners of war are slaves of the victors and sold as merchandise to the whites [meaning Arabs] ... Unfortunately, however, the whites always demanded more black slaves, especially children; they came to their borders, even travelled to the princes in the middle of Africa, to incite them to wage war against their brothers ... For many centuries now, a very large number of slaves have been exported annually from Afnu/Hausa and Bernu/Bornu to the Barbary States and Egypt, perhaps also to the southeast coast of Africa, if not to Guinea.[1]

By the eighteenth century, the first traces of the Hausa language were to be found in the city of Tunis, suggesting that Hausas were being traded across the Sahara to supply slaves as soldiers to the ruler.[2] Some routes led directly northwards from Kano to Tripoli.[3] Others took their human cargo via branch routes to Morocco, Algeria, Tunisia, Tripolitania and Cyrenaica.[4] The majority of the Hausa slaves marched to North Africa were women, while most of the Hausas who were transported across the Atlantic were men.[5]

Other routes led southwards and over time became more important in terms of numbers transported. The jihad had expanded the Sokoto Caliphate as the warriors attacked their neighbours, particularly the ancient Yoruba empire of Oyo, which had dominated what is today central and southern Nigeria since the fourteenth century. The imposition of a strict interpretation of Islam was just one element of the Caliphate's motivation; the other was the enslavement of the conquered. Their capture provided the slaves, who were then distributed among the elite, while also being used as commodities to be traded.

> Some slaves from Benue and the Niger-Benue confluence hinterlands were 'disposed of to the Arabs' (Tripolitanian Arab traders who traveled to the confluence areas as guests of Muslim rulers trading horses, weapons, and other goods of the Mediterranean for slaves, ivory, and other tropical goods); others were 'sold at towns on the banks' of the rivers and 'eventually reach[ed] the sea-side, where they [were] shipped on board Spanish slavers.'[6]

The trade to the coast began soon after Usman dan Fodio's jihad commenced in 1804. His wars produced thousands of slaves every year, many of whom were sold through Yorubaland and by Yoruba merchants into the Atlantic trade.[7] The fate of some of these slaves has been documented. One, named 'Bernard', was a Hausa trader from Gobir who was travelling to a salt market when he was captured. His route took him from Gobir in the far north of the Caliphate, on a journey southward via Yauri, Nupe, Oyo, Ilorin, Ajase Ipo to Ijebu, where he was sold to a Portuguese trader at Ijaye, a lagoon port on the outskirts of what is today Lagos.[8] The march took five gruelling months, with Bernard and the remainder of the slaves allowed to rest for one day a week, and sometimes even less. Others were taken on a more westerly route, which came to be dominated by the Asante. By the middle of the nineteenth century, slaves were taken to the Fante coast in what is today Ghana, where they were sent across the Atlantic via the English castle at Anomabu, or the Dutch fort at Kormantin.

Paul Lovejoy estimated the numbers taken in both directions. He suggested that some 3,000 to 6,000 slaves were also 'sold northwards across the Sahara from 1810 to 1870, representing a northward volume of about 250,000 to 300,000 for the century as a whole.'[9] Between 100,000 and 150,000 were sent south across the Atlantic from the end of the eighteenth century until the middle of the nineteenth. Portuguese traders took the majority to Brazil, and particularly to the region of Bahia, where the Portuguese sugar plantations required large numbers of slaves.

> The origins of Muslim slaves in Bahia [Brazil] can be traced to the interior of the Bight of Benin and the jihad of Shuhu Uthman dan Fodio that established the Sokoto Caliphate. As is well known, the ethnic configuration of the Bahian population changed significantly in the last decades of the eighteenth century and continuing into the nineteenth, as Hausa, Nupe and other Muslims became more common among slaves, and most especially with the arrival of Yoruba-speaking slaves in the nineteenth century.[10]

The importation of slaves into Brazil brought that nation on a collision course with Britain, which was by the middle of the nineteenth century using its navy to try to enforce an end to slavery. In 1850 the Royal Navy seized ships in Brazilian waters, in 1862 Britain instituted a five-day blockade of Rio de Janeiro, and by the following year the two nations were close to war.[11] In the event, the issue was settled by arbitration and the payment of reparations by Brazil for the sinking of a British warship, the *Prince of Wales*.

The Portuguese were not the only Europeans to engage with the Caliphate. Britain was active in what became Nigeria, with commercial interests leading the way. The Scottish explorer Hugh Clapperton reached Sokoto in 1825 and engaged in months of discussions and negotiations with Bello. Clapperton and Bello came to an understanding that the Trans-Atlantic slave trade would be ended. In exchange Sokoto would receive arms, ammunition and other goods.[12] The British government refused to ratify their agreement and commercial interests replaced negotiations. By the mid-nineteenth century, trade in goods had replaced the trade in slaves. The Inland Commercial Company, founded in 1883, sent an expedition to the confluence of the Niger and Benue rivers, opening the way to relations with the Nupe Emirate.[13] Other companies followed, becoming intense rivals until they were unified under the Royal Niger Company, which succeeded in conquering Nupe in 1897. The Company's strength allowed them to resist French and German calls for access to the Niger River, and in 1885 the sultan granted the Company all rights to both banks of the River Benue, in return for an annual payment.[14] The Company negotiated a similar deal to control the Niger River.

These events coincided with the Conference of Berlin of 1884–1885, which unleashed the 'scramble for Africa' between the European powers and intense competition for control of West Africa. Initially the British attempted to allow the commercial interests to resist the French and Germans. However, with Germany taking areas of Cameroon and France taking Dahomey, London decided that the region was too important to be left to a private company. In 1899, the Company's Charter was revoked and a Protectorate of Northern Nigeria established. Colonel Frederick Lugard was instructed to end slavery once and for all.[15]

Lugard had previously been a captain in what was called 'the Slavers War' against Mlozi in Nyasaland a decade earlier.[16] After training local tribesmen, he led an attack on the stockades of slavers in northern Nyasaland on 16 June 1888, during which he was seriously injured. Lugard transferred to West Africa and headed a contingent of the West Africa Frontier Force—formed in 1900 to enforce British interests in its West African colonies of Sierra Leone, the Gambia, Gold Coast (Ghana) and Nigeria. The troops engaged in a series of actions against the Caliphate that concluded with battles at Burmi in May and June 1903. These clashes illustrated what modern military technology could achieve. The West African Frontier Force, of just twenty-one officers and 500 troops, but armed with machine guns and artillery, defeated the caliph's army of 2,000 cavalry and 4,000 infantry.[17] For Sokoto the British victory was terminal. 'When the sun set that day on the smoking ruins of Burmi, with the dead lying thick in the trenches, on the ramparts, and among the houses, the Fulani Empire came to an end.'[18]

Although the Caliphate had fallen, the question of slavery was unresolved. Britain inherited one of the largest concentrations of slaves in the world, at a time when slavery across the British Empire had been illegal for the past seven decades. How to deal with them was to exercise London for years to come. Lugard, appointed high commissioner of the newly created Protectorate of Northern Nigeria, wrote: 'The British flag is now hoisted over the whole of Northern Nigeria … and organised slave-raiding has become a thing of the past in the country where it existed lately in its worst form.'[19] This was certainly what many locals believed.

As the British advanced—even before the fall of the Caliphate— slaves started deserting their masters in droves. In November 1901, two years before the battles of Burmi, a British officer reported that in Agaye and Lapai alone, some 30,000 slaves had crossed the Niger River to flee from their enslavement, and that in the towns, 'Things were ... bad: farms were being deserted by the slaves and such was the state of unrest that cultivation had almost ceased. The Fulani ruling classes were rapidly becoming desperate at the state of the country.'[20] If the Fulani elite were deeply worried, the slaves were rejoicing. When the British captured Kano, slaves gathered at the palace, where the British hoisted the Union Jack. There they gathered and rejoiced, singing:

> A flag-touching dance,
> Is performed by freeborns alone,
> Anybody who touches the flag,
> Becomes free,
> He and his father [master],
> Become equals.[21]

For Lugard and his officers, the situation was far from ideal. They had inherited a state almost entirely reliant on slavery. Suddenly the British government—which had been attempting to suppress slavery for decades—found 2 million slaves on its hands.[22] It has been estimated that as many as 200,000 slaves deserted their masters during the British invasion and colonial consolidation. Lugard's dilemma was acute, since eradicating the final vestiges of slavery was part of their mission.

> The conquest of the Sokoto Caliphate was undertaken as an anti-slavery campaign against a Muslim state in which slavery was essential to its economy and the bedrock of its society. Yet neither the Royal Niger Company nor the Protectorate government wanted to end slavery or encourage any dislocation that might impede the consolidation of colonial rule.[23]

How were Lugard and his colleagues to end enslavement without seeing the economy collapse? Even before the final conquest, this was something that Lugard, as high commissioner, was becoming increasingly concerned about. When he found that slaves were deserting the masters as early as 1897, he wrote that the slaves did so because they simply wanted 'to lead a life of vagrancy in Lokoja, or of comparative idleness in the surrounding country.'[24] Lugard was by no means alone in these views. Others, who became known in British circles as 'the movement', took an even more unsympathetic view, arguing that freeing all slaves would be disastrous. 'I can assure you most positively that if a policy of wholesale liberation of domestic slaves is pursued it will mean the ruin of this Protectorate at no distant date,' wrote Lugard's former private secretary Reginald Popham Lobb.[25] In a speech to the elders of Sokoto on 21 March 1903—just six days after the city had fallen to British troops—the high commissioner laid out his policies towards the community, assuring them that their religion and customs would be respected. He then declared:

> Every person, including slaves, has the right to appeal to the Resident, who will, however, endeavour to uphold the power of the native courts to deal with native cases according to the law and custom of the country. If slaves are ill-treated they will be set free as your Koran orders, otherwise Government does not desire to interfere with existing domestic relations. But slaves set free must be willing to work and not remain idle or become thieves.[26]

Lugard, who was not as conservative, worked hard to find a means of ensuring the slaves were freed without bringing about the collapse of the region's economy. As late as 1936, the census suggested that over 121,005 former slaves were 'still living in their previous mode.'[27] It was only in 1936 that Britain, under pressure from the League of Nations, introduced a Slavery Ordinance which went a long way towards abolition, although some trading in children and concubinage continued.[28]

The impact of slavery in northern Nigeria and Niger, as well as the surrounding regions, continues to be felt. This is hardly surprising. Well into the twentieth century in French-controlled areas of the Sahara, Tuareg and Arab groups allied to France were permitted to keep their slaves.[29] For some, however, in Niger, little has changed, even to this day. Houssa Aboubakar, a farmer of slave descent in northern Ader, said in 2005: 'Before we used to work for the Abzinawa [elites], who sat and did nothing; then the White [colonialists] controlled our labour; now project agents tell us what to do. Someone is always sitting and watching us work for nothing.'[30]

Nor has there been an end to the involvement of the Fulani in jihadist movements across other areas of the Sahel.[31] The Fulani currently play a significant role in several Islamist groups from Mali and Burkina Faso to Niger and Nigeria and are involved in a series of complex alliances and shifting relationships that few outside the region have grasped. There are many reasons for this, but status is one of them. A Fulani leader is quoted as saying:

[J]oining an extremist group is often associated with elevated status. Having weapons gives you a kind of prestige—young people from the villages are very influenced by the young armed bandits who drive around on motorbikes, well dressed and well fed. Young herders are very envious of them, they admire their appearance.[32]

Conclusion

What can we learn from these examples of indigenous African slavery? First, enslavement was not always forced upon African societies by external actors. In the case of Ethiopia, the practice goes back to the beginning of recorded history. In the case of Sokoto, it was extended in the nineteenth century at the point of the sword.

Secondly, foreign powers certainly had an impact on the trade. Without the Egyptians and Arabs, slavery would have been a local Ethiopian phenomenon, practised by the nobility and the courts, but not on the scale that it reached. The trade routes and the goods that were brought by foreign merchants vastly enhanced enslavement. Without the demand from North Africa and Europeans (the Portuguese in particular), the Sokoto Caliphate would also have used slaves primarily for domestic purposes. It was trade that allowed slavery to grow to become so profitable, helping to embed the practice deeply into the Caliphate's institutions. Neither Ethiopian Christianity nor Sokoto's Muslim faith halted the practice, although faith may, from time to time, have ameliorated a slave's suffering, in certain circumstances. In this regard, African societies were neither better nor worse than others across the globe.

Thirdly, enslavement led to predicable results. In West Africa, areas that provided slaves were depopulated, agriculture decayed and civilisation fell away. Many villages simply ceased to exist.[33] Equally, trading with outside powers left wealth in the hands of the local elites. 'In the coastal, slave-selling societies, the trade led to a concentration of capital and power in the hands of a few chiefs and traders, and to a certain extent to specialization in certain crafts.'[34]

Fourthly, external pressure, particularly from Britain, played an important role in ending slavery. London saw extinguishing the trade as a major goal of foreign policy for much of the nineteenth century. Pressure was brought to bear on Ethiopia to end enslavement, while the defeat of the Sokoto Caliphate put an end to the practice, even if British administrators were slow to bring this about. The League of Nations also placed international pressure on both administrations to end enslavement. Emperor Haile Selassie and the British in Sokoto found this distinctly uncomfortable, and both acted to try to comply with the League's demands.

PART 4

TRANS-ATLANTIC SLAVERY

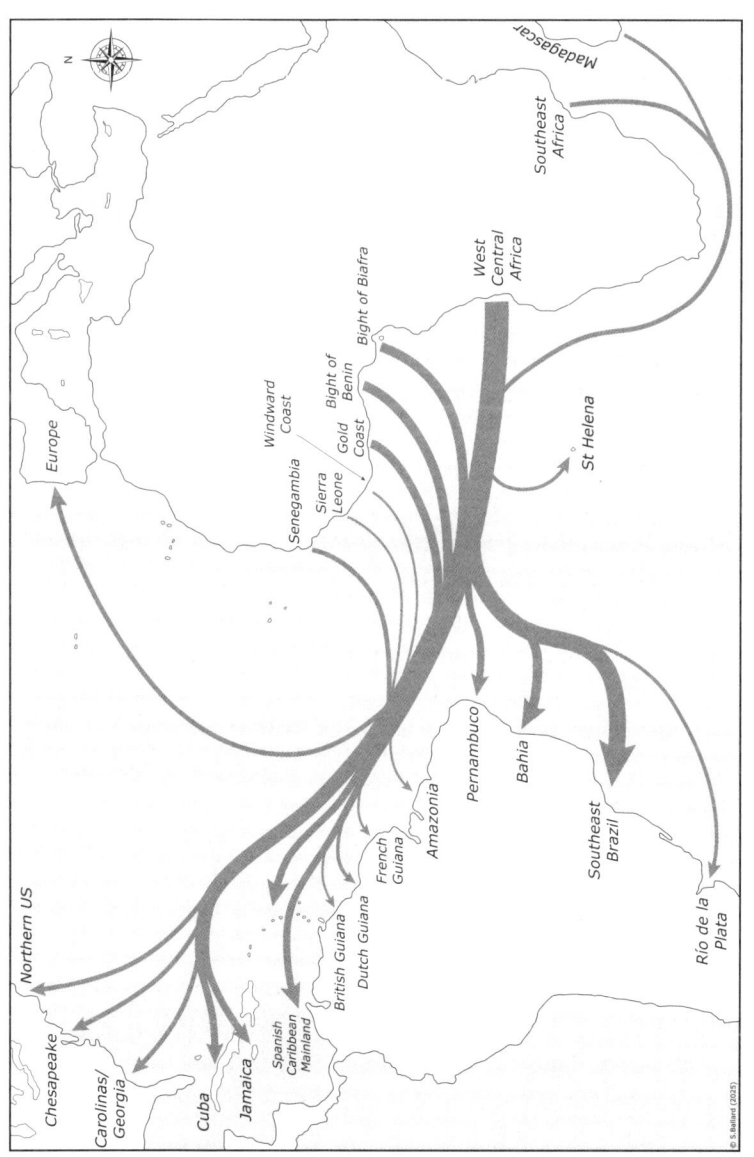

Map 5: Trans-Atlantic slave routes

The map is adapted from David Eltis and David Richardson, *Atlas of the Transatlantic Slave Trade*, Yale University Press, 2010, Map 11, pp. 18–19.

'In 1441 Antao Goncalves, the young captain of a small vessel dispatched by the infante Dom Henrique of Portugal to take on a cargo of seal skins and oil, put ashore a landing party on the coast of northern Mauretania for the express purpose of capturing blacks.'[1] So began the trade that would continue for the next four centuries. During that period, over 12 million men and women were transported from Africa to the Caribbean and the Americas. When Goncalves returned to Portugal, he had a lukewarm reception: there was little interest in his slaves. However, this soon changed. Within three years six vessels—caravels—had brought no fewer than 235 African slaves to Portugal. 'This event heralded a new era in the social, economic, and ideological history of Portugal,' wrote Anthony Russell-Wood.[2] Indeed, the shipments initiated a trade that would transform the social relations of Africa, Europe and the Americas, with effects being felt down the centuries.

What can be said that sheds new light on Atlantic slavery, a subject so well researched and so well known? The answer lies in the context. In the preceding and succeeding chapters, I have attempted to show how slavery evolved before the Trans-Atlantic trade, how it developed alongside these events, and what took place in Africa after it ceased. As we have seen, Africans were being enslaved and trafficked long before the arrival of the Portuguese and long after Lisbon ended the trade. This is frequently overlooked. Even after formal abolition, European powers continued to benefit from enslavement, in the form of imports produced by slaves in Africa whose unpaid labour subsidised their production. The succeeding chapters will also show how Europeans—as well as Africans—were taken captive by the Ottomans and their North African colonists: the Barbary corsairs.

The slave trade was not the result of a mere whim. Rather, it developed alongside the growing demand for products associated with rising living standards that came with the Industrial Revolution: cotton, coffee, tobacco and sugar. None were vital to European life, but their importance grew as wool was replaced by cotton and a taste for tea, and the sugar with which it was drunk, gained in popularity. These commodities were to transform global trade and re-shape nations, from China to the Americas. Spurred on by this demand, the European Trans-Atlantic slave trade grew rapidly. For this period, it was larger than the Islamic slave trade across the Sahara, the Red Sea and the Indian Ocean. All data has its weaknesses, but Table 4 below provides one of the most reliable estimates.[3]

Table 4: The Trans-Atlantic Slave Trade and the Islamic Slave Trade Compared

Century	No. of Trans-Atlantic Slaves	No. of Islamic Slaves	Total No. of Slaves
Sixteenth	338,000	750,000	1,088,000
Seventeenth	1,876,000	900,000	2,776,000
Eighteenth	6,495,000	1,300,000	7,795,000
Total	8,709,000	2,950,000	11,659,000

As outlined previously, these statistics only reflect a partial picture since they ignore the trade across the Sahara, the Red Sea and the Indian Ocean that began many centuries earlier and continued until this time. African societies had a lengthy experience of their populations being enslaved prior to the arrival of Europeans. It was a history that underlay the rapid rise in the Trans-Atlantic trade.

> The whole of the Atlantic slave trade was founded on the willingness of Africans to sell other Africans to Europeans, and on the ability of African rulers to conduct such sales without facing local rebellion. The conduct of trade generally followed African dictates until European colonialism began in earnest from the late nineteenth century, by which time the Atlantic slave trade had largely ended.[4]

The story of the Trans-Atlantic trade is very well known. Rather than simply re-tell it, I will attempt to explain aspects that are less understood, without denying any aspect of the fate of the African slaves when they reached the Caribbean and the Americas.

14

THE DEVELOPING TRADE

Portugal and Spain were steeped in slavery. The Romans had taken Iberian slaves, and so had the Goths after the establishment of the Visigothic Kingdom, which existed from the fifth to the eighth century. Following the invasion of the Iberian Peninsula in the eighth century by Arabs and Berbers (or Moors as they became known), the Spanish and Portuguese were persuaded, or forced, to convert to Islam. Some were enslaved. Al-Istakhri, an Arab in the tenth century, wrote of the sources of slaves to be purchased in North Africa: 'From the Maghrib there come black slaves (khadam) from the land of Sudan, and white slaves from al-Andalus and highly valued slave girls. An unskilled slave girl or man will fetch, according to her or his appearance, 1000 dinars or more.'[1] Once the Moors were routed in the fifteenth century, the boot was on the other foot. They were enslaved in their turn and traded across the straits of Gibraltar.

After the Islamic conquest of North Africa, Europe's relations with the continent were very limited. Europeans found it difficult to contact or visit Africa. For the next 700 years, the Islamic world was 'virtually the only external influence on the political economy of Africa.'[2] At the same time, the peoples and societies of the Sahara and the Sahel were linked to the outside world in a way they had never been before. The Islamic world was extensive and complex. Conflicts and trade were just part of these relationships. Ideas and innovations flowed along these routes, just as they did across the more famous Silk Route linking China and Japan with Europe. Slaves were very much part of this trade. The exclusive Islamic relationship with the rest of the continent ended when Portuguese carvels reached the Senegal River in 1445. It provided the Europeans with an entrée into the existing systems of human trafficking. As Basil Davidson put it: 'the Portuguese, having sailed round the Muslim monopoly, established along the North African coast, had now entered the trans-Saharan slave trade by the back door.'[3] These links were facilitated by Sephardic Jews, who had fled to North Africa following Spanish persecution in the fourteenth century.

Spanish and Portuguese ships began probing expeditions down the African coast in the second half of the fifteenth century. At first the Portuguese had little competition from other European states for relations with the North Africans. Initially the Portuguese were hoping to acquire gold.[4] Over time this changed, and Portugal was able to benefit from the pre-existing culture of enslavement.[5] The first Portuguese base was established at Arguin in Mauritania and became a means of connecting with the Trans-Saharan caravan routes.[6]

> When the Portuguese voyagers first arrived at Senegambia, Benin and Kongo, they found a thriving commerce in slaves. These kingdoms represented the southern extremity of an extensive trade conducted by Islamic nations that involved the capture and sale of Europeans and North African Berbers as well as black people from south of the Sahara Desert. Although Arabs nurtured antiblack prejudice, race was not the major factor in this Islamic slave trade. Arab merchants and West African kings, for example, imported white slaves from Europe.[7]

At first the Portuguese travelled along the coasts taking about 800 slaves a year—slightly fewer than were traded along each of the six major Trans-Saharan routes in this period.[8] However, demand grew rapidly. The reason for this was the colonisation of the Americas by the Spanish, which began in the 1490s.[9] The 'discovery' of the Americas gradually brought the Caribbean and the Americas within Europe's sphere of influence. This followed the pioneering exploration by the Italian explorer Christopher Columbus, who made four voyages on behalf of the Spanish monarchy between 1492 and 1504. In that short space of time, he came across the Caribbean islands as well as Central and South America. These tropical lands could provide a new range of crops to meet the public's growing taste for exotic products that could not be cultivated in the cooler European climates. The plantations that the European powers established led to a huge demand for slave labour. The fall of Constantinople to the Ottomans in 1453 also contributed to rising demand in Africa, as the flow of slaves from the Black Sea region into the Mediterranean was reduced.

The rising demand for slave labour

What had at first been an insignificant engagement with African slaves turned into a flood. Between 1441 and 1505, some 140,000 to 170,000 men and women were trafficked between Africa and Portugal.[10] Some would have been sold onwards, but by 1552 there were 32,000 slaves among the Portuguese population of 1,000,000, the majority of whom were Africans.[11] So numerous were they that an Italian visitor to the Iberian Peninsula in circa 1580 commented that 'there are such numbers of [black African] slaves that cities resemble games of chess, with equal numbers of white and black people'.[12] A Flemish visitor proclaimed in a letter: 'I felt as though I had been transported to a city in hell; I came across black people everywhere.'[13] Over time the numbers of slaves being exported to the Americas would far outweigh those retained in Europe.

As Europe recovered from the devastation of the Black Death of the fourteenth century and the agricultural depression that followed, the population increased. This was accompanied by a growth in trade, and by the sixteenth and seventeenth centuries there were rising standards of living, which encouraged people to begin to develop new tastes. The novel commodities they hankered after were sugar, coffee, tobacco, chocolate, rice and cotton.[14] The combination of a rising demand for luxury goods, new territories to conquer, the lure of gold and innovative technologies was to transform the global economy. These exotic products could be cultivated in the tropics, but they were most effectively grown at scale on plantations, and this required huge numbers of people to do the backbreaking labour.

The colonisers were not prepared to do this themselves, so they attempted to enlist the native peoples in this work, but to little avail. They fled or died after the Spaniards arrived in Hispaniola in 1492. The population of Native American Taino people who lived in the Caribbean was dramatically reduced. Raids, executions and diseases, to which the local people had no immunity, led to a catastrophic collapse in the population of the Caribbean.

> The greatest part of this decline occurred within the first few years of the encounter with Europeans, with the years 1496 and 1497 probably the worst. In this short period, the population of Hispaniola was almost halved each year. The rate of decline then slowed but the result was equally catastrophic. In 1508, only 60,000 Taino were counted in Hispaniola; in 1514, some 30,000; and in 1518 just 11,000 survived.[15]

This decimation was produced by a combination of attacks, forced labour, poor diet and diseases such as smallpox to which the indigenous populations were exposed for the first time. It almost resulted in their elimination.

> The period 1420–1804 was marked by epidemic disease, subsistence crises, and generally poor standards of public health. European imperialism created the conditions for the more rapid spread of disease around the world and more directly exposed people to new disease environments. Thus, the native peoples of the Americas, lacking immunities to diseases such as smallpox and influenza, died in great numbers when they came into contact with Europeans.[16]

African slavery, on a vast scale, was seen as the answer to the needs of plantation owners. They were resistant to the diseases brought from the Old World and could, therefore, be expected to yield longer service.[17] They were also unlikely to try to escape by fleeing into an interior that they had no knowledge of. Even so, the work was so brutal that death rates among Africans remained extraordinarily high. As one observer of the Cuban sugar plantations wrote, they were simply 'worn out'.[18]

Two other commodities would later have as transformative an impact on the international political economy: tea and opium. Britain's taste for tea was so insatiable that it drained the country's finances, to be replaced by opium grown in India for sale in China. When the Chinese resisted, London sent in the Royal Navy. The wars with Beijing of the nineteenth century resulted in the transfer of Hong Kong to British control.[19] In the sixteenth and seventeenth centuries, it was sugar and tobacco that were to drive the demand for labour. To obtain the slaves they required, the Europeans did not generally raid the African coastal communities they encountered— although this did take place. Rather, they established relationships with the local rulers, with whom they traded. This became an enduring pattern.

> [U]sually the Portuguese and the other Europeans and white Americans who succeeded them did not capture and enslave people themselves. They instead purchased slaves from African traders. This arrangement began formally in 1472 when the Portuguese merchant Ruy de Sequeira gained permission from the Oba (king) of Benin to trade for slaves, as well as for gold and ivory, within the borders of the Oba's kingdom … The rulers of Benin, Dahomey, and other African kingdoms restricted the Europeans to a few points on the coast, and the kingdoms raided the interior to supply the Europeans with slaves.[20]

The Portuguese king, João II (r. 1481–95), sent diplomatic missions to Senegal, Benin, Kongo and inland to Mali, Mossi, Songhay and Timbuktu.[21] The Europeans got to know the customs and traditions of the African elites, while establishing forts along the Atlantic coast from which to engage in the commerce. They had to 'inform themselves of the political practices prevailing along the Atlantic littoral, including the rituals of rule, gift exchanges, and customs that would foster a local sovereign's goodwill.'[22] In so doing the Europeans relied on local guides and translators, since they were intent on trade, rather than colonisation.

At the same time, the Europeans were creating a demand for slaves, which local rulers were keen to answer because of the goods they were being offered. As early as 1462, it was evident that the Senegambian military needed the horses that the Europeans brought with them for their cavalry, so the local rulers captured slaves as their currency of exchange.[23] Access to the horses allowed competing elites to out-perform each other on the battlefield. Very soon this trade led to the depletion of village populations along the coast.[24] The trade grew rapidly, and by 1505, the region from the Senegal River to Sierra Leone was exporting 3,500 slaves annually.[25]

Gradually the Europeans moved around the African coast, extending their search for human cargoes. This was far from being the backward region of European imagination. A Dutch visitor was stunned by what he saw in Benin City on the Guinea coast in 1602, one of the few towns open to Europeans before the nineteenth century. He found an urban landscape comparable to those he had left in the Netherlands.

> The town seemeth to be very great; when you enter into it, you go into a great broad street, not paved, which seems to be seven or eight times broader than the Warmoes street in Amsterdam, which goeth right out and never crooks … The houses in this street stand in good order, one close and even with the other, as the houses in Holland stand … The King's Court is very great, within it having many great four-square plains, which round about them have galleries, wherein there is always a watch kept … There are also many men slaves seen in the town, that carry water, yams and palm-wine, which they say is for the King; and many carry grass which is for their horses; and all of this is carried into the court.[26]

The region from the River Volta to the Lagos Lagoon was a particularly rich source of slaves and was referred to by the merchants as 'the Slave Coast'. In the 240 years between 1616 and 1850/51, it was to produce some 2 million slaves: 20 men and women taken every day.[27]

For the African seized and taken aboard, it was a tragic and deeply frightening experience, from which many never recovered. Some even thought they were about to be eaten by white cannibals. The vast majority would never see their families or communities again. The conditions on board ship and the brutality with which they were treated was truly savage. European captains, sailors and surgeons commonly referred to the slave ships as 'slaughter houses', 'coffins', or 'floating tombs'.[28]

Their captors found the enslavement no easy task. They did not have safe harbours in which to anchor, instead operating from offshore, away from the surging surf. They faced numerous hazards, from diseases that took high tolls in mortality to man-eating sharks.

When they ventured ashore, to maintain the forts they established along the coast, they took their life in their hands. This was the recollection of Justly Watson, who made the journey in 1755:

> The landing is the worst I ever saw, and I believe one of the worst in the whole world (yet we arrived in the best season.) I was informed, sometimes ships have been four or five weeks before anybody could get ashore or any boat go off to them. There is a bar before the shore, in which the sea breaks prodigiously, & the canoes frequently overset in what is called good weather. After one gets ashore there are several rivers to pass over, which makes it tiresome & dangerous.[29]

The European forts can be seen to this day along the coast. The Portuguese led the way, but they were soon joined by the Dutch, English, French, Danes, Germans and Swedes. The oldest portion of what is Ghana's current presidential palace was a former Danish fort (Christianborg) dating from 1661.[30] However, the Europeans were there by sufferance, and paid the local rulers for being able to establish their operations.[31] Even then, the combination of the climate, disease and the hostility of local peoples posed a constant threat.

> Aside from rotting in the humid climate, these bases were vulnerable to attack: the Dutch position at Offra and the French one at Glehue were destroyed in 1692, the Danish base at Christianborg fell in 1693, and the secondary British base at Sekondi fell in 1694. In contrast, the leading British base at Cape Coast Castle, the overseas headquarters of the Royal African Company, which was gained from the Dutch in 1652, was never taken by Africans and was successfully defended against African attack in 1688. Nevertheless, the British were well aware of the weakness of their position. The garrisons of European forts were indeed very small and, both for their own security and for the capacity for intervention in local conflicts, relied upon the forces of African allies.[32]

The rulers of West Africa provided the slaves that the European traders sought. A combination of severe droughts in the late seventeenth and eighteenth centuries and incessant wars meant there were plenty of people who could be taken captive and then sold.[33] Both Muslim and non-Muslim states participated. The men and women they seized were sold across the Sahara in this period, but also taken to the coast to be exported overseas. Hausa states in what is today Nigeria participated as did states further west, on the upper Niger and the Senegambian basins. There are many examples of this, including the pagan state of Segu on the Niger River, which engaged in this practice from the early seventeenth century.

> Its first ruler, Kalajan Kulubali, attracted a following of young men who ravaged the countryside, sometimes as mercenaries in the employment of petty rulers and at other times as enslavers interested in the profit and glory to be gained from military action ... Bands of men would waylay caravans or kidnap children and the occasional farm in his field. This tradition was carried to its logical extension under the grandson of Kalajan, the noteworthy Mamari Kulubali, whose military career led from raiding to organised warfare. Mamari Kulubali attracted escaped slaves, debtors, criminals, as well as his own age-mates, whose quest for adventure had provided the nucleus of his army. Before Mamari Kulubali died in the mid-1750s, Segu had raided north to Timbuktu, occupying it briefly in 1727, and south to Kongo, near the forest edge. So many slaves were taken in these campaigns that Segu became a major source of slaves for the European slave ships in the Sengambia basin.[34]

15

EUROPEAN POWERS AS SLAVING NATIONS

Portugal was at first the largest Trans-Atlantic slave trader, although Britain overtook it for a period. Table 5 is informative for two reasons: showing how the British elbowed the Portuguese out of some of the trade in the mid-eighteenth century, and how rapidly British enslavement fell after the abolition of the trade in Britain in the nineteenth century.

Table 5: Main Trans-Atlantic Slaving Nations, 1676–1850[1]

Dates	Portugal	Britain	France	Other Powers	Total
1676–1700	41%	38%	4%	17%	718,200
1701–1725	43%	38%	11%	9%	1,089,100
1726–1750	36%	38%	18%	9%	1,471,800
1751–1775	27%	43%	17%	6%	1,926,200
1776–1800	34%	37%	22%	8%	2,008,400
1801–1825	62%	15%	7%	17%	1,877,700
1826–1850	73%	0%	4%	25%	1,771,300
Total	4,971,000	3,102,000	1,372,000	1,417,700	10,862,700

Portugal, Angola and Brazil

An exception to the pattern of ships anchoring off the West African coast, supplied by local rulers, was to be found further south, where the Portuguese came into contact with the Kingdom of the Kongo in the area of the Congo River mouth. The rulers relied on thousands of slave soldiers, who lived in special villages.[2] The Kingdom of the Kongo had been weakened by civil wars, and the Portuguese seized the opportunity that this afforded them to send expeditions into the interior to capture slaves. The 1560s saw a transformation from what have been described as the 'relatively peaceful former methods of transferring dependents' which had characterised the early intra-African slave trade to more direct, brutal slave raiding.[3] Portuguese enslavement would devastate Angolan societies over the centuries.

> The trade in slaves impacted all aspects of life in central Africa. The demand for captives fueled wars of conquest, and the importation of firearms to execute those wars led to the collapse of states, such as Kongo and Ndongo, while creating new alliances, such as the ones between the Angola and the Kingdoms of Kasanje and Matamba.[4]

The Portuguese developed relationships with local communities. As they followed the Kwanza River into the interior, the Portuguese came across Imbangala warlords who 'roamed the countryside living off what they could plunder.'[5] Informal relations between these raiders and the Portuguese were transformed into permanent alliances in the second decade of the seventeenth century, with the Imbangala becoming mercenaries for their Portuguese allies. Living in fortified camps, they recruited members through raids, as well as selling them on to the Dutch or Portuguese. Further into the interior, other states, including Kasanje and Matamba, fulfilled similar roles.[6]

The result was a bonanza for the Portuguese, who were able to extract some 1.3 million people between 1500 and 1700.[7] So lucrative was this trade that it was replicated in what became the Portuguese colony of Angola, centred on the city of Luanda which was founded in 1576.[8] For the Portuguese this was fortunate, since they found it increasingly difficult to pursue their activities in West Africa after the 1640s because of the rise of powerful Dutch and English private companies, which exercised political as well as commercial influence. This competition was so severe that it forced the Portuguese to develop new sources of slaves.[9] Unlike much of the rest of Africa, Angola became a moving frontier, with the Portuguese—rather like the Omanis in East Africa—pushing deeper and deeper into the interior.[10] By the 1880s, they had penetrated over 500 kilometres into central Africa. In so doing, they co-operated with African rulers to produce the slaves Portuguese were seeking.[11]

The towns the Portuguese established—Luanda and Benguela—became hubs from which the settlers operated, lived and gradually became integrated into the local community. Although some Portuguese remained aloof, many engaged in marriages of convenience with local women. They produced Luso-Africans, who became an influential section of society.

> During the eighteenth century, Luanda lost its flavor as an African city where passing ship captains and supercargoes loaded captives belonging to Luso-African slavers, agents of the clans dominant in the colony's interior. It became a more heterogeneous entrepot, with an influential community of immigrant traders who supervised the European commercial capital that swelled the arteries of trade and slavery inland.[12]

From the sixteenth century, Portuguese colonialists, whether they were traders, missionaries or officials, all owned slaves. They did not simply traffic in these men and women. Plantations were developed in the interior and near Luanda, although there was a constant flight of slaves from the city.[13]

However, the main axis of this commerce was westwards: to export men and women to the islands off the African coast, the Caribbean and the Americas. The Portuguese were not just the largest Atlantic slavers—they started first and ended last.[14] The demand for slaves in Portugal's Brazilian colony grew almost unabated with the discovery of gold in the late seventeenth century and then with the development of sugar plantations. Slaves were transported from Africa and primarily from Angola, with over 5.8 million being taken mostly to Brazil. There was a strong demand for labour in the country, accounting for 52 per cent of all the men and women taken via the Middle Passage.[15] The conditions on the vessels on which they were transported were vile.[16]

The Africans were used throughout Brazilian society, but were predominantly deployed to the sugar plantations, for which the country was ideally suited. Building on the expertise that they had gathered from their highly profitable plantations on Madeira and Sao Tome, the Portuguese developed plantations in their Brazilian colony.[17] Its rich black soil was so fertile that it could produce crops for sixty years or more. A plantation owner would simply stamp his boot into the ground; if it sank up to the ankle, it was deemed right for the crop.[18] Fertile soils, plentiful rainfall and slave labour ensured a highly profitable industry. As early as the 1580s, Brazil was supplying most of Europe's needs.[19] From 1600 to 1650, sugar accounted for 95 per cent of Brazil's exports, and slave labour was relied upon to provide the workforce to maintain these earnings.

For the Africans, the conditions on the plantations were nothing short of purgatory.

> 'A mill is a hell and all the masters of them are damned', wrote Father Andres de Gouvea from the city of Bahia in 1627. Time and again observers who witnessed the roaring furnaces, the boiling cauldrons, the glistening black bodies and the infernal whirling of the mill during the 24-hour day of the sugar *safra*, or harvest, used the same image of hell.[20]

Sugar was not the only commodity that was cultivated using slave labour. Coffee grew in importance, and by the 1830s coffee exports surpassed sugar.[21]

A fresh source of slaves began to emerge. The expansion of the Sokoto Caliphate in 1804 saw an outbreak of raids and hostilities across what is today northern Nigeria. This, in turn, provided the slaves—some Muslim—who were transported by Brazilian traders from the Bight of Benin. Many were taken to the Brazilian region of Bahia, where they came to form a substantial community.[22] They participated in a series of revolts in Bahia between 1807 and 1835, drawing on their military experience and adopting amulets and white Muslim robes to strengthen their Muslim identities.[23] On Sunday, 25 January 1835, they rose against their masters in the city of Salvador da Bahia to free a jailed leader and marched through the streets, gathering support. The authorities responded with predictable brutality, condemning sixteen of the leaders to death, of which four sentences were carried out and the rest commuted. Others suffered imprisonment or flogging. Hundreds of the survivors were deported back to Africa.[24]

The slave trade continued well into the nineteenth century and more than 2 million African slaves were imported into Brazil between 1800 and 1850.[25] Attempts to end Brazilian slavery were slow to take effect. It was only after the British sent the Royal Navy into Brazilian waters in an attempt to end the trade that it was finally halted in 1850–1851.[26]

Britain, the Caribbean and the Americas

The Portuguese had pioneered the slave trade off the West Coast of Africa, but others followed in their wake. When the British and Dutch established their presence in the second half of the seventeenth century, they followed the Portuguese practice of relying on locally hired Africans or African slaves to ply their trade.

> Local canoe men ferried goods and passengers, including slaves, to and from English and Dutch shipping, and supervision of captives designated for export was among the tasks assigned to 'castle' or 'company' slaves owned by Dutch and English trade forts on the African coast.[27]

To make the system viable, the British traders came up with an ingenious scheme. Thomas Clarkson, an abolitionist, explained in 1788 that African merchants took trade goods on credit from the British.[28] To secure the transaction, African traders were 'obliged to leave a pledge or security for their return.' Invariably, those pledges or pawns were required to be 'their own relations, who are detained till they come back.' If the slaves who had been promised by the African traders were provided, the 'pawns' were freed, but if they were not then their own children were taken as slaves themselves and sold.

The growth of the British slave trade coincided with the demand for the luxury goods described earlier, particularly sugar, cotton and tobacco, but it began with English pirates preying on the Portuguese and Spanish fleets. Men like John Hawkins (1532–1595) and Walter Raleigh (1552–1618) made their names as what were politely termed 'privateers'—raiders licenced by the British state.

Between 1586 and 1603 ... there were an estimated 235 privateers flitting around the Caribbean, easily hidden in the myriad island hideaways, ready to pounce on stray vessels and on the treasure fleets heading home to Spain ... This piratical phase, supported by the Crown, soon gave way to long-term interests in settlements and colonization in the region. The seizure of St Kitts (1624) and Barbados (1625) launched a new phase in the regional (and British) history.[29]

Over time this collection of colonies grew, as Britain ousted its rivals. The 'privateers' were replaced with a monopoly company endorsed by the state: the Royal African Company of 1672. By 1763 Britain owned eleven 'sugar islands' in the Caribbean, as well as colonies in North Africa: all required slaves.[30] The French were not far behind, settling on St Kitts, Guadeloupe, Martinique, Haiti and St Dominique. By 1700 the French had transported 124,000 slaves to their islands. Tobacco and sugar plantations on the American mainland also had to be served, and by 1790 some 700,000 Africans had been taken from their homelands to the newly formed United States.[31]

The demand was voracious and the cost to their African cargo was huge. Many of the ships carried far more slaves than they were designed for, and their human cargoes were packed so tightly there was barely room to breathe.

The slavers' cargo space was generally only five feet high. Ships' carpenters halved this vertical space by building shelves, so slaves might be packed above and below on planks that measured only 5.5 feet long and 1.3 feet wide. Consequently, slaves had only about 20 to 25 inches of headroom. To add to the discomfort, the crew chained male slaves together in pairs to help prevent rebellion and lodged them away from women and children.[32]

Fed twice a day on a diet of vegetable pulp, porridge and stew, the men and women were frequently hungry, their rations insufficient. Diseases such as malaria, yellow fever, smallpox, scurvy and dysentery took a terrible toll. It is little wonder that the death rates on board ship were high. It is calculated that 1.8 million, more than 14 per cent of all those who embarked in Africa, never disembarked in the Americas.[33] These death rates—comparable with those of slaves crossing the Sahara—were unsurprising: conditions on board ship were notorious.

So terrified were Africans when captured, and so terrible were conditions on board the slave ships, that there were many instances of suicide, revolt and resistance. Careful examination of the data has suggested that there were no fewer than 485 'acts of violence by Africans against slave ships and their crews.'[34] These included ninety-three attempts to liberate captive Africans by attacks from the shore. There were a further 360 insurrections on board ships, during which at least one person died. Slave masters were well aware of the danger of revolt. In 1725, William Barry, captain of the Bristol based *Dispatch*, advised that slaves taken in the Bight of Biafra should be chained: 'keep [the slaves] shackled & hand bolte[d] fearing their rising or Leaping Overboard.'[35] Failed slave mutineers were treated with the utmost brutality: flogged and scarred. Captain Harding of the *Robert* is reported to have hoisted a woman who joined the revolt 'by the Thumbs, whipp'd and slashed her with Knives, before the other Slaves, till she died.'[36]

To maintain their control, traders kept weapons ready and loaded, but they regarded this as an insufficient guarantee of their security. The threat of resistance was so serious that slavers employed African 'guardians', who were chosen from among the slaves, and armed them to ensure that their human cargoes did not rise up against their masters. This was perhaps not surprising; the slaves outnumbered the crew by eight to one on board English ships in the late seventeenth century.[37] A detailed description of the duties of the guardians was provided by Captain Phillips during the voyage of the *Hannibal* in 1693–94. He bought 'some 30 to 40 gold coast negroes' to act as guardians. Their role was to 'sleep among them to keep them from quarrelling; and in order, as well as give us notice, if they discovered any caballing or plotting among them, which trust they will discharge with great diligence.'[38] To enforce discipline, the guardians were armed with whips—the 'cat of nine tails as a badge of his office, which he is not a little proud of, and will exercise with great authority.' The guardians were not always men: between a third and a half were women.[39] The defiance did not end once the slaves reached their destinations. There were rebellions in many colonies, including British Guiana, Barbados, Jamaica and

Antigua, as well as Brazil, Cuba, North America and—perhaps most famously—Haiti, led by the legendary Toussaint Louverture.[40]

The plantations served Europe's insatiable demand for sugar, tobacco and other exotic goods. To cultivate these, trade routes were established linking Africa, the Americas and Europe. This was the 'triangular trade'. Manufactured goods would be taken from ports in Britain, France or the Netherlands and sailed down to the African west coast. The Europeans would visit the forts or 'slave factories' they had established and enter into a trade with the local ruler for the human cargo they required. This was done to coincide with the harvest or dry season, when wars between Africans were more frequent and captive slaves were plentiful. With their hold filled, they would sail for the Americas—to European colonies in the Caribbean, Brazil or North Africa. There the slaves would be sold and sugar, tobacco and cotton purchased for transport to Europe for consumption or processing. The entire trade could take as long as a year to complete, but was enormously profitable.[41] Returns on such voyages for British ships were between 8 and 10 per cent, twice what could be obtained from investing in government bonds.[42]

Recently, the triangle trade metaphor has been questioned; perhaps it would be more accurate to consider it a diamond-shaped trade. Giorgio Riello suggests that textiles from the Indian subcontinent were critical to this commerce, pointing out that these imports had been transported across the Sahara for generations before the arrival of the Europeans and that they continued to be a substantial part of the goods offered for African slaves.[43] As he argues: 'By the 1790s ... cottons sold to Africa accounted for 58 percent of all traded commodities (or 80 percent of all textiles). British cottons were worth £2.9 million while Indian cottons were worth £3.4 million.' This link between the Trans-Atlantic and Indian Ocean trades is still being explored, but it is intriguing and underlines why considering slavery only from the perspective of the Middle Passage is a mistake.

The impact on African societies

The men and women brought to the coast were traded with Africans for cloth, beads and horses, but there was another, more deadly product that was on offer: guns. For local rulers they were an invaluable addition to their arsenal, one that could transform their relationships with surrounding communities. Basil Davidson outlines the scale of the operation in Dahomey (present-day Benin):

> Huge quantities of firearms poured into West Africa during the major period of the slave trade; and the state of Dahomey, increasingly a militarized autocracy, was among those that had the doubtful benefit. At the height of the eighteenth century commerce, gunsmiths in Birmingham alone were exporting muskets to Africa at the rate of between 100,000 and 150,000 a year, and it was common talk that one Birmingham gun rated one negro slave. This last was Birmingham sales talk rather than a statement of fact, since African traders were seldom willing to sell a captive only for a gun and demanded other goods as well; yet the spirit of the saying was true enough. Firearms were indispensable to the Guinea trade.[44]

Guns and horses for African cavalries became an integral part of the slave trade.[45] Official records showed that between 1796 and 1805, no fewer than 1,615,309 firearms were exported by English manufacturers to West Africa.[46] The weapons that were supplied had an immensely destabilising impact on the region. Conflict between rulers intensified, and with it the number of captives that could be taken and sold. Guns were used to kill and capture opponents, producing further slaves for the market.[47] An econometric study summed up the relationship in this way: '[P]ushing guns and gunpowder was the most effective way to produce enslaved Africans for American plantations and mines. This is why colonial planters thought there existed an unlimited supply of African slaves at their disposal.'[48]

At the same time, slave soldiers enhanced the power of African elites. They performed a range of roles, including bodyguards, militarised retainers, and soldiers.[49] The Asante in Ghana, for example, used slaves in the seventeenth and eighteenth centuries to strengthen their armed forces.[50] The rulers also benefitted from the taxes and dues they were paid; these finances allowed elites to dominate their regions. 'The rise of the Imbangala state of Kasanje in the Angolan interior represents such a case as do the Asante.'[51]

Patrick Manning argues that the dramatic extraction of vast numbers of Africans as slaves transformed social orders.

> Gradually and systematically, if not consciously, Africans made institutional changes which led to a more regular stream of slave deliveries. Overall, Africans decided to supply slaves to meet the new European demand: this conclusion is supported by the fact that the number of slaves exported in 1690 was nearly double that of 1640, but the price of slaves had not increased.[52]

It was by no means universally true that slavery benefitted the existing social hierarchy. Political fragmentation improved the lot of some rulers, but others fell away. Nathan Nunn cites the collapse of the Jollof Confederation in Senegambia in the sixteenth century, and the impact of slavery on the Kingdom of the Kongo, which left the local ruler, Affonso, writing to the Portuguese in 1526, complaining that 'there are many traders in all corners of the country. They bring ruin to the country. Every day people are enslaved and kidnapped, even nobles, even members of the king's own family.'[53]

The preceding chapters have provided details of how deeply slavery had been embedded in Africa long before the arrival of the Portuguese. European patterns of enslavement had a transformative impact on local societies, sometimes strengthening rulers, at other times sending them into decline. It strengthened ties with the outside world, although, as we have seen, the Trans-Atlantic trade did not initiate commerce with countries as far afield as India; rather, it consolidated these transactions. Africa would never be the same again. How it was altered depended upon the circumstances in particular locations.

16

ABOLITION AND THE RETURN TO AFRICA

Opposition to slavery grew gradually in Europe and the United States. There was no sudden dawning of awareness that this was a practice that could not possibly be justified. In Britain, it was the result of years of political agitation, led by men like William Wilberforce and work by Christians, particularly the Quakers. Two events stand out. The first was the judgement of Lord Mansfield, the Lord Chief Justice, in June 1772, which ruled that a master could not seize a slave and remove him from England against the slave's will, and that a slave could secure a writ of habeas corpus to prevent that removal.[1] The ruling was a narrow one, which was widely assumed to have outlawed slavery in England, even though this was not the case. The judgement was seized on by British abolitionists and the American anti-slavery movement and celebrated by the poet William Cowper, who wrote:

> We have no slaves at home—Then why abroad?
> Slaves cannot breathe in England; if their lungs
> Receive our air, that moment they are free.
> They touch our country, and their shackles fall.
> That's noble, and bespeaks a nation proud.[2]

The importance of Lord Mansfield's judgement has been extensively debated over many years. It has been argued that the Chief Justice was genuinely ambivalent on the question of slavery. 'He accepted and endorsed the widely assumed mercantile importance of the slave trade, yet he doubted the validity of theoretical justifications of slavery, and he sought to redress instances of individual cruelty to slaves.'[3] Whatever Mansfield's intentions, his judgement certainly stimulated the growing movement against enslavement.

The second was a horrific, but by no means isolated event: the treatment of 450 slaves being carried by the *Zong* to Jamaica in 1781. Running short of water, Captain Luke Collingwood had 131 of the weaker slaves flung into the Atlantic to drown.[4] Two years later the case came to court, not for murder, but as a claim against the ship's insurers, who were refusing to pay compensation for the 'cargo' that had been lost.[5] The atrocity received only limited coverage at first, but gradually become infamous, inspiring the abolitionist movement.

'The importance of the Zong lies beyond the simple facts of the case. It became the cause celebre that galvanized the anti-slavery movement from being a minor campaign by a set of marginal figures infected by evangelical enthusiasm to becoming the most significant moral campaign in British history.'[6] It led to the first debate in Parliament in 1788, but progress was slow. Resistance to reform remained fierce: far too many in the British establishment were deeply invested in slavery. In 1805, an abolition bill failed in Parliament, for the eleventh time in fifteen years.[7] However, the campaign was relentless and finally led to the passing of the Slave Trade Act in Britain on 25 March 1807. The law prohibited the trade across the British Empire, even if it did not free existing slaves. Any captain continuing the practice on a British vessel would be prosecuted with a fine of £100 for every slave found aboard his ship. The law had an immediate impact on West Africa.

> The last English slaver, the Kitty's Amelia, sailed from the port of Liverpool on July 27, 1807. When her master, Captain Hugh Crow, reached the Slave Coast on the Gulf of Guinea and told the King of Bonny that Britain had abolished the trade the latter was undisguisedly depressed. But he soon brightened; for, he said, 'We tink the trade no stop, for all we Ju-Ju-men tell we so, for dem say you country can never pass God A'mighty.'[8]

How right the king was. It would take many years, and many lives, before slaves were no longer transported over the seas. Slavery itself was only to be abolished in 1833, leading to the end of the practice across the British Empire.

Fig. 1: Nubian prisoners sit on the ground in an act of submission, guarded by Egyptian soldiers armed with sticks, circa 1330 BCE. The first evidence of Nubian slaves taken up the Nile for enslavement in Egypt was carved into stone in 2900 BCE on the second cataract.

Fig. 2: In 1781, Captain Luke Collingwood, claiming the ship was running low on drinking water, had 133 Africans thrown live overboard from the British slave ship *Zong*. The case came to court for the loss of 'property'—the slaves. The public outcry helped transform Britain from a leading enslaver into the most important nation campaigning against slavery.

SLAVE-DEALERS AND SLAVES—A STREET SCENE IN ZANZIBAR

Fig. 3: Slaves and slave dealers, Zanzibar. So lucrative was the trade that Oman's Sultan Sayyid Said bin Sultan al-Busaidi (1791–1856) transferred his capital to Zanzibar, bringing Baluchi troops and Indian administrators. Oman sent caravans as far as Angola, returning with slaves and ivory and becoming one of the largest enslaving nations in the Indian Ocean.

TIPPOO TIB

Fig. 4: Hamad bin Muhammad al-Murjabi, better known as Tippu Tip, was the most important Zanzibari slave trader. He was tall, shrewd and generally immaculately dressed, controlling large areas of central Africa until his troops were defeated by Belgium's King Leopold in 1893.

Fig. 5: Lord Frederick Lugard, governor of Northern Nigeria, meeting the Emir of Katsina, Muhammadu Dikko, 1907. In 1903 the British were welcomed by the emir, having already conquered most of the Sokoto Caliphate. The defeat of the Caliphate left Britain with two million slaves, decades after slavery had been abolished across the Empire.

Fig. 6: Ethiopian slaves accompanying their masters to present Emperor Haile Selassie with funds for defence, following the invasion of Italian fascists in October 1935. There were between 300,000 and 500,000 slaves in Ethiopia at this time. Italy used the freeing of the slaves as propaganda to justify their occupation.

Fig. 7: President Barack Obama and Michelle Obama at the 'Door of No Return', Gorée Island, Senegal, June 2013. Michelle Obama commented: 'Standing there, I thought about the terror and grief these people must have felt as they took their last steps through the doorway, knowing they would never again see their families or their country.'

Britain's naval squadrons off West and East Africa

To enforce the legislation, the Royal Navy established the West Africa Squadron in 1808 to patrol the Atlantic, dispatching two vessels to police the African coast. It was an extremely ambitious assignment, driven by a succession of British abolitionist foreign ministers, who believed passionately in the cause.[9] 'For much of the next 50 years Britain stood alone among [European and North American] nations in its determination to enforce its abolitionist law.'[10] The law was slowly extended after 1815 to non-British slave ships.

A vast area of the Atlantic had to be patrolled, including 2,000 miles of the West African coastline. These measures were reinforced in 1819 when a 'Preventative Squadron' was given the task of ending the practice. 'Soon,' wrote *The Times*, as the first seven ships left for West Africa, 'we shall hear no more of the slave trade.'[11] This proved to be far too optimistic.

By the end of the 1840s, Britain had thirty-five warships off the West African coast.[12] The patrols were expensive, frustrating and dangerous. Many sailors died of disease while at sea. This extract from an unnamed officer gives a flavour of what life was like and how difficult it was to halt the trade:

> Her Majesty's Ship [blank], West Coast Africa, July 26, 1845. Here we are, on the most miserable station in the wide world—nigger hunting—attempting the impossibility—the suppression of the slave trade. We look upon the affair as complete humbug. You may make treaties in London and send the whole combined Squadrons of England and France to this coast, and then you will have gained your object. So long as a slave, worth only a few dollars here, fetches $80 or $100 in America, men and means will be found to evade the strictest blockade.[13]

The cost to Britain was huge: possibly the most expensive humanitarian campaign of all time. The West Africa Squadron was estimated to have cost as much as £2 billion in today's money.[14] 'At its peak in the 1840s and 1850s, British operations off the West African coast involved up to 36 vessels and more than 4,000 men, costing an estimated half of all naval spending—amounting to between 1 per cent and 2 per cent of British government expenditure.'[15] This sum is comparable with the compensation Britain paid out in 45,000 awards to slave owners for the 'loss' of their assets: the 800,000 enslaved people who were freed.[16] According to a 2022 Bank of England staff working paper: 'A sum of £20 million (approximately £1,958 million in August 2022 prices) was allocated and payments were made to slave owners for the loss of their "property".'[17]

Britain's naval efforts did not end the trade, although they were not without effect. Over time the Royal Navy captured a total of 566 slave ships.[18] Paul Lovejoy summed up the outcome: '[A]bolitionist efforts failed to stem the flow [that] was maintained until 1850 ... After 1850, however, the trade dropped off rapidly, with slightly more than 225,000 slaves exported in the 1850s and 1860s, before ceasing altogether.'[19] The cost to Britain was more than monetary. Thousands of sailors lost their lives patrolling the African coast: 'one sailor died for every nine slaves freed—17,000 men over the 52-year period—either in action or of disease.'[20] They are remembered by the Navy to this day.

Britain's attempts to contain the West African enslavement was only one aspect of the story. In 1858, Britain expanded the blockade to the other side of the continent: the Indian Ocean. In that year, HMS *Lyra* arrived off Africa's east coast to begin enforcing anti-slavery treaties in the western Indian Ocean.[21] These patrols proved to be at least as difficult as the West Africa blockade. The dhows which they were attempting to intercept were nimbler and better suited to slipping into coastal shallows and rivers to avoid detection. Yet the Royal Navy's work again had results, even though the numbers of slaves rescued were not as large as those freed in the Atlantic. It is calculated that 198,710 Africans were released from ships in the Atlantic alone between 1808 and 1863. This represented 6.2 per cent of the estimated 3.2 million Africans who were taken from West Africa during this period.[22] The successes in the Indian Ocean were very much smaller. Between 1860 and 1890, the Navy seized 1,000 dhows, and released approximately 12,000 slaves from their Arab captors.[23]

Britain had been transformed from one of the nations most deeply involved in slavery to an active opponent of the trade, even though enforcing the law was exceptionally difficult. Britain had no right to board and inspect the vessels of other nations without specific treaties. These were slowly and painfully negotiated.

> Treaties signed in 1817 and 1835 between Spain and Britain, and in 1826 between Brazil and Britain made slave trading illegal between Africa, Cuba and Brazil. France began enforcing suppression in its colonies from the 1830s, and in 1836 Portugal was the last nation in the Atlantic world to abolish slave trading.[24]

At first the United States refused to allow other nations to board its vessels. However, in 1820, the nascent U.S. Navy began deploying warships off the West African coast. Enforcement was sporadic until a permanent Africa Squadron was sent in 1842.[25] Yet the system of patrols only really became effective seven years later, when President James Buchanan expanded the fleet and negotiated the reciprocal right to search British and American vessels. Special courts were established in New York, in Sierra Leone and at the Cape of Good Hope, presided over by an American and a British judge. In 1862, Captain Nathaniel Gordon of the slave ship *Erie* was hanged in New York for his role in the crime, the only person ever executed for being 'engaged in the slave trade' under the U.S. 1820 Piracy Law.[26] Abolitionism had finally found its teeth. Other commissions to deal with the liberation of slaves were established in Cuba, Brazil and Angola.[27]

The very last slaves to make the Trans-Atlantic crossing to America were put on board the *Clotilda* on 15 May 1860 off the coast of Dahomey (present-day Benin), bound for the port of Mobile in the American South.[28] Slavery and the slave trade had long been illegal, with naval vessels patrolling the Atlantic attempting to bring the trade to an end. Despite this, partly because of a notorious wager, and partly because of the profitability of the slave trade, the *Clotilda* was sent to collect her human cargo. The men, women and children had been captured in April by Fon warriors from the Kingdom of Dahomey. The king's troops, armed with machetes, axes, clubs and flintlock muskets, smashed down the gates of their town, Tarkar. One of the captives, Kossula, wept as he recalled how he attempted to flee, but 'they too strong for me. They take me and tie me. I don't know where my people at. I never see them no more.'[29] Among those in the town were slaves: people who had been unable to pay their debts, criminals and captives seized in warfare.[30] They were marched southwards in chains before being held in fetid prisons. Tarkar's ruler was brought before the king of Dahomey, but he refused to be taken to America as a slave and was instead beheaded with a giant razor.

After an intimate inspection, the slaves were taken across the breakers in canoes and put on board the *Clotilda* for the brutal trip across the Atlantic. Finally, after six weeks at sea, the 103 captives who had survived the crossing arrived in the United States. They had been smuggled past blockades, only to spend the rest of their lives serving their masters, mostly in the Alabama cotton plantations. Their settlement, called 'Africatown', was founded by thirty-two survivors and still stands on the outskirts of Mobile.[31]

Freed slaves

Those who were freed, and who survived the journey back to Africa, had their lives transformed. Britain's naval flag, the Union Jack, was to many Africans a symbol of liberation. On 20 June 1897, a large crowd assembled outside the colonial government house in the Seychelles.[32] The 2,000 who gathered were among 2,667 individuals who had been freed by the Royal Navy. Like many throughout the British Empire, they were celebrating Queen Victoria's Diamond Jubilee. The crowd held large Union Jacks printed with the words, 'The Flag that sets us free.' Once they had assembled, a message translated from Créole was given to the colonial administrator, Cockburn-Stewart. The message read:

> We members of the different tribes of Africans living in the Seychelles, take the occasion of the Diamond Jubilee of Queen Victoria to express to you—Her Representative in these Islands our thanks for all that She and England have done for us. ... Kindly, Sir, express to the Queen our thanks for our freedom and to England our gratitude to those English Sailors who were killed and wounded, fighting that we might be free.[33]

The archive of Cockburn-Stewart contains photographs showing flags displayed in the procession.[34] However, by no means were all the rescue attempts successful. Many freed former slaves died before they could be returned to their country of origin.[35]

What to do with the slaves liberated by the British was a constant problem, since it was far from clear where they had come from, or how to return them. Four out of five Africans who were freed in the Atlantic after 1807 were initially taken to British colonies, such as Sierra Leone.[36] There were other destinations for the slaves freed by Britain: the remote island of St Helena in the central Atlantic and the South African port of Cape Town. The Royal Navy's intervention led to the capture of large numbers of vessels taking slaves from Africa to Brazil, with St Helena receiving over 25,000 slaves who had been liberated from 450 vessels.[37] The 1,410 shipped to the Cape in the 1840s were subsequently joined by thousands of others.[38] On their arrival they hardly received a warm welcome. They were described in a debate in the Cape Legislative Assembly to be 'a very inferior species of labour' and their arrival declared to be 'a measure of unmixed evil'.[39] Their reputation was not improved by the fact that they brought smallpox, which left almost a thousand Capetonians dead. The former St Helenian slaves were only a fraction of those who were taken to the Cape, having been freed in both the Atlantic and the Indian oceans: some 5,000 to 6,000 in total. The treatment of the former slaves in the colony was distinctly poor. Many were indentured or apprenticed, or fell into debt bondage. In some cases, their treatment was said to be even worse than enslavement.[40] Other 'liberated Africans' were taken to the port of Durban. Between 1873 and 1877, Durban received 502, some just six months old.[41] They were put to work, given employment by Natal farmers, planters, big companies and business families. Seventy-six of them were assigned to the Durban Public Works Department, the port captain, and the hospital, and were generally regarded as good workers.[42]

The drive to abolish the slave trade led to its suppression not only in the British Empire, but also in other areas of European influence. The French conquest of Madagascar in 1894–1895 was followed by the ending of slavery in 1896. The British defeat of the Sultanate of Darfur in 1916 saw a similar outcome.[43] Britain conquered the Sokoto Caliphate in 1903 and London inherited its vast residue of slaves, a subject explored in Part 3. However, abolition was a long, complex and sometimes contradictory process. In London the abolitionists held sway, but abroad it was often the local British official, the 'man on the spot', who made the decisions. What to do about local African slaves was a particular problem. For example, in the 1850s, Britain refused to extend prohibition over areas of Lagos. Benjamin Campbell, British consul in Lagos from 1853 to 1859, reassured local slave owners that 'the British Government had no disposition to interfere with the state of domestic slavery existing in Africa.'[44] This was only reversed when Lagos became a British protectorate in 1861.

African colonies for freed slaves

Freed Trans-Atlantic slaves were found places to live along the coast of West Africa. London's 'Black Poor' were settled in Sierra Leone in 1787. Many were African Americans, who had sought refuge with the British Army during the American Revolution, but they also included other black Londoners from the West Indies, Africa and Asia.[45] They were followed by Americans in Liberia in 1822 and by the former French slaves in Gabon in 1849. How the freed slaves interacted with the local Africans is a complex subject, which can only be touched on. However, the integration (or re-integration) of former slaves into societies they had seldom come from was no easy task. A Royal Naval vessel landed 411 men and women.[46] The black settlers had a torrid time of it: half of them died during the voyage, or in the first four months of arrival. Soon there were clashes with local people.[47] The development of Sierra Leone continued to be troubled, with attacks by the French (1794) and clashes with other black settlers from Nova Scotia (1800). By 1833, nearly 40,000 'recaptives' (as the slaves rescued by the Royal Navy were known) had joined the original 2,000 emancipated slaves from Britain or North America.[48] Tensions remained between the liberated former slaves and the locals, but over time they became an integral part of Sierra Leone's society. By 1867, Sierra Leone had received just over half of all freed slaves. Many were subsequently moved to other colonies. 'Ultimately, close to half of all Africans removed from slave vessels ended up in the British Caribbean, and over 40 percent remained settled in Sierra Leone.'[49]

The establishment of Libreville—the capital of Gabon—
followed a different trajectory. In 1839 a French naval officer,
Édouard Bouët-Willaumez, cruising down the West African coast,
persuaded the local ruler at the mouth of the Gabon estuary to
cede land to France, acting entirely on his own initiative.[50] The
French navy founded Gabon as a place from which to combat the
slave trade in the Atlantic. Six years later, in 1849, the village which
became Libreville was established by fifty former slaves who were
resettled from Senegal.[51]

In Liberia, the 'Americo-Liberians', as freed slaves were
known, became an elite. They came to dominate local peoples
and were bitterly resented. One of the problems was their origin:
most of the settlers had not come from Liberia, but were Nigerian
or from further south, from Congo or Angola.[52] They were
brought from the United States by the American Colonization
Society, an organisation dedicated to ridding America of freed
black men and women.[53] They were housed in compounds known
as 'receptacles' in Monrovia, Grand Bassa, Cape Mount and
Greenville. Conditions were poor, and those who arrived were
worried that their fate was uncertain and their troubles by no
means over. This sentiment was captured in a song recorded by a
Lutheran minister who visited an overcrowded, dirty receptacle
in Monrovia in 1860.

Thus far we've haply come
But here we cannot stay,
Soon must we go again,
Nor can we tell which way,
Tell which way,
Tell which way,
Nor can we tell which way.

Perhaps to a slaver sold,
Perhaps it is not so,
This ask us not to tell,
Because we do not know,
Do not know,
Do not know,
Because we do not know.

Here food & drink we find,
And pity too is shown,
But now we end our song,
The future is not known,
Is not known,
Is not known,
The future is not known.[54]

By 1867, the American government had deposited approximately 5,700 'recaptives'. It was not conducive for the establishment of a new society, and clashes were inevitable.

> The first violent confrontation between Afro-American settlers and Africans occurred during the now legendary Battle of Fort Hill on December 1, 1822. Tradition maintains that the first settlers in Monrovia were outnumbered and on the verge of being overwhelmed by the attacking Africans. At that crucial moment a settler woman, Matilda Newport, fired a cannon with her pipe. The blast is said to have killed and wounded many of the attackers, causing the rest to retreat in disarray. This early victory against great odds has become an important element in settler ethos. It marks the triumph of 'civilization over barbarism; of enlightenment over gross ignorance; and of Christianity over paganism.'[55]

Conflict between the settlers and the locals continued into the 1860s and 1870s, with tensions lasting well into the twentieth century. The Americo-Liberians did have one benefit from their time in the United States. They had witnessed democratic systems in action. Soon after their arrival, they pressed for the establishment of constitutional, representative government.[56] By 1834 they had been given six elected councillors, and five years later a formal constitution, which the Liberians ratified.[57]

A rather different situation existed in Portuguese colonies when slaves were freed. In Angola and Mozambique, they were known as '*libertos*', and until recently received little attention. In Mozambique, almost 55,000 slaves were registered by the colonial authorities as *libertos*. However, their conditions were often little better than they had been when enslaved. 'Most were still beholden to their masters, or to the colonial government, and enjoyed neither fewer or greater possibilities for exercising individual movement or agency.'[58] In Angola, although no longer slaves, they nonetheless remained bonded labour for seven years.[59] Some were freed by the Portuguese navy off Angola, while others were released from enslavement in Angola itself.[60] While the treatment of the former slaves was very poor, at least they had a real chance of finding their way to their original home areas.

On the other side of Africa, freed slaves encountered similar problems. The British may have—as we have seen—released some 12,000 slaves they found on board Arab dhows, but they had to find a home for them. There was no single answer. As has been mentioned in Part 3, some Ethiopian children were taken to Yemen after they were released and then sent onwards to South Africa. In 1874, the British Church Missionary Society (CMS) committed itself to caring for slaves freed by Britain in East Africa.[61] Previously, former slaves had been taken to Bombay, where they were cared for by British families before being transferred to a CMS station nearby. They became known as the 'Bombay Africans' and were educated in English, Hindi, reading and arithmetic, as well as practical skills such as weaving, carpentry, cooking and dressmaking. At the same time, the former slaves were encouraged to use their original languages and prepare themselves to return to Africa.[62]

In 1864, seven of the most promising 'Bombay Africans' were sent to Rev. Johannes Rebmann, who lived just west of Mombasa at the oldest CMS station in East Africa. He had been at the station since 1846 and is perhaps best known as the first European to see Mount Kilimanjaro two years later. However, Rebmann was a poor choice, since he disliked much of his work and spent most of his time in the more congenial settings of Mombasa or Zanzibar. The priest made it clear to the 'Bombay Africans' that he had little interest in their training. He refused them a salary and insisted that they lived at a standard similar to the Africans around them. Rebmann removed their privileges of shoes and tea and repeatedly humiliated them.[63]

It was hardly an auspicious beginning. However, other former slaves were ready to leave Bombay, and the CMS appointed the head of their 'African Asylum', William Price, to build a new freed slave station in Mombasa. In 1874, Price reached the port and bought land near Mombasa. He began constructing a settlement there, which he named 'Frere Town', after Sir Bartle Frere, who had fought the slave trade. By March 1876, Frere Town had a population of 342, all of whom were freed slaves, as well as seventy 'Bombay Africans'. Another sixty remained in the previous settlement at Rabai.[64] Life was not easy. Some of Price's fellow missionaries criticised him for his leniency towards the former slaves. Frere Town soon became well known and local runaway slaves 'streamed into the station begging for asylum'. Price intervened where he could, but he decided to co-operate with the authorities and 'remained within Islamic law', returning the 'runaways' to their masters.[65]

Price was the most liberal of the missionaries, supporting slaves in litigation against brutal masters and giving the 'Bombay Africans' increasingly responsible positions within the station. When his staff complained about the treatment of a slave-girl in June 1876, there ensued a full-scale confrontation with the Mombasan townspeople. They complained that the mission's 'negroes are arrogant, finding themselves supported by missionaries and are reckless as to the consequences.'[66] Several hundred Mombasans gathered to attack the station and the former slaves were only saved by the intervention of Baluchi troops serving the sultan of Zanzibar. In July 1876, Price resigned and was replaced by a far less sympathetic administrator, James Lamb, who reversed many of Price's policies.

The plight of the 'Bombay Africans' fluctuated, according to the missionary that the CMS appointed. The 1876 clashes with locals were not the last; a further confrontation took place in June 1880.[67] By 1882, Frere Town no longer received CMS support, and although the older settlement at Rabai continued, it too went into decline. When Ugandan railways were being built, many former slaves took jobs as porters, cooks, guides and servants. The consul-general of the British East African Protectorate followed a policy of allowing slavery on land to die out gradually—a position also adopted in the Sokoto Caliphate. It was not until the abolition of the legal status of slavery in 1907 that the practice was finally ended, with 7,683 slaves claiming freedom papers.[68]

Conclusion

The Trans-Atlantic is by far the best-studied aspect of the African slave trade, yet it is also misunderstood. The links with North

Africa and Iberia, which preceded the arrival of the Portuguese off West Africa in the fifteenth century, are seldom included in the discussion. As the Portuguese and other European powers pushed further down the African coast, their collaboration with the African rulers they encountered is also little acknowledged. This is no exoneration for the immense suffering that enslavement inflicted on West Africans; rather it is the context within which it occurred. Similarly, it is important to understand the links with the Indian Ocean trafficking, which saw so many people from what is today Mozambique transferred round the Cape into the Atlantic, to work on the plantations of Brazil and other American colonies. Portugal did not simply engage in trade; it settled large areas of what became Angola and Mozambique, imprinting enslavement, as well as Portuguese culture, on existing societies. European powers must take their share of responsibility for what ensued, but African elites cannot look back on their past contributions to the slave trade with pride.

Finally, there is the long, complex and finally successful attempt led by Britain to abolish slavery, first in its own empire and then across the world. London campaigned from the Ottoman and Ethiopian empires to the Americas. The Royal Navy spent decades trying to enforce abolition, losing thousands of sailors in the attempt. The slaves they freed had a torrid time of it. While the Union Jack was, indeed, the 'flag that set them free', their fate was not always a happy one. British pressure for abolition was not always maintained, but by the late nineteenth century it had borne fruit, in the form of international agreements and conventions designed to end enslavement. 'Given that policy was framed by treaty law and the desire to maintain stability, the process of suppressing the trade and abolition was gradual, but the trend was unmistakeable, as slavery became a moribund institution in large parts of Africa in the late nineteenth and early twentieth centuries.'[69]

PART 5

THE OTTOMAN EMPIRE AND BARBARY SLAVERY

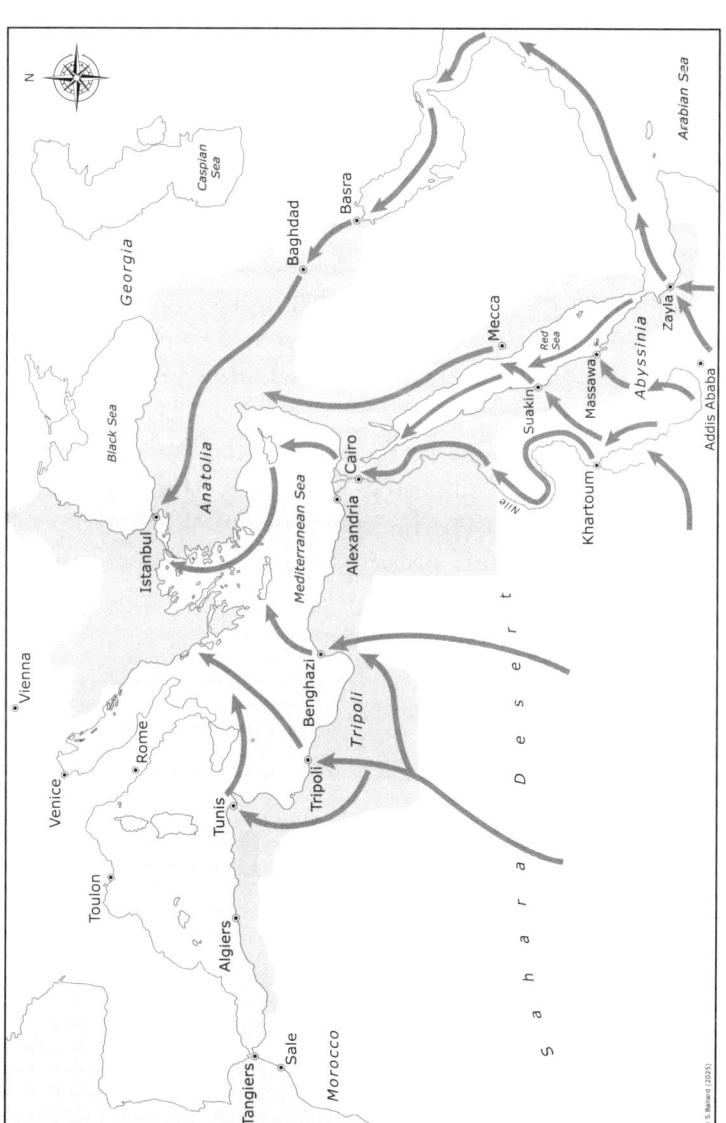

Map 6: Ottoman slave routes from Africa at the height of the empire, c. 1683

The map is largely adapted from Ehud R. Toledano, *The Ottoman Slave Trade and its suppression: 1840–1890*, Princeton University Press, 1982. Darker shading indicates the extent of the Ottoman Empire, c. 1683.

The Ottoman Empire and its colonies along the North African coast, the Barbary states, may seem tenuously related to African slavery, yet they are not. As we saw in the Introduction, the Ottomans enslaved some 1,167,000 Africans, whom they brought to various parts of their empire, while the Barbary corsairs took at least 1,000,000 Europeans to North Africa. Algiers alone is said to have imported 625,000 Europeans between 1520 and 1830.[1] It is important to remember that captives were transported in both directions: to and from Africa. The slave trade across the Mediterranean began in the time of the Greeks and Romans and continued down the centuries.[2]

The Ottomans were by no means alone in practicing African enslavement in Europe. Slaves from Africa were used extensively across Europe, although far fewer than the numbers that were transported to European colonies. Nations such as Portugal, France, Spain and the Netherlands used slaves at home, as well as on their tropical plantations. It is estimated that in the late eighteenth century there were more than 14,000 black people living in Britain as servants, pages and launderers, some of whom were nominally free, but unpaid and subservient.[3] At the same time, slave caravans across the Sahara continued to be received by the Barbary states throughout this period, as discussed in Part 1. Understanding this has not been made easier by the reluctance of North Africans to examine their role in this history. Slavery remains a 'taboo subject ... [in] contemporary Algeria', with what is described as an 'overwhelming silence' surrounding the topic.[4] This is an attempt to bring together some of these complex inter-relationships.

17

THE OTTOMANS

The Ottoman Empire grew out of a Turkoman tribe that left Central Asia before establishing themselves in the thirteenth century in Anatolia, the Turkish peninsula forming the western extremity of Asia. Osman I (r. 1280–1324) founded the dynasty and the empire took his name.[1] Over time the empire's Muslim troops became the scourge of Christendom, capturing Constantinople in 1453, capital and final vestige of the Holy Roman Empire. The city's magnificent cathedral (Santa Sophia) was transformed into a mosque (Hagia Sophia), encapsulating the transformation. The Ottomans drove the Venetians out of the eastern Mediterranean and moved northwards through the Balkans until their army stood at the gates of Vienna in 1683. There, the Hapsburg emperors finally halted their advance with assistance from Poland, Bavaria and other German states. Despite this setback, the Ottomans remained a vast, sprawling and mighty empire.

> At its height in the sixteenth and early seventeenth centuries, the Ottoman empire linked three continents: Asia, Europe and Africa. The empire stretched from the southern borders of the Holy Roman Empire through Hungary and the Balkans to Yemen and Eritrea in the south, controlling much of North Africa and western Asia, and encompassing an array of cultures, languages, peoples, climates and social and political structures.[2]

The Ottoman Empire became more than just an extended state with a vast bureaucracy. It has been described as 'arguably the most important Islamic power on the face of the earth. At the height of its expansion, it ruled a vast territory from the western Mediterranean to the Persian Gulf, from southern Poland to southern Sudan.'[3]

African slaves

This is not a history of the Ottoman civilisation. These chapters only explore their trade in African slaves and how this was extended into North Africa under the Barbary corsairs. Yet Africa was not the only source of slaves for the Ottomans; they also seized Europeans from the Caucuses, as well as from eastern and south-eastern Europe.[4] But the sultanate also turned to Africa. Ehud Toledano, one of the few academics to examine the African connection, has combed available archives to provide an assessment of the trade.

> Scattered data and reasonable extrapolations regarding the volume of the slave trade from Africa to the Ottoman Empire yield an estimated number of approximately 16,000 to 18,000 men and women who were transported into the empire per annum during much of the nineteenth century. Estimates for the total volume of coerced migration from Africa into the Ottoman territories are as follows: from Swahili coast to the Ottoman Middle East and India—313,000; across the Red Sea and the Gulf of Aden—492,000; into Ottoman Egypt—362,000; and into Ottoman North Africa (Algiers, Tunisia, and Libya)—350,000. If we exclude the number going to India, a rough estimate of this mass population movement would amount to more than 1.3 million. During the middle decades of the nineteenth century, the shrinking African traffic swelled the numbers of enslaved Africans coerced into domestic African markets, as well as into Ottoman ones.[5]

Despite the substantial numbers of Africans enslaved by the Ottomans, the subject has received little attention from scholars, both Turkish and international. 'Research that has been done on African Turks in general is very limited, whereas scholarly research on African Turks in Antalya is nonexistent,'[6] another author remarked. The subject has been considered too sensitive, and 'no big, conscious, and sociopolitically important community of people who consider themselves as descendants of enslaved people or slaveholders such as in the United States of America or South America exists in Southwest Asia and Turkey.'[7] This situation is gradually changing, but there is much work to be done.

African slaves became increasingly important for the Ottomans following the Russian conquest of Georgia and Circassia (1801–1828), which prevented the Ottomans from raiding these territories for European slaves.[8] The sources of the Africans were complex and their routes to their destinations in the Ottoman Empire were arduous. It is sometimes argued that Ottoman slavery was milder than enslavement in the Americas (for example) as there were no plantations and the slaves were offered an opportunity to integrate into Ottoman society through marriage or manumission. Ehud Toledano challenges that assumption.

> Evidence from various parts of the Ottoman Empire … suggests that even domestic slavery, especially for women, could not be described as 'mild.' The intimacy of the home, family, or household did not guarantee good treatment of the enslaved, and concubinage was a far cry from the ideal manner in which it was depicted by contemporary witnesses and later scholars who use their accounts.[9]

A letter from the Grand Vizier Mustafa Reşhid Pasha (effectively the Ottoman prime minister) to the empire's governor of Tripoli in November 1849 acknowledged the suffering that could be endured by the slaves in transit. The letter referred to the death from thirst of 1,600 black slaves, on their way from Bornu in northern Nigeria to Fezzan in southern Libya: 'While our Holy Law permits slavery it requires that slaves be treated with fatherly care, and those who act in a contrary manner will be condemned by God.' The governor was ordered to punish the slave dealers and to ensure that similar disasters did not recur.[10]

The Africans were acquired by the means described throughout this book: captured in wars, held after raids and kidnapping, or purchased from neighbouring powers.[11] Many were Ethiopian. The constant wars in southern and eastern Ethiopia provided slaves from among the Oromo and Sidama peoples. Ethiopian lords regularly exported their own subjects, and the Ottomans were willing recipients. Finally, there was the ancient practice of shipping slaves up the Nile or by caravan to Egypt.

> In the Upper Nile, Bahr al-Ghazal, and the White Nile areas, the activity of the European and Ottoman ivory traders quickly

developed in the 1850s into a massive slave-raiding and slave-trading operation … The raids were led by 'northern traders,' or Syrian, Egyptian and north-Sudanese merchants, most of whom were Ottoman subjects.[12]

The arduous caravans across the Sahara were described in Part 1, 'The Trans-Saharan Slave Trade', but other routes were also used to move the human cargo from Ethiopia and Sudan, and on to Ottoman cities across the empire. The first was by sea. In 1840, a British naval officer conducted a survey of traffic on the Gulf and found that 100 dhows were engaged in the slave trade in just two months—August and September. Each carried between fifty and 200 slaves. The officer described conditions on board dhows coming from Zanzibar to the Committee on the East African Slave Trade in graphic terms: 'The slaves, when taken from the slave-dhows, are generally in a filthy state, and ripe for an outbreak of an epidemic disease; it is, therefore, necessary that our cruizers [sic] should be relieved from their custody as quickly as possible.'[13]

When the Suez Canal was opened in 1869, it provided a direct route from Yemen and the north-eastern Mediterranean. Toledano explained that:

> The abundance of slaves in southwestern Arabia and their cheap prices created sufficient incentives for exportation … The slaves were invariably presented to the [Suez] authorities and to unfamiliar inquirers as servants or domestic slaves of the passengers and often carried certificates of manumission. Many slaves accompanied their masers out of their own free will, hoping to enjoy the amenities of life in a large Ottoman metropolis.[14]

The slaves, who were used in many roles, made up one fifth of the entire Ottoman population in the sixteenth century.[15] Some were given domestic labour, while pretty girls were sent to the harems. Female slaves were an integral part of the life of Egyptian cities under the Ottomans. Edward Lane, a British traveller who visited Egypt between 1833 and 1835, explained how they provided sexual services. Few Egyptians kept more than one wife, instead taking African women.

> [S]ome prefer the possession of an Abyssinian slave to the more
> expensive maintenance of a wife; and keep a black slave-girl, or
> an Egyptian female slave, to wait upon her, to clean and keep in
> order the apartments of the hareem, and to cook ... The white
> female slaves are mostly in the possession of wealthy Turks. The
> concubine-slaves in the houses of Egyptians of the higher or
> middle classes are, generally, what are termed 'Habasheeyehs,' that
> is, Abyssinians, of a deep brown or bronze complexion.[16]

Thomas Reade, Britain's acting consul-general in Cairo, gathered information by visiting slave markets in the Egyptian capital and its environs in August 1867 dressed as an Arab. He found 5,000 slaves for sale in Cairo itself and another 2,000 at the Tantah fair outside the city.[17] Reade recorded that up to 15,000 enslaved Africans annually were brought down the Nile to be sold in Cairo. This steady stream was kept up from 'Jalabat, on the Abyssinian frontier, [where] an enormous Slave Mart is constantly open,' as Reade put it.[18] In cities like Bursa, an important centre of silk production, the enslaved made up half the inhabitants, but the ethnic makeup of slave populations varied from city to city. In the Syrian port of Aleppo, for example, in the period 1640–1700, there were only sixteen Ethiopian slaves out of a slave population of almost 300.[19] The majority were Georgian or Russian. Some African slaves were eventually freed, but even then, they were regarded as inferior.

> One might argue that the key event of cultural and social integration
> for the female slave was mothering a child by her master, which
> gave the woman *umm al-walad* ('mother of the child') status. By
> law, her child was a free-born Muslim, and after the birth she could
> not be re-sold. In practice, however, the treatment of women with
> *umm al-walad* status varied considerably.[20]

Mothers could be separated from their children, even if they were manumitted.

> This was a practice that Islamic juridical literature and the Ottoman
> law courts permitted. Hence, in 1664 Ibrahim b. Halil el-Urfali,
> after acknowledging before the qadi that he had manumitted his
> pregnant Abyssinian female slave Fatima, delegated another man,
> Yusuf b. Murtaza, to marry her off to 'whomever she pleased'—

but only after she had given birth to the child that Ibrahim had fathered. While the court record indicates that Fatima had a choice in whom she might marry, it is probable that she paid a high price, that of separation from her child.[21]

Men who were castrated to become eunuchs had a particularly difficult time. An Ottoman woman, Leila Hanum, wrote in her memoirs in the 1920s of how they:

> were captured in the depths of Africa by men without a heart or pity, who then emasculated them between the ages of 8 and 12 years, sold them secretly to Arab slave traders who, in turn, sold them secretly to others with considerable profit. They were taken secretly to Istanbul.[22]

There the eunuchs were given an education in hygiene, writing, reading and mathematics, as well as being taught to pray. They were then put to service in the homes of the Ottoman elite. There were as many as 800 in the Ottoman court and palace alone, with many holding positions of considerable influence.

Istanbul's largest and busiest Ottoman slave market was a major attraction for European travellers. It did business every day from 8 a.m. until midday, except Fridays. Charles White published a vivid description of the market in 1845:

> In the center is a detached building, the upper portion serving as lodgings for slave dealers, and underneath are cells for *ajamee* (slaves newly imported). ... Under the colonnade are platforms, separated from each other by low railings and benches. Upon these dealers and customers may be seen seated during business hours smoking and discussing prices ... The platforms are divided from the chambers by a narrow alley, on the wall side of which are benches, where black women are exposed for sale. ... Underneath ... are ranges of cells, or rather vaults, infectiously filthy and dark. Those on the right are reserved for second-hand males; the furthest and worst of these dens being destined for those who, from bad conduct, are condemned by the kihaya to wear chains.[23]

It was not until 1877 that the Istanbul market was finally closed, but the trade itself did not cease. Instead, the market was transferred to the homes of the dealers, with the authorities taking care to look the other way.[24] Britain exerted considerable pressure on the Ottomans to end the slave trade, but with limited success. It was not until the 1880s and 1890s that there was a significant decline in the slave trade to the empire, as colonisation spread across Africa. 'Though still carried on to a limited extent, the [African] traffic certainly lost much of its force … European advances in Africa sharply reduced slave trading on the continent and, in the last decade of the nineteenth century, the sources of supply were severely curtailed.'[25]

18

THE BARBARY CORSAIRS

The Ottomans had risen to power as a land-based empire, but gradually acquired naval assets. This was particularly true after 1453 and the capture of Constantinople, renamed Istanbul. 'When need dictated, they became a sea power,' wrote Andrew Wheatcroft.[1] Over time the Ottomans' naval strength grew as they challenged the great Christian navies of the time: Venice, Genoa, the Knights of St John, Spain and France. This culminated in one of the most significant naval engagements of the age: the Ottoman victory at the battle of Zonchio in 1499.[2] It resulted in the banishment of the Venetian admiral, Antonio Grimani, for his failures.

This was by no means the last naval confrontation between the Christian states and the Ottomans. Aruj Reis and his brother Khizr would plague their rivals for years to come.[3] They became known and feared across the Christian world. The brothers, from the island of Lesbos, were born in the 1470s to a Turkish father and a Greek mother.[4] Aruj was captured in the 1490s by the Knights of St John and forced to row as a galley slave. It left Aruj with a visceral loathing of Christians.[5] Aruj became a prominent figure by transporting Muslim and Jewish refugees from Spain to North Africa after the capture of Granada by Ferdinand and Isabella in 1492, earning him the nickname 'Baba Aruj' (Father Aruj), which evolved into 'Barbarossa' (Redbeard) due to his red beard. The brothers worked together, attacking Christian vessels from Anatolian ports and later from Egypt, before moving operations to the island of Djerba, just off the Tunisian coast. It is the largest island off North Africa, an ideal base from which to raid Christian shipping. Aruj was badly wounded in clashes with the Genoese and lost an arm, but managed to rebuild the fleet and launched fresh attacks on the Italian coast. In 1516, the Muslim ruler of Algiers called on the brothers to help him capture a Spanish fortress just off the entrance to the port. This they agreed to, but when the fortress proved impregnable, Aruj changed tactic and overthrew and killed the ruler of Algiers, adding the city to his growing chain of territorial possessions.[6] In 1517, Aruj was attacked by Spanish forces and North African Muslims, but he defeated them both, extending his influence once again. In further fighting around Algiers against Spanish forces, the following year Aruj was killed. Control of his possessions, and the name 'Barbarossa', passed to his younger brother Khizr.[7]

In 1519, threatened by Spain, Khizr decided to formally submit to the Ottoman sultan, Selim I, who had asked for his assistance. The sultan had recently completed the conquest of the Mamluk Empire, which included Egypt, and was looking to extend Ottoman control west to Algiers. The sultan gave Khizr the honorary rank of *Beylerbey* (meaning the 'commander of commanders') and sent him 2,000 elite troops and artillery.[8] It was a moment of real significance. Not only had the Ottomans acquired the services of one of the most skilled naval officers of the period, but they had also extended their influence across the Mediterranean. In May 1529, Khizr once again laid siege to the Spanish fortress at the entrance of Algiers harbour. After a bombardment lasting three weeks, and with just twenty-five troops left alive, the Spanish commander Don Martin de Vargas finally surrendered.[9] The sultan accepted Algiers as a province of his empire, appointing Barbarossa as governor.[10] Although the link was sometimes tenuous, Barbarossa and the Barbary corsairs had become an integral part of the Ottoman Empire.

Over time the Barbary lands would extend from Morocco eastwards along the North African coastline, giving them access to the Atlantic as well as the Mediterranean. The single Ottoman governorship existed until 1587 when the sultan decided to establish three separate rulers for Algiers, Tunis and Tripoli, each appointed for a three-year term of office.[11] The sultan provided elite troops, known as janissaries, to bolster these states, drawn from Anatolia and the Levant. Gradually, real power ebbed away from the rulers (pasha) to their armies. The janissaries, operating an assembly of officers, became the real power in the Barbary states. They became 'an army of occupation' that 'jealously guarded their position, treating the indigenous Moors and Arabs with contempt.'[12] After 1659, the pasha of Algiers lost what little was left of his power and with it his claim to a share of the corsairs' booty. By this time, the authority of the Ottoman sultan had also become nominal, but it suited both parties to preserve the notion that the Barbary states were part of the wider empire.

Confronting Christians

Relations between the Ottomans and the Christians were far from straightforward. The sultan engaged in bitter fighting against the Hapsburgs and the Order of Knights of St John, then based in Rhodes, but this did not prevent an informal alliance between King Francis I of France and Sultan Suleiman I. The alliance allowed corsair vessels, with some 30,000 sailors, to seek protection from the Hapsburgs in the French port of Toulon in the winter of 1543–1544.[13] In return, the Barbary navy refrained from attacking French vessels. Indeed, there was a brief period (1533–1538) when there was overt Ottoman–French naval co-operation, with their fleets jointly raiding Italian ports.[14] The Hapsburgs were outraged.

> The sight of Christians fighting Christians with the help of Infidels was shocking enough to many people at the time, but there was worse to come … Toulon consequently became a Turkish colony for eight months … The transformation of a Christian town into a Moslem one, complete with mosque and a slave market, did not fail to amaze those who witnessed it.[15]

Although the Barbary fleet had found sanctuary in Toulon for a winter, as time passed their attacks on French vessels increased. Sultan Suleiman I ordered the North Africans to lay off the French, but ten galleons and a large number of smaller vessels were captured in the 1560s. The French, then under Charles IX, established a consulate in North Africa, yet still there were complaints that it was 'raining Christians in Algiers' as the number of French captives surged.[16] The corsairs were accused of practising 'the most detestable vices' on their captives, including sodomy, theft and pederasty, with the aid of renegades of Christianity who had gone over to Islam from Spain, Italy and Provence.[17] A treaty, or 'Capitulation', was signed between France and the Ottomans in 1604, allowing the French to chase, capture and punish corsairs who did not desist from pillaging French cargo, and requiring that the French slaves be freed.[18] France and Algiers reaffirmed this in 1619, but neither side displayed good faith; neither freed the other's slaves, who were valuable rowing in the galleys.

Agreements, formal and informal, were reached with other European powers over the centuries. As a result, the Barbary corsairs might attack certain foreign vessels in some periods, but offer them protection in others. These relations were cemented by Ottoman ambassadors who were sent to represent the sultan across Europe. '[T]he Ottoman Empire, Morocco, Algiers, Tunis, and Tripoli sent numerous embassies—probably more than three hundred—to Europe. They generally came with a considerable retinue of secretaries, interpreters, stewards, and others, including slaves.'[19]

The Kingdom of Naples exchanged envoys with the Barbary state in Tripoli in the 1740s. Hardly surprisingly, given this history, the consul's reception in Naples was distinctly cool. 'Frequent incursions, sacking, seizing of booty, and enslavement left indelible traces in the popular memory such that, when Haci Hüseyin Efendi and Mustafa Bey arrived in Naples, perceptions of the "Turks" were essentially negative.'[20] However, over the years the closer contacts began to soften these sentiments. The Barbary ambassadors came to be seen as:

> emissaries from a world full of every kind of rarity, luxury and marvel. Neapolitans even adopted new cultural practices such as drinking coffee, encouraged by their contact with Islamic worlds. The 'Turkish' drink inspired a growing number of new coffee houses across Italy and Europe where the bourgeois culture of the Enlightenment had begun to take root. In this regard, Bourbon political diplomacy enhanced the Neapolitans' cultural interest in the Islamic world.[21]

Despite their best efforts, these Barbary diplomats were unable to prevent their relations with European powers from gradually deteriorating. Raids by the Barbary states and attacks by European forces led to repeated confrontations. When two survivors of a particularly horrific Algerian attack made their way into Marseilles in March 1620, they had a terrible tale to tell. A ship had been captured, its goods seized, and the crew beheaded, one by one, and tossed into the sea.[22] An enraged crowd, two or three thousand strong, formed around the Algerian consulate in Marseille, which was finally invaded and the ambassador and his staff killed—forty-eight in all. The French authorities, aware that the diplomatic code had been broken, ordered the arrest and punishment of the perpetrators. Algiers was not placated. For the next eight years, the two powers were unofficially at war.[23] Finally, the European powers, together with the United States, extinguished the Barbary corsairs, but not until well into the nineteenth century.

African slaves in Europe

Our concern here is the fate of the slaves who were captured by the corsairs and transported to Africa, but this was no one-sided affair. European powers seized and enslaved thousands of Ottomans and North Africans, who were forced to row Maltese, Italian, Spanish and French galleys.[24] Estimates of the numbers of these galley slaves include 1,500 to 2,000 in Malta; 20,000 in Italy, principally Livorno; and 25,000 to 30,000 in Spain. The French also used Africans as oarsmen, but often they were recruited voluntarily.[25] Exactly how many Africans were held by European powers has yet to be accurately estimated. As Kate Lowe observed: '[T]he black African presence has been so completely ignored. The reasons for this are manifold, but an absence of material is not one of them. Far from being genuinely invisible the traces of these fifteenth- and sixteenth-century black Africans can be found in almost every type of record.'[26]

Some indication of the numbers of African slaves in the Iberian Peninsula was provided in Part 4, 'Trans-Atlantic Slavery'. There are also estimates of the numbers of Muslim slaves in central and western Europe, but they do not identify which of these were African. The number of Islamic slaves was put at '2,525 million of all origins between 1500 and 1800—most of those, about 2,250 million, between 1500 and 1649.'[27] From the 1500s, most slave labour was transferred from the European mainland to colonies in the Americas, but not all of it. There is fragmentary evidence of African slaves in the Italian territories, from Sicily to Tuscany, the Republic of Genoa, Venice and Rome itself.[28] Smaller numbers were to be found in northern Europe, from Britain to Germany and Poland. The 1570s saw African slaves brought to Britain to serve as domestic servants, entertainers and prostitutes, with Africans in the courts of Henry VIII, Elizabeth I and James I.[29] The duke of Medina Sidonia had seven black slaves in his stables in Seville, while Catherine of Austria was given a black pastry chef and confectioner named Domingos de Frorenca as a wedding present in 1526 by her Portuguese husband, King Joao III.[30] The Dutch captured 132 men from the Barbary port of Sale in 1636 and subsequently sold them as slaves.[31] However, the numbers involved were small when compared with the slave labour used in the colonies: European industries and agriculture did not need the constant supplies of labour that the plantations in the colonies required.

The slave markets of Malta, run by the Knights of St John, were the largest in this period. The number of slaves fluctuated from the mid-sixteenth century, peaking in the 1700s at 3,000, only to gradually decline.[32] But here again, some were North Africans and some were Turks. They rowed the Order's galleys, worked in their shipyard and constructed Malta's massive fortifications. Some were ransomed, while most were not. Their lives were brutal and all forms of dissent were swiftly crushed.[33] Slave revolts were recorded in 1531, 1596 and 1749. None succeeded. In the Barbary states there was resistance as well. In Algiers in 1763, 4,000 'Christian slaves ... rose and killed their guards and massacred all that came in their way. All the ... gates of the town were shut; a general massacre was apprehended, but after some hour's carnage, during which the streets ran with blood, quiet was restored.'[34]

19

SLAVES OF THE BARBARY STATES

The situation in Europe was replicated on the other side of the Mediterranean, as the Barbary corsairs came to dominate the seas. The three North African states—Algeria, Tunisia and Tripoli—were part of the Ottoman Empire. Istanbul had a significant influence until the early eighteenth century, although this gradually waned. The northern European states sometimes signed treaties with their Barbary counterparts, obtaining guarantees of safe passage (or letters of marque, as they were known) from the rulers. In exchange, the Barbary vessels were able to pass through European waters unmolested on a reciprocal basis.[1] The result was a complex web of alliances and conflicts that spanned nations, religions and decades.

The Barbary corsairs attacked their opponents across a vast area, from the Mediterranean to the Atlantic and the North Sea, while simultaneously trading successfully with their allies.

> In order to join this international enterprise of privateering, Morocco and the three regencies developed fleets of varying size and effectiveness, the largest operating out of Algiers and Sallee [in Morocco] and the smallest out of Tripoli. An unwritten agreement seems to have divided the spheres of operation: Tripolitanian privateers stayed close to home, attacking Maltese and Neapolitan ships, while Tunisian brigantines and galleys roved the eastern Mediterranean and particularly targeted trade in the Adriatic Sea. On the Atlantic coast of Morocco, Sallee grew as a privateering harbour soon after its settlement by embittered Moriscos, refugees from Hornachos in Spain, who arrived there in the early seventeenth century.[2]

In the 1600s there was a gradual change in technology as the Barbary corsairs moved away from galleys (and the slaves that were required to row them) to square rigged ships. The new technology was largely provided by Europeans, who either joined the corsairs willingly or were captured during raids. The defeat of the Spanish Armada by England's Elizabeth I in 1588 brought peace, but left large numbers of sailors in northern Europe out of work and seeking alternative employment. Some, including Dutch and English mariners, found an alternative in North Africa. It is estimated that between 1580 and 1680, half of all Barbary captains were of European origin.[3] They went over to the Barbary powers, bringing with them concepts of rigged ships that could navigate the Atlantic. This allowed for a sharp reduction in the number of sailors on each vessel. The largest war-galleys had required banks of oarsmen, five men to an oar, with a total of 250 per vessel. It was estimated in 1676 that of 18,000 European slaves then employed in Algiers, only 900 were still rowing on galleys.[4]

The new technology, using sails and the power of the wind, allowed for voyages well beyond the Mediterranean. By 1627, Barbary vessels were raiding as far away as Iceland. By 1630, they were attacking the Atlantic coasts of Portugal, Spain, France and England while also raiding across the Atlantic, in the Azores and the Newfoundland fisheries off North America.[5] In these expeditions the corsairs were joined by Europeans who had gone over to their side. The idea of raiding Iceland is said to have come from a Dane called Paul in 1627, Iceland then being a Danish possession. During the raid, 242 men, women and children were captured and between thirty and forty killed. 'The ship finally reached Algiers on 17 August 1627. In all the expedition had yielded 400 Icelandic and Danish captives, who were all sold as slaves in Algiers.'[6]

British slaves

The Barbary corsairs raided all around the British Isles, with slaves taken from Cornwall, Devon and Scotland, as well as Ireland. Some Scottish ports were so severely attacked that the king ordered 'general contributions' to provide relief for the families of the captives and the townspeople.[7] Devon and Cornwall suffered repeated assaults in the seventeenth century. In August 1625, Mount's Bay in Cornwall was attacked and sixty men, women and children were taken into slavery. Fishing boats from Looe, Penzance, Mousehole and other Cornish ports were boarded, their crews taken captive and their empty vessels left to drift ashore. As many as sixty Barbary men-of-war prowled the Devon and Cornish coasts and attacks occurred almost daily.[8] In that year, the mayor of Plymouth, Thomas Ceely, complained to the authorities of the scale of the Barbary threat. He explained that in one year a thousand sailors were taken from the region. Twenty-seven ships and 200 people had been seized during one ten-day period alone. Eighty were captured in the port of Looe:

> [O]ne poore Maritime Towne in Cornwall call[ed] Loo [sic] hath within ten dayes last past lost 80 Marryners and Saylers which were bound in fishing voyages for the deepes, and there have ben taken by the turks within the sayd tyme 27 Shipps and barkes at least, and in them there could not be lesse that [sic] 200 persons.[9]

The island of Lundy, in the English Channel, was occupied intermittently by the corsairs from 1625 until 1636 and used as a base to carry out raids along the English coast. Their activities had such a severe impact that in 1636 the merchants and ship owners of Plymouth, Barnstable and Southampton wrote that they would no longer attempt to go to sea, as the waters were 'much infested by Turkish pirates from Algiers, and especially from Sally in Barbary.'[10] This was no exaggeration: eighty-seven ships and around 3,000 seamen had been taken captive. The pirate who led these operations was a Dutch privateer, Jan Janszoon, who went over to the Barbary corsairs and became known as Murat Rais the Younger.[11]

Murat Rais is best known for his attack on the Irish village of Baltimore in County Cork.[12]

> Shortly before midnight on Sunday the 19 June 1631 two Algerian ships dropped anchor just outside the entrance to the harbour of Baltimore, south-west Cork, Ireland. At 2 a.m. armed men in the ships' boats rowed quietly into a muddy cover a quarter of a mile south of the main village. Here the fishermen's houses were set on fire and 111 captives were seized, together with some booty. Early next morning two elderly were sent on shore, and at four in the afternoon the Algerians sailed away.[13]

This was the most devastating attack the British Isles endured.[14] Efforts were made to free them for years. In 1640, the English Parliament passed an Act to redeem captives 'taken by Turkish, Moorish and other pirates from the cruel thraldom which they lay under.'[15] Edward Cason was sent to Algiers with funds provided by Parliament to pay for their release. His mission was plagued with bad luck; he was attacked en route and had to return to England to replenish his funds. It was not until September 1646 that he arrived in Algiers to meet the local ruler and bargain for the 650 British captives that were being held, including the Irish. It was no easy task. 'The greatest part of the inhabitants had rather keep their slaves than permit them to be freed,' he explained to Parliament.[16] 'They come to much more per head than I expected … Here be many women and children which cost £50 per head, first penny [whose investors] might sell them for an hundred.' Men were cheaper, going for £38 by the time they were on board. In the end, Cason only had sufficient funds to pay for some of the slaves, and after further funds were sent from London he returned home with the 264 men, women and children that he had managed to free. Of these, only Joane Broadbrook and Ellen Hawkins finally returned to the village of Baltimore.[17] The rest had died in servitude in the previous fifteen years, or converted to Islam and 'gone Turk'. William Okeley said of his captivity: '[We were] so habituated to bondage that we almost forgot liberty, and grew stupid and senseless from our slavery.'[18]

The numbers taken by the corsairs across the Mediterranean dwarfed those captured during attacks on the British Isles. Barbary fleets would often wait offshore until they found an opportune moment to attack.

> One tried and true strategy used by the Barbary corsairs was to lie in wait in bays or inlets and on islets close to the community that was to be attacked, and to wait until night to catch the local population unawares; the same 'surprise effect' could be achieved if the attack coincided with a religious holiday, when military vigilance was relaxed.[19]

The complexity of the relations between the corsairs and the Europeans is captured by Franca Pirolo, who investigated Barbary raids on the Italian states.

During the 16th and 17th centuries, Turkish pirates and Barbary corsairs continuously attacked the coasts of Southern Italy. Both foreign threats wielded expanding power; the increasing naval supremacy of the Ottoman Turks heralded the era of their empire's greatest power and glory, while the Barbary corsairs—pirates and privateers who operated from North Africa under the protection of the Ottoman Empire—extended their maritime dominance by increasing the size of the fleets with which they besieged the coasts of Mediterranean countries, especially Italy and Spain. Southern European nations responded to this period of the so-called 'corsair wars' by seeking new methods to secure peace. This, in turn, stimulated diplomacy, commercial exchange, and religious conversion as well as slavery between Muslim and Christian powers across the Mediterranean Sea. [20]

Conditions of slavery in the Barbary states

The enslavement of Europeans by Barbary corsairs reached its peak in the first half of the seventeenth century. The corsairs were at their most active, capturing hundreds of ships and thousands of Europeans, mostly at ports along the Mediterranean coastline. Once they arrived in one of the Barbary states, the captives were brutally treated.

> Upon returning to their home ports, captors customarily paraded their human commodities who were chained and nearly naked, having been robbed of their clothes. The port population, along with the officials who had financed the privateers, came out to inspect the captives and their booty. The captives were then led before the local ruler (who was also the chief shareholder in all privateering ventures), and he chose the best for himself. [21]

For the women, the inspection was an experience of utter humiliation. So repulsive was the prospect that some female captives begged their husbands to kill them. Another pleaded with her mother to slash her face with a knife so that she would be grotesquely disfigured. [22] Virgins were highly valued and particularly sought after by the rulers for their harems. This, of course, required an intimate examination of the women. The prospective purchasers 'have liberty to view their Faces, and to put their Fingers into their mouth to feel their Teeth; and also to feel their Breasts. And ... they are sometimes permitted by the Sellers (in a modest way) to be search'd whether they are Virgins.'[23] Once the initial rituals were over, the slaves were taken to public bathhouses which were used as holding pens for the captives. Conditions were terrible. A naval officer described the jails in Algiers as 'most resembl[ing] a house where the negroes of the West India Islands kept their pigs.'[24]

Slaves entered households which might consist of very large numbers of slaves. An Italian convert, Ali Bicnin, who led the Algerian corsairs in the second quarter of the seventeenth century, could boast two palaces. He was served by up to 800 slaves—in addition to those that rowed his boats and worked on his farms.[25] Men who were despatched to the galleys suffered some of the harshest conditions: fed on bread and water, naked to the waist, and flogged if they failed to row with sufficient vigour. Few lasted very long. 'Attrition rates for white slaves were estimated at 20 per cent a year in the seventeenth-century Maghrib, and this meant that large inflows of newcomers were necessary to sustain the existing population.'[26] So harsh were the conditions that it has been estimated that 'the crude mortality rates among whites were probably higher than among blacks in the Americas, even on sugar plantations.'[27]

The enslaved who were kept in town generally had better prospects. Skilled slaves were put to work in their professions. Some rose to become merchants and might be well treated by their new masters. Others were allowed a degree of freedom in their movement and were permitted to worship together as Christians three times a week in Algiers.[28] If they were lucky, some came to run taverns, selling wine to Ottoman troops and renegade soldiers, as well as their fellow captives. Others went into surgery, while some became scribes, writing the letters home for fellow captives. This was encouraged by their captors, who were keen to see what ransoms could be extracted for the men and women that they had seized. There were also important roles that slaves fulfilled as clerks, keeping a tally of other slaves: how many there were, what work they were given and how many had died. 'The highest ranking administrative slave role was the Christian Secretary to the [Algerian] Dey, who kept accounts related to Christian slaves and their ransoms and corresponded on the ruler's behalf with Europeans and American powers.'[29]

Those captives who were sufficiently high-born were treated better than others, in the expectation that they might be ransomed for a large sum.[30] Some noble women were even allowed to marry. For the rest, there was just the hope that people from their home village or region might rally round and raise cash to buy their freedom. Friends and families, sometimes backed by senior members of the clergy, would raise what funds they could. Religious orders in Spain and France, the Mercedarians and the Trinitarians, organised the fundraising.[31] In Britain, local initiatives to raise ransoms were taken up by the state. In one instance, 1,000 women appealed to the Privy Council.[32] There were also appeals to the king in 1632 to send the fleet to free the captives.[33] Then, in October 1640, a petition signed by about 3,000 of Charles I's subjects who were being held captive in Algeria came before Parliament. It drew attention to their 'most unsufferable labours, as rowing in galleys, drawing in carts, grinding in mills, with divers [sic] such unchristian like works most lamentable to express and most burdensome to undergo.'[34]

Their repeated pleas were finally heeded, and in the seventeenth century the English fleet attacked the harbours of Morocco, Tunisia, Algeria and Libya. Yet still the British continued to be taken captive and rot in servitude. Although large sums of money were raised, the numbers that ever returned were low. Perhaps as few as 3 or 4 per cent of all slaves were actually ransomed. The rest remained in slavery until they perished, joined their captor or were freed by force.[35]

Slaves belonging to the most senior officials were kept in slave pens, or *bagnios*, overnight, with a narrow entrance and few windows. In 1666, a Flemish captive wrote of being held with more than 500 slaves in Algiers in just such a *bagnio*, with more than twenty languages being spoken. These were stinking holes, infested with fleas and baking hot in the summer.[36] Slaves who worked for the state were provided with no more than a shirt, shorts and a pair of sandals per year, and given bread to survive on.[37] Conditions in Moroccan towns were said to be even worse.[38] At times the imprisoned slaves were left to starve, with Moors shouting at them to eat stones to survive. Dead dogs and cats would be thrown into the dungeons to humiliate them.[39] These stories were recounted by those who were ransomed or managed to escape. Were the accounts accurate, or exaggerations? It is hard to tel. As Nabil Matar concludes: 'With the authority of experience behind them, the captives-turned-writers presented opinions readers must have viewed as accurate and objective.'[40] They certainly coloured relations between the Christian and Muslim worlds.

20

FIGHTING AND DOING DEALS WITH THE BARBARY STATES

As we have seen, the Barbary states were founded in battle. The corsairs established them as a bastion of the Ottoman Empire in the western Mediterranean. Gradually these links waned, but the states continued to contest control of the seas, including the Atlantic. All the old powers—France, the Italian states, Spain, Britain and the Netherlands—fought the Barbary states, when they were not making deals with the corsairs. These complex relationships were illustrated by the close co-operation between the British and the Barbary rulers when it suited both parties. 'All Barbary corsairs posed a threat to all European trading nations which, in theory, could have combined against them. In practice, co-operation proved impossible, with operations against Barbary scaled down or abandoned whenever war broke out in Europe.'[1]

This pattern of disrupted co-operation between the Europeans occurred notably during the French Revolutionary Wars (1792–1802) and the Napoleonic Wars (1803–1815), as Caitlin Gale has shown by reference to the comprehensive data kept by London insurers in the Lloyd's Lists.[2] British ships visited the North Africans, returning with corn and meat that was vital to Britain when wars meant that other markets were closed.

> The Barbary States were a crucial part of the British military strategy in the Mediterranean and a vital part of their supply chain … Correspondence between the admirals in the Mediterranean and the British government demonstrated the importance Barbary's trade and friendship held for Britain. Barbary provided supplies

and food. Their necessity increases with each new force and garrison established there.[3]

This was one side of the relationship, but there was conflict as well. As the corsair raids spread across the Atlantic, other powers were drawn in. The Danes had been involved since 1627 when Algerians raided several places in Iceland, then under the Danish crown. This was just the beginning of these attacks.

> They landed, for instance in 1627, in several places in Iceland and made more than a hundred people captives after having robbed and destroyed the villages. The same year Algerians killed at least thirty-four people and took with them as prisoners 242 inhabitants from the small island of Heimaey off the southern coast of Iceland. In 1629, they carried off thirty women from the settlement of Hvalba in the Faroe Islands.[4]

The Danish kings attempted to do deals with the Barbary states. From 1748, it was compulsory for all ships flying Danish colours and destined for ports beyond Cape Finisterre to carry an Algerian sea pass. This held true for voyages to Spain, Portugal and all ports in the Mediterranean.[5] Despite the passes, the scourge of enslavement did not end. In 1753 the Danish kingdom finally resorted to sending a fleet to Morocco to demand the return of Danish captives.[6] This did not put an end to the issue, and war erupted, from 1769 to 1772, this time with Algiers. The Danish fleet was unsuccessful. Plagued by illness and poorly equipped, the ships were forced to return home empty-handed. It was only in 1772 that a treaty was finally concluded, with both sides freeing the captives that they had held.[7]

The newly independent United States of America also became a target for the Barbary corsairs. The first encounter took place in 1625, just five years after the early puritans on board the *Mayflower* had landed in Plymouth. Two American ships were captured and the captives taken to the Moroccan port of Salee.[8] Despite appeals to the English crown for protection, the clashes and enslavement continued, as the corsairs spread their activities across the Caribbean and onwards to the Americas. The American War of Independence from Britain (1775–1783) left the United States free, but without the protection of the Royal Navy. The Americans had no fleet of their own and were even more at the mercy of the Barbary states, who were seizing growing numbers of captives. By 1793, Algiers alone held 119 American sailors in its prisons.[9] Ransoms were paid for their freedom, but their prices continually rose. This could not continue indefinitely. In January 1794, the U.S. Congress resolved to establish a navy for the purpose of protecting American commerce abroad. Passing a resolution was one thing; having deployable warships was another. It would take two years before the first would come off the drydock; with a forty-four-gun frigate, the *United States* launched on 10 May 1797.[10] The year before, the Americans had been forced to pay the astronomical sum of $642,000, one fifteenth of all federal spending, for the release of 107 Americans held in Algiers, some of whom had languished there for more than ten years.[11]

In 1800, Tripoli gave the U.S. an ultimatum: pay $225,000 or face war. Newly elected President Thomas Jefferson had had enough. He despatched a squadron to blockade Tripoli. At the end of the Tripolitan War (1801–1805), the U.S. signed treaties with all three Barbary states and freed some 300 American prisoners.[12] It was during this war that a force of eight U.S. marines, bolstered by 500 Egyptians, Greeks and mercenaries of other nationalities, marched across the desert from the Egyptian port of Alexandria to capture the Tripolitan city of Derna. It was an extraordinarily arduous expedition, during which they were said to have seen 'neither house nor tree, nor hardly anything green ... not a trace of a human being.'[13] When they reached Derna, they seized it. The pasha of Tripoli, Yusuf Karamanli, who had previously successfully extorted vast sums from the Americans, capitulated. It was the first victory for the United States on foreign soil and is still recalled in the Marines' Hymn, in the line, 'to the shores of Tripoli'. The American presence in Derna was soon abandoned and Washington paid $60,000 dollars for the release of all American prisoners, after which no further tribute would be paid to Tripoli.[14] It was a huge sum, but the whole war against the Barbary states had cost over 3 million dollars, or a third of the entire budget of the U.S. government.[15]

By 1807, Algiers was once more attacking American vessels. Britain had suffered down the years from corsair raids, but in the early nineteenth century the British were more concerned with crushing Napoleon and trying to end the rebellion of their American colony. During the 1812 war between London and Washington, Algeria sided with the Americans.[16] This relationship was short-lived. In May 1815, U.S. President Madison sent another fleet, this time ten-strong, to attack Algiers. The expedition was a success and terms were dictated in which all captured American slaves and ships would be returned and no further tributes paid. In 1816, the Algerians attempted to renege on this agreement. In response, Madison deployed the U.S. Mediterranean Squadron to protect American ships. As the Napoleonic Wars came to a close, the demand for action against the Barbary states became too strong for European politicians to ignore, and they joined the American navy's assault. The Congress of Vienna, held in 1814–1815, pledged to put an end to their raiding and enslavement.[17] At the time there were still 600 white slaves in Tripoli, most of them Italian.[18]

'Anglo-Dutch and Anglo-French naval forces attacked Barbary ports in 1816 and 1819 respectively, and the United States forcefully imposed a treaty on Algiers in 1815. The French seizure of Algiers in 1830 ended a process of cajoling, intimidating, or battering the Barbary states into freeing their Christian slaves.'[19] French colonisation of North Africa finally extinguished the Barbary corsairs and the states they had established. In 1881, France imposed a protectorate over Tunisia after the British withdrew objections to French expansion at the Congress of Berlin in 1878.[20] France maintained the administration of the bey of Tunis, but under French supervision, imposing the same rule over Morocco. The threat that the Barbary corsairs had represented to nations from Norway to Newfoundland and across the Mediterranean was finally at an end. No longer would European sailors sight a sail on the horizon with apprehension and dread. Once an arm of the Ottoman Empire, the corsairs had unleashed a terror which was ingrained in European legend and myth.

Conclusion

Perhaps the clearest lesson to be drawn from the Ottoman Empire and the Barbary states is the inter-dependence of Mediterranean nations and their ability to affect states as far afield as the Americas. The Barbary corsairs preyed upon their northern neighbours, bringing Europeans to the shores of North Africa, few of whom ever returned. They became part of the social fabric of Algeria, Morocco and Tunisia, just like the African slaves whom they continued to bring across the Sahara. However, the scale of European enslavement cannot be overlooked.

> On Barbary galleys or Ottoman ships there were more Christian slaves than there were volunteers, condemned criminals, or Janissaries. In the centre or Algiers or Tunis and throughout the suburbs, the workshops, shipyards and warehouses functioned on the backs of a slave workforce. There was a vast pool of slave labour, constantly renewing itself and being renewed, underpinning the entire economic life of such communities.[21]

All slaves endured terrible suffering, whether they came from Africa or Europe. Some managed by skill and good fortune to rise up the social hierarchy. A few even obtained their freedom. The vast majority were permanently deprived of their families, from which they had been so cruelly separated. Africans transported by France, Portugal, Spain and Italy to Europe as captives also gradually became integrated into European society. Much research is still required if this story is to be fully fleshed out.

It is argued that perceptions of the cruelty of the corsairs laid the groundwork for future European attitudes towards North Africans and Islam. 'Barbary's slavery, piracy, cruelty and vengefulness reinforced the connotations of barbarism and built up through the centuries a system of beliefs which became the ideological expression of a would-be dominant European society, turning history into myth, creating a specific social disposition, inducing attitudes, and inculcating ways of behavior.'[22] There appears to be some truth in this view, although it fails to acknowledge the comparable manipulation of the term 'crusaders' by contemporary Islamic societies. The troubled relationship between Europe and Africa is too complex to be reduced to a single historical factor.

PART 6

SLAVERY TODAY

'Thinking that slavery has a five-thousand-year history in the region perhaps one is less surprised that it should not have ended,' wrote Richard Lobban.[1] If slavery were just an ancient phenomenon, consigned to humanity's past, it would be bad enough, but it is not. Although most people assume enslavement is over, it continues to be found in countries across much of Africa. It is a little-acknowledged fact that it is still possible to own, buy and sell, capture and ransom, trade in and become rich from African slaves to this day. This is not a reference to what is termed 'modern slavery', but the old-fashioned kind: chattel slavery. This has been masked.

> [S]ince the independence of African countries in the 1960s and 1970s, slavery has become largely a subterranean force, no longer legal in most countries but continuing in various contexts, just as slavery has persisted elsewhere in the world. Some countries that include territory in the Sahara, such as Mauretania [sic], Niger, and elsewhere, have been particularly reticent in ending slavery, and when slavery has been suppressed, dependent relationships arising from former servitude have persisted, limiting the access of the descendants of slaves to land and other resources. ... A preoccupation with trans-Atlantic slavery or the African diaspora in the Americas risks losing perspective on the long trajectory of slavery in Africa and indeed the Indian Ocean.[2]

Contemporary enslavement takes many forms, with African slavers controlling lives across the continent. Yet the two organisations established to represent African states and their peoples, the African Union and the Arab League, do not appear keen to investigate these practices. Even the United Nations has made only limited efforts to highlight contemporary slavery. While aspects of the European slave trade have been researched in detail, and issues of reparations have begun to be discussed in the West, the same cannot be said of the Arab world. 'In contrast to the Atlantic slave trade and the allied chattel slavery of Africans in the Americas, the subject of Arab slavery of Africans is one which many would prefer to be buried and about which there is curiously an unspoken understanding that we should generally be silent.'[3]

Slaves can still be found in at least five African states: Mauritania, Mali, Niger, Libya and Sudan. A combination of history, societal pressures, conflict, poverty, greed and corruption keep diverse forms of enslavement alive. I will examine each nation in turn, before considering the reaction of international organisations. However, some forms of enslavement cross borders and can be found in more than one nation. This is particularly true among the Tuareg, who live in large parts of the Sahara and the Sahel, including Algeria, Libya, Niger, Mali and Mauritania. I will deal with this briefly under 'Mali', while acknowledging that it is more widespread.

21

CONTEMPORARY AFRICAN SLAVERY

Mauritania

Anyone who is sceptical about contemporary enslavement need look no further than Mauritania. Its social makeup is complex, leading a commentor to remark that: 'Slavery in Mauritania is also a racial slavery.'[1] The social structure of the country is divided between the dominant Arab–Berber minority—the so-called 'white' Moors, or Beydane—and the subservient 'black' Moors, or Haratine, who are slaves or descendants of slaves. The 'white' Moors form about 30 per cent of the population and the 'black' Moors 40 per cent.[2] The remaining 30 per cent of the population are African migrants from states bordering Mauritania, some of whom have also been enslaved.

Tomoya Obokata, UN special rapporteur on contemporary forms of slavery, produced his latest report on Mauritania in May 2022.[3] Professor Obokata summed up the findings of his recent visit:

> Slavery exists within Arabic-speaking communities, also known as Moors, as well as within Black Mauritanian communities such as the Soninke, Wolof and Fulani. The Moor community consists of two groups, the dominant Beydane, of Arab-Berber background, and the Haratine, descendants of enslaved persons originating from Black communities in the south of Mauritania who now share the culture of the Beydane. The Haratine have historically been subject to chattel slavery, and this practice persists, although it is perhaps less prevalent than in the past. Even where there are no formal ties of 'ownership', many Haratine remain economically, socially and culturally dependent on their historical enslavers owing to

a lack of viable economic alternatives and the multiple forms of discrimination they face.[4]

There is no official information on the numbers of enslaved Mauritanians. The government actively discourages the collection of this data and does not collect information about the race or ethnicity of the population.[5] Indeed, the government has flatly denied any enslavement. An official representative told the UN Committee on the Rights of the Child in September 2001 that: 'Mauritanian society had never known servitude, exclusion or discrimination, either in the pre-colonial or colonial period or since independence, and so no vestiges of such practices could thus persist.'[6] At other times the official stance is that laws have eliminated the issue. One of the few estimates of the numbers of Haratine (but not of the non-Moorish Mauritanians) who live in slavery was provided by the U.S. State Department in 1994.

> The most common situation involves Haratine who live independently but continue, from a sense of fear and duty, to perform unpaid labor for their former masters. Anecdotal accounts indicate that there still may be individuals forcibly held against their will in urban areas as well as in isolated communities. Their numbers are difficult to quantify, although credible reports indicate that there are from 30,000 to 90,000 people living in slavery.[7]

Mauritanian governments, both colonial and post-colonial, have attempted to ban enslavement, but to little effect. Mauritania declared independence from France on 28 November 1960, and laws and decrees outlawing slavery were passed in 1981, 2007, 2014 and 2016.[8] Although recognising slavery as a crime against humanity, the laws have had only limited impact. As Professor Obokata made clear after his 2022 visit:

> Despite the strides that the leadership of Mauritania has made in acknowledging the continued existence of slavery and the important measures implemented to strengthen the country's anti-slavery legislative framework and facilitate the integration of victims, descent-based slavery continues to persist in Mauritania alongside contemporary forms of slavery and other slavery-like

practices. Victims of slavery face social exclusion and significant barriers relative to other Mauritanians in terms of accessing basic services, land rights, and decent work.[9]

This is the formal situation. Yet it is easy to lose sight of the individuals trapped in servitude. In 2018, the British *Guardian* newspaper published an in-depth article by Seif Kousmate, a photojournalist who spent a month with the slaves. Tens of thousands remain trapped in these conditions, he reported, with 'darker-skinned inhabitants beholden to their lighter-skinned "masters"'.[10] 'Slave status is passed down from mother to child, and anti-slavery activists are regularly tortured and detained. Yet the government routinely denies that slavery exists in Mauritania, instead praising itself for eradicating the practice.' Even freed slaves are restricted to poorly paid jobs and have no access to education. Others remained in servitude.

> Mabrouka, 20, was a child when she was taken from her mother, also a slave, to serve with a family in the south-western Rosso area. Around the age of 11, when she was cooking for her masters, she was badly burned on her left arm. She still suffers from the pain. Mabrouka was 14 when she was freed in 2011, but was never able to go to school. She got married at the age of 16 and is now the mother of Meriem, four, and two-month-old Khadi.[11]

Since independence, political movements have developed to take up the cause of these oppressed. El-Hor ('The Freeman') came into being in 1978, after droughts had driven many into the cities, undermining the hold the elite had over their slaves.[12] El-Hor fought for the rights of 'black Moors'. The wider black population remained excluded from their work. El-Hor has been gradually accommodated by the government. In 1986, black Africans formed FLAM—Forces de libération africaines de Mauritanie.[13] They called for an armed uprising against the state.[14] Ethnic tensions rose. In 1989, the Mauritanian government unleashed repression against the Africans, forcing some 80,000 to flee to neighbouring Senegal and Mali. This was accompanied by the executions of several hundred black African troops and officers who had been associated with FLAM.[15] Further movements, including SOS Esclaves, were founded to take up the cause. SOS Esclaves has formed partnerships with international organisations, including Anti-Slavery International, which says it provides financial aid and education and helps bring cases against slave masters.[16]

Slaves and former slaves are not just found in rural areas, but also in the capital, Nouakchott, especially since the exodus from the countryside following the famines of the 1970s. Shanty towns and squatter settlements dot the city's neighbourhoods. In 2013, Biram Dah Abeid, president of the IRA (Initiative pour la résurgence du mouvement abolitionniste) and a descendant of slaves, told a Belgian newspaper that:

> We fight in the capital, Nouakchott, in the rich, residential and administrative neighbourhoods where the ruling class lives. Those we have managed to take before the courts are part of the dominant bourgeoisie that has studied in Europe … The latest case IRA worked on is a business man, cousin of the President, whose house is 30 metres away from the Presidential palace … How can we say that slavery is present only in rural areas? Slavery continues in these well-off circles. There are more cases of slavery in the cities than in the rural areas.[17]

Activists who have taken up their cause continue to be repressed and even killed.[18] At the same time, Professor Obokata was able to record limited progress after his 2022 visit to the country. There was also progress in the question of recognition. 'Official denials of slavery are now the exception rather than the norm, and the Special Rapporteur is encouraged by the steps that the country's leaders have taken to acknowledge, prevent and address slavery.'[19] Professor Obokata urged Mauritania's government 'to do more to tackle the root causes of slavery, including the deep-rooted societal and cultural acceptance of slavery and marginalization of victims.'[20]

Mali

There are hundreds of thousands of slaves in Mali, a fact that has repeatedly been brought to the attention of the international community through the work of Professor Obokata and Alioune Tine, the UN independent expert on human rights in Mali. They described enslavement as 'widespread' in 2023 and remarked that:

Nothing can justify slavery, whether it be culture, tradition, or religion ... While there is no data on the number of people born into slavery according to Mali's National Commission on Human Rights, the experts' statement highlighted estimates from some organizations of at least 800,000 victims, including 200,000 living 'under the direct control of their "masters"'. [21]

The UN experts pointed out that there was no legislation in Mali specifically covering slavery by descent, and called for action: 'Slave "masters" must be held accountable for their actions, compensate victims and restore their rights and dignity.'[22] To understand the scope of the current practices in Mali (and its neighbours), it is necessary to look at the development of slavery over centuries.

In 1591, Moroccan Sultan Ahmad al-Mansur's army invaded the Songhay empire (which spanned present-day Mali, Niger, and parts of Mauritania, Senegal and the Gambia) carrying away massive amounts of gold and tens of thousands of slaves to Morocco, despite the fact that the majority were Muslim. Some of those enslaved were conscripted into the army while others were sent to southern Moroccan oases to produce sugar that al-Mansur traded in Europe for weapons and lumber. In Algeria, slave labour was also used in agriculture, especially in the south. [23]

The invasion initiated the conflict between Mali's Arab and Berber north and the African south, mentioned earlier. In Mali, it has produced deep divisions. On the one hand there is a section of the population that considers itself to be 'white': the Arabs, Tuareg and Fulbe or Fulani. On the other hand, there are the Songhay, Bambara and Dogon, who are referred to as 'black'.[24] These divisions are often described as ethnic divisions by expatriates, but locals consider them racial.[25] The slaves held by the Tuareg are traditionally referred to as *Bellah*, although the Tuareg themselves used the term *Ilkan*, which means male slave. This has produced a complex hierarchical pyramid, which reflects both race and bondage.[26]

Slavery was outlawed in principle by the French colonial law in 1905, even as the authorities continued to turn a blind eye to the practice, which they referred to as 'domestic slavery'. The French feared that abolition would destabilise the Malian economy, lead to unrest and threaten colonial rule. At independence in 1960, it was the African south of Mali that provided most of the army and, indeed, the government, further alienating the Tuareg north. The Tuareg rose in rebellion in 1962, a revolt which lasted for two years before being brutally repressed.[27] There was a fundamental belief among Mali's African rulers that northern Tuareg and Arabs were 'inveterate racists and slaveholders'.[28] The repression left 'a deep mark of racial grievance on many Tuareg and Arabs in northern Mali. It confirmed what many feared in the 1950s about being incorporated into a black-ruled postcolonial country.'[29] Baz Lecocq summed up the problem pithily: '[B]oth sides were equally obsessed with race ... While the Keita regime perceived the [Tuareg] as white, anarchist, feudal, lazy, pro-slavery nomads who needed to be civilised, the [Tuareg] elite saw the Malian politicians as black, incompetent, untrustworthy slaves in disguise who came to usurp power.'[30]

These tensions can be clearly seen in the history of clashes between Dogon farmers and Fulani or Tuareg herders. The Dogon originated in southern Mali, but moved northwards during the Mali Empire of the thirteenth and fourteenth centuries until they occupied an escarpment and plateau area above the Seeno plains in central Mali.[31] From the nineteenth century the Fulani military dominated the plains, chasing the Dogon onto the escarpment and enslaving many of them.[32] The escarpment soils are poor and good farmland is scarce, so when the French arrived, the Dogon felt secure enough to move down onto the plains. They grew in numbers and strength and began demanding fees from Fulani herders for grazing around their hamlets. This led to repeated clashes. However, in the post-colonial period the Dogon contributed 25 per cent of the army, while the Fulani represented just 0.5 per cent of recruits and were forced onto the defensive.[33] The Dogon began attacking Fulani villages, resulting in Fulani fleeing to Burkina Faso and joining Islamist jihadi groups.[34]

This complex relationship between oppressed and oppressors, with power shifting between the 'white' and 'black' Malians, is an important element in the interactions between the Arab–Berbers and the African groups. It underlies both the problem of enslavement and the issue of Islamist jihadi groups that has come to dominate life in so much of this part of the Sahara and the Sahel.

Niger

Some of the history of Niger has been dealt with in the preceding chapters on Trans-Saharan slavery (Part 1) and indigenous slavery (Part 3), with the rise of the Sokoto Caliphate. Yet the story of enslavement in Niger is complex and contested: while the government insists that slavery is a practice from the past which no longer takes place, campaign groups like Timidria are equally adamant that it still exists. Timidria's careful census found 870,363 slaves as recently as 2004.[35] At the same time, academic sources suggest all figures should be treated with considerable caution.[36] This is, of course, an important caveat, but it does not get us very far.

The Timidria survey provided a wealth of evidence pointing to the enslavement of men and women who were interviewed. Timidria travelled across six of Niger's eight regions visiting 'villages, neighbourhoods, camps, tribes, groupings, cantons, and urban centres.'[37] Some 11,000 questionnaires were completed, capturing a range of experiences. For initiating the survey, the president of Timidria was imprisoned.[38] The group's research quoted examples from other sources as well. One was from a newspaper, *Alternative*, which published a dossier on slavery on 28 July 2000.[39] The journalists interviewed a runaway slave, Tumajet Ghousmane, who described herself having been given to her owner 'as a wedding gift'. She was subsequently beaten and abused. 'As far as the master is concerned, we are just objects, like a chair, a pestle, or a mortar,' she said.[40]

Similar testimonies appeared in a lengthy article in *The Guardian*, in which a young woman, Al-Husseina Amadou, described the attitude of her master: 'he bought me like a chicken.'[41] Benedetta Rossi, an academic who has written widely on slavery in Niger, described the treatment of another woman:

> The case of Hadijatou Mani is emblematic. Hadijatou was born to an enslaved mother in Southern Niger in 1984. When she was twelve years old she was sold to El Hadj Souleymane Naroua, a friend of her mother's master, for the equivalent of £250. She thereby became Souleymane Naroua's concubine, and as such she was sexually accessible to him without restriction and had to carry out domestic work without pay for her master. On

18 August 2005, Souleymane Naroua granted Hadijatou a ransom certificate after Hadijatou had given birth to a child. She refused to remain with him and left. Souleymane Naroua argued that (in his interpretation of Maliki Law) she was automatically his wife. The case was brought to Konni's local tribunal, which on 20 March 2004, ruled that there had been no marriage because no bride wealth had been paid, and that consequently Hadijatou was free to walk away from Souleymane Naroua.[42]

The case went to appeal, which Hadijatou lost. However, refusing to accept defeat, she took her case to the Court of Justice of the Economic Community of West African States, which heard her appeal on 7 April 2008. It was the first time a case of slavery had ever been considered by the court, which ruled in her favour. Following the judgement, a lawyer for the government of Niger announced that: 'A ruling has been made, we have taken note of it and it will be applied.'[43] Hadijatou was awarded the equivalent of $19,000 in damages. She was jubilant:

> I am very thankful for this decision. It was very difficult to challenge my former master and to speak out when people see you as nothing more than a slave … With the compensation I will be able to build a house, raise animals and have farm land to support my family. I will also be able to send my children to school so they can have the education I was never allowed as a slave.[44]

How is it possible that, despite such clear evidence, there is confusion about the nature of enslavement in Niger and the numbers involved? The answer lies in the complex social hierarchies that have developed over generations, rather like those in Mauritania. In 2021, the U.S. State Department provided a summary of how ingrained enslavement is in Niger's local culture.

> The Tuareg, Zarma, Fulani, Toubou, and Arab ethnic minorities throughout the country, and particularly in remote northern and western regions and along the border with Nigeria, practiced a traditional form of caste-based servitude or bonded labor. Persons born into a traditionally subordinate caste or descent-based slavery sometimes worked without pay for those above them in the social order. Such persons were forced to work without pay for their

masters throughout their lives, primarily herding cattle, working on farmland, or working as domestic servants.[45]

Practices like this have come about over many generations, although before the nineteenth century slaves were relatively few in number, used mainly in the home and apparently not for broader-scale economic purposes.[46] Enslavement developed along with the wave of jihads that spread across West Africa in the eighteenth and nineteenth centuries. The Sokoto Caliphate was only one of several jihads in the region.[47]

Today some women continue to be traded, used in the home and for sex. A dwindling number are the result of capture and conflict. However, a far larger proportion of the population are what are termed *horso* within the Zarma society of south-western Niger.

> A slave who has been assimilated into the master's lineage— usually after his line has been connected to a noble family for three generations—achieves the status of *horso*. The *horso* experiences little of the violence and overt repression that a Westerner associates with slavery. He wears no chains, and according to cultural norms may not be beaten, exchanged or sold ... He is free to wander through the community without restraint and may even live in a separate village and simply pay a tax or tithe (*laabu albarka*) to the master at the end of each harvest. But in spite of this lack of physical restraint, the *horso* is on the other side of an impenetrable social barrier, and is never assimilated into Nigerien society ... The *horso* ... never progresses beyond the status of child. He spends his entire life remitting a percentage of his harvest to his master, never becomes an *alfari* (farmer) or *dotigi* (elder), and therefore never claims control of agricultural land. Indeed, the ideology of Zarma slavery closely associates the *horsos'* servile status with their landlessness. Ask any Zarma noble or *horso*, how *horso* arrived at their station and he will tell you that they descend from men who were defeated in battle, were given the choice between a warrior's death and enslavement, and chose the latter.[48]

Dismantling such a complex, embedded social hierarchy is no easy task, and although these forms of labour have been known about for years, they continue to be tolerated, whatever their legal status may officially be.

Sudan

The early history of Sudanese slavery was explored in Chapters 1 and 3, but to understand enslavement as it is practised today, we have to consider how it developed during the nineteenth century and the Anglo-Egyptian condominium which ruled Sudan between 1899 and 1956.

> In the 19th century the institution of slavery was deeply entrenched in the social structure of the Sudan, and most of the slaves used or exported from this country were procured from the peripheral tribes and other African countries. This was the great reservoir of manpower where they were captured in wars or raids; kidnapped, paid as tax or tribute, presented as gifts, or simply bought. Slaves came from different places and often travelled great distances ... From the Sudan and Abyssinia, they came northwards, overland or down the Nile to the North African Littoral or were shipped north and eastwards, as were the Somalis, to Arabia, the Persian Gulf and India.[49]

The slaves were put to use in the ways that have been discussed throughout this book: women generally in the home or the harem, men in the fields or in the army. Exactly how many were enslaved in Sudan is not clear, but the numbers ran into the tens of thousands. One estimate suggests that 'Egypt and Arabia drew an annual supply of 15,000 to 20,000 slaves from the East Sudan and Abyssinia, not including the trade within the Sudan. Besides those procured for the foreign trade, many slaves were retained in the Sudan for domestic and agriculture purposes.'[50] In November 1895, a comprehensive Anti-Slavery Convention was signed between Britain and Egypt in Cairo. Then, following the Anglo-Egyptian conquest of Sudan, Britain put considerable effort into abolition. However, the practice continued well into the twentieth century, and the recent instability in Sudan has allowed a resurgence of enslavement.

Since Sudanese independence in 1956, the country has suffered dozens of plots and attempted and successful coups, which made any serious suppression of enslavement difficult to enforce. Animosity between Arabs and Africans, a legacy of the slave trade, has exacerbated the situation. Zeinab Mohammed Salih, a Sudanese journalist, told the BBC, 'The superiority complex of many Arabs lies at the heart of some of the worst conflicts in Sudan.'[51] This played a part in the rise of the Sudan People's Liberation Movement in the 1980s, a southern-based movement that fought for the rights of the African population. 'The successive Khartoum regimes since the start of the current civil war between the North and the South in 1983 have been notorious for encouraging enslavement of southern blacks, and increasingly Christian Sudanese, by northern Arab Muslims,' wrote Professor Jok Madut Jok in 2001.[52]

This finally led to the division of Sudan in 2011, with South Sudan emerging as an independent state. The rupture did not end political tensions within Sudan; the military seized power in October 2021. However, rifts within the military elite soon appeared, leading to the most recent and, at the time of writing, on-going Sudanese civil war that erupted in April 2023. Anarchy and violence rippled across the region, bringing chaos that only strengthened opportunities for repression and slavery. There is a powerful ethnic element to the conflict, which has been highlighted by experts reporting for the United Nations. The Rapid Support Forces led by Mohamed Hamdan Dagalo, generally referred to as 'Hemedti,' grew out of the notorious Janjaweed militia, which plagued Darfur and is frequently cited as the perpetrator of atrocities there precisely because a section of the population is African. 'Neighbourhoods and homes were continuously attacked, looted, burned and destroyed, targeting the neighbourhoods where Masalit and other African communities were harassed, physically assaulted, sexually harassed, sexually abused and, at times, executed.'[53]

In 2024, Katharine Houreld and Hafiz Haroun visited Sudan for *The Washington Post*. Their findings revealed how widespread slavery has become since the eruption of war the year before, which pitted the Sudanese Armed Forces against Hemedti's Rapid Support Forces.

> Elements within the Rapid Support Forces, which have captured most of the capital, Khartoum, and swept across most of the western region of Darfur, have made these abductions a lucrative source of revenue, said victims, other witnesses and activists. Some of the victims said they have been enslaved and sold to work on the

farms of RSF commanders, and others recounted being held while their families were forced to ransom them. Some victims said they were seized several times. Among those abducted, witnesses and activists said, have been girls and young women who were chained, bound and sold as sex slaves.[54]

The Washington Post's findings have been replicated by others.[55]

In 2023, Arab militia of the Rapid Support Forces attacked Africans from the Masalit ethnic group in El Geneina, capital of Sudan's West Darfur. *The Guardian* reported:

> Gamar al-Deen was visiting a friend when gunmen poured into his neighbourhood on 27 April 2023. 'I came back to find they were all dead,' he says. 'My mother, my father, uncles, brothers, sisters. I wanted to die myself in that moment.'
>
> Deen, a teacher, lost a dozen members of his family that day. Several of his neighbours were killed too. At his friend's during the carnage, he saw a group of fighters strip a woman naked and then rape her in the street. 'They told us, "This area belongs to us, not you, you are slaves,"' he says.[56]

Nicholas Kristof, an American journalist who is no stranger to conflicts, went to see the civil war for *The New York Times*. 'I just went to Darfur. Here is what shattered me,' he wrote.

> When an Arab militia rampaged through Maryam Suleiman's village in the Darfur region of Sudan last year and lined up men and boys to massacre, the gunmen were blunt about their purpose. 'We don't want to see any Black people,' a militia leader said, adding mockingly: 'We don't even want to see black trash bags.' To make his point, Maryam recalled, he shot a donkey because it was black.[57]

Libya

Libya differs from other contemporary African states in which enslavement is practised. Slaves in the rest of the continent are generally the result of war, capture or generational enslavement from birth. Adults and children who become ensnared in Libyan slavery are most frequently held because they embarked on lengthy and hazardous attempts to escape war, poverty and abuses in their home countries. Libya is their route to Europe. The hope of a better, more peaceful life in which they can fulfil their potential leads them to cross deserts and mountains and face hostile border guards and criminal gangs in an attempt to find a route across the Mediterranean. Each stage of these journeys is fraught with risk. They turn to traffickers who promise them safe travel in return for money. Some refugees are successful and do, indeed, make lives for themselves in Europe or the Americas. They act as magnets for the many thousands who follow them, drawn by the promise of prosperity and the hope that they can send funds home to their families. Only too often the outcome is the exact opposite: they leave their bones in the Sahara, jettisoned by human traffickers, who are bent on making money. Or they drown as they attempt to cross the Mediterranean. If they, and the families who support them, run out of funds, the refugees and migrants face another peril: enslavement.

Many of those who arrive in Libya are not African. Frontex, the European Union's border agency, recorded unregulated crossings of the central Mediterranean in the period January to October 2024. A total of 55,227 made the journey. The top five countries of origin were Bangladesh: 11,141; Syria: 10,495; Tunisia: 7,283; Egypt: 3,606; and Guinea: 3,031.[58] The nations from which the refugees or migrants come varies over time. While recognising this, our focus is on the Africans who travelled from countries as far apart as Ghana and Eritrea only to find themselves held in Libyan detention centres. The verdict of the United Nations is clear: official detention centres serve as jails in which enslavement, torture and sexual violence are inflicted on the captives.

> There are reasonable grounds to believe that migrants were enslaved in detention centres of the Directorate for Combatting Illegal Migration in Abu Salim, Zawiyah and Mabani, as well as in places of detention in al-Shwarif, Bani Walid, Sabratah, Zuwarah and Sabha. The Mission considered that enslavement, including sexual slavery, had occurred when, for example, there was an element of ownership or there were actions imposing a similar deprivation of liberty.[59]

The circumstances surrounding the overthrow of Libyan leader Colonel Muammar Gaddafi in 2011, ending his forty-two-year dictatorship, are complex. A Libyan uprising, supported by some NATO forces, led to a collapse of central authority and a standoff between competing centres of authority. Khalifa Haftar, a former general in the Libyan National Army, controlled the east of the country while a Government of National Unity, backed by the UN, held the capital, Tripoli, and surrounding areas. Rival militias roamed large parts of the south and centre of the country. While the insecurity unleashed by ending Gaddafi's rule laid the groundwork for the current insecurity, the Colonel had exploited the threat of mass migration to Europe over the years. He did this 'to gain concessions and bolster [Libya's] international standing ... It has uniquely mobilized the fear of a "migrant invasion", essentially "blackmailing" the European Union.'[60] Enslavement in the country's detention centres took place 'during and after the Gaddafi era.'[61]

Slavery in Libya had been discussed for some time, but following a report by CNN in November 2017 it gained wide international attention.[62] After receiving grainy footage of a slave sale, CNN sent journalists to Libya to gather evidence. They uncovered nine slave auction sites.

> Carrying concealed cameras into a property outside the capital of Tripoli last month, we witness a dozen people go 'under the hammer' in the space of six or seven minutes.
>
> 'Does anybody need a digger? This is a digger, a big strong man, he'll dig,' the salesman, dressed in camouflage gear, says. 'What am I bid, what am I bid?'
>
> Buyers raise their hands as the price rises, '500, 550, 600, 650 ...' Within minutes it is all over and the men, utterly resigned to their fate, are being handed over to their new 'masters.'
>
> After the auction, we met two of the men who had been sold. They were so traumatized by what they'd been through that they could not speak, and so scared that they were suspicious of everyone they met.[63]

These findings have been replicated by other investigations.

The twenty first century slave trade dealers operate with impunity. Some migrants are helplessly auctioned off in private. Shamsuddin

Jibril, a Cameroonian who lived through this experience, said that 'They took people and put them in the street under a sign that [reads] "For Sale". They tied their hands just like in the former slave trade, and drove them … in the back of a Toyota Hilux.'[64]

One of the largest groups seeking to reach Europe via Libya are Eritreans. Many flee enforced, indefinite conscription and the hazard of being sent to fight in Eritrea's regional wars, which have resulted in tens of thousands of deaths. The conditions that the Eritreans encounter along the route to Libya are brutal. Once they arrive in Libya their situation can deteriorate still further, with enslavement a real prospect. It is a reflection of just how severe the situation is in Eritrea that refugees leave their country knowing full well what hazards they are likely to encounter. This young Eritrean woman had no illusions about what she might face before setting off.

> I heard that there are many dangerous things on the road to Libya and in Libya itself, but at that time, I was not thinking about all these problems when I decided to go. … I heard that the Libyans deal with people in a very tough way. Some detain people and some beat them. And I also heard that the sea is very difficult, that people die there. … I heard that the Libyans haven't got respect for people, especially for girls and especially for foreigners.
>
> Question: So, when you decided to go to Libya and you heard that, was there anything you did to protect yourself?
>
> No. … No-one was thinking about those things. The main thing is how we can leave. I have not thought for a long time. Just, I heard that one girl from Wedsherify had reached Italy. The girls here are depending on the stories from Europe, people who are successful in reaching Europe, who are writing on social media or calling … So, we are thinking about when we reach it [Europe], not about the journey.[65]

There is evidence that the slavery practised in detention centres is officially sanctioned.[66] Eritreans described conditions in the Tajoura Detention Centre, where Libyans come to select people to work. Often, they openly referred to the labourers as slaves: 'Every morning when someone comes there, he says: "We need five eubayd", which means 5 slaves. "I need five slaves." Everybody that is hearing that one, they are feeling angry.'[67]

Some refugees manage to raise funds from friends and families to escape captivity. Others do not and remain trapped in enslavement, often in official detention centres. Slaves can be held in the centres and sent to work during the day. Their forced labour ranges from farm and construction work for Libyans to providing official services for the authorities such as road maintenance and garbage collecting.[68]

There is one final aspect of these forms of captivity that is seldom discussed. Migrants have also been captured and recruited into terrorist organisations and other criminal networks. These forms of enslavement mirror much earlier use of slaves in military service.[69]

22

CAN AFRICAN SLAVERY BE FINALLY ENDED?

Will it be possible to put an end to Africa's enslavement and the slave trade, after so many decades of frustrated attempts at abolition? We have to be sceptical. While there are indeed examples of African movements fighting to achieve just this end, some of which have been mentioned here, it is also true that the international organisations that are meant to speak for the continent's people have been remarkably silent. The United Nations has a special rapporteur who investigates the subject, but works with limited resources. His investigations can hardly be said to be well known. Other UN bodies, such as its education arm, UNESCO, have ignored present-day slavery. The undoubtedly important work that UNESCO does focuses almost exclusively on the slavery of the past, when people were transported across the Atlantic, and on how the descendants of those slaves have fared since.

International organisations: The United Nations

The contemporary plight of Africa's enslaved is an uncomfortable reality that the African Union, the Arab League and the United Nations appear unwilling to confront. All three of these international organisations, having pledged to guard human rights, continue to ignore the reality of chattel slavery in Africa today, or minimise the problem.

> Slavery, not post-slavery, is alive and well in some African societies—although not quite as 'well' as it used to be, and increasingly under threat. By contrast, the main post slavery

discourse that informs public commemorations of 'African slavery' focuses narrowly on the legacies of Atlantic slavery. It silences the legacies of the more recent enslavement of Africans by Africans and the slow process of emancipation that has been taking place in the twentieth century. There exists no consolidated post-slavery discourse about this chapter of African history, not even amongst the victims of past abuses.[1]

As outlined above, the UN special rapporteur on slavery has worked hard to investigate and publicise the plight of enslaved people in Mauritania and Mali. However, it is difficult to find this research reflected in the work of the UN more widely, and in particular in the publications of the UN's scientific and educational organisation, UNESCO.

UNESCO has done a great deal to make African enslavement more widely recognised and understood. The UNESCO Slave Route Project has been developed for the past thirty years since its foundations were laid in 1994.[2] 'At the international level, the programme has thus played a major role in "breaking" the silence surrounding the history of slavery and placing this tragedy that has shaped the modern world in the universal memory,' UNESCO proudly boasts. However, the silence it wishes to break is selective. Reading UNESCO materials, one cannot ignore that their overwhelming focus is on the Trans-Atlantic slave trade. Vital as this is, it is only a part of the story, reflecting once again the 'tyranny of the Atlantic'.

This bias is apparent in the July–September 2024 special edition of the *UNESCO Courier* celebrating the thirtieth anniversary of the Slave Route Project.[3] Articles included features on Gorée Island in Senegal, the last surviving Cuban slave, black women in the Caribbean, a Haitian dancer and the Caribbean's call for restorative justice. Only in the lead article, by Myriam Cottias, was there any indication that indigenous slavery was a question that required addressing.

'Breaking the silence.' Thirty years ago, in 1994, this was the main objective of UNESCO's Slave Route programme, now known as Routes of Enslaved Peoples, namely to expose the memory of this human tragedy, which led to the deportation of 12.5 million men, women and children from Africa to the Americas between the 16th and mid-19th centuries. On the coasts of East Africa and the Indian Ocean, it has been estimated that over a million men and women were deported. In addition to this appalling figure, which is based on an international analysis of the archives, some seven million captives died on the internal slave trade routes in Africa.[4]

Where are the UNESCO investigations into the descendants of Africans on the Indian subcontinent, like the Sidis of India or Pakistan, who trace their origins to the slave trade from Africa? What work is under way into the fate of the hundreds of thousands of Africans who were abducted by the Ottoman Empire or enslaved in Arabia over the centuries? UNESCO, despite its mandate for scientific and educational work, has little to say about indigenous slavery across the African continent, or the ongoing enslavement continuing to this day.

The African Union and the Arab League

If the United Nations' response to contemporary slavery has been desultory, the response of the African Union and Arab League is even less evident. When the plight of Africans trapped in Libyan detention centres was first made public, the African Union did participate in an emergency airlift in 2019 of the most vulnerable refugees—mostly women and babies—to Rwanda.[5] The same year, the organisation adopted an Action Plan to eradicate child labour and what it termed 'modern slavery' on the continent. It makes no mention of chattel slavery, or the capture and enslavement of refugees.[6] The AU's African Committee of Experts on the Rights and Welfare of the Child published a well-researched report on the situation in Mauritania.[7] The report was clear about what was described as 'the repression of discourse around the pervasive issue of slavery and slave-like practices in Mauritania.'[8] The experts called for multidimensional measures to be adopted to challenge these endemic problems. So far there is little sign of progress in this regard, nor much indication that the African Union's leadership is really confronting the issue.

On the question of reparations for the slave trade, the African Union has built on the declaration of the World Conference against Racism, Racial Discrimination, Xenophobia and Related Intolerance, held in Durban, South Africa, from 31 August to 8 September 2001.

> The Conference agreed that slavery and the slave trade are a crime against humanity, and should have always been so. It was further agreed that slavery and the slave trade, including the transatlantic slave trade, were appalling tragedies in the history of humanity, especially in their negation of the essence of the victims. The Conference also recognized that colonialism had led to racism and caused suffering and that its consequences persist to this day. [9]

This has been taken up recently by the African Commission on Human and Peoples' Rights, which at its 2022 conference adopted a resolution on 'Africa's Reparations Agenda', '[r]ecognizing that the human rights situation of Africans in the diaspora and people of African descent worldwide remains an urgent concern.' [10] The resolution noted the emergence of 'contemporary forms of enslavement of Africans and people of African descent globally including in the Middle East and Arabo-Persian Gulf states.' This was something of a breakthrough. How far this will develop, or receive the priority it deserves from African leaders, is another matter. However, it is a beginning.

If the African Union has begun to tackle some of the questions relating to contemporary African slavery, it is difficult to find any similar acknowledgement from the Arab League. Yet the League has ten African member states, ranging from Mauritania to the Comoros. There appears little appetite in Egypt, Africa's oldest confirmed slaving nation, to discuss its role or responsibility, while the Saudi response has been to close its archives and discourage research. [11] This has not prevented the question of Arab responsibility for enslavement from being raised sporadically. For example, the Caribbean scholar Shaun Flores argued that: 'The Arab world owes us reparations as well.' [12]

The most concerted attempt to discuss Arab involvement in the slave trade came at a conference arranged by Professor Kwesi Kwaa Prah, founding director of the Centre for Advanced Studies of African Society at the University of the Western Cape in South Africa. The conference, held in Johannesburg in February 2003, concluded with a declaration.[13] The statement began by describing the legacy of African slavery as:

> one of the most vexatious problem areas in the conscience of the human community. At a time when people of African descent, particularly in the Diaspora, are calling for reparations for the chattel slavery of Africans in the western hemisphere and its effects, Africans on the continent are making similar demands for Ottoman and Arab-led slavery and its outstanding historical and sociological implications.

The declaration continued by remarking that other forms of African slavery were relatively well known, but that:

> Arab-led slavery of Africans continues to be an area of silence and darkness in African and non-African perceptions of African society and history. The painful reality of this history is profoundly aggravated by the fact that slavery continues to the present day in the Afro-Arab borderlands, an area that encompasses the broad stretch of Africa running roughly between the 10th and 30th degrees of latitude across the African continent, and particularly in Mauritania and the Sudan.

The conference then proceeded to condemn Arab slavery in the strongest terms and to call for the whole subject to be more intensively researched. There was also a call for reparations from the Arab world, as well as an explanation that this was in no way an anti-Arab position. 'Does the demand of reparations for the Atlantic slave trade amount to anti-Europeanism?' Kwesi Kwaa Prah asked rhetorically.[14]

If the sources quoted in this chapter are correct—and there is no reason to doubt them—then hundreds of thousands of Africans (perhaps as many as a million) remain enslaved today. These are chattel slaves who are owned by a master or mistress. This does not include those who are held in 'modern slavery'. At the same time, it is hard to resist the conclusion that African and Arab leaders have limited interest in their fate. The African Union and the Arab League appear only marginally concerned about those who are held in some of the worst conditions known to mankind. UNESCO's attention has concentrated on the Trans-Atlantic slave trade. The

Arab League and its member states seem determined to look the other way. Perhaps none of these responses should come as any surprise. The fate of contemporary slaves is an indictment of the leaders of these organisations. Why would they want to scrutinise their treatment, or attempt to free them, when this would only highlight their own inadequacies? How much easier is it to pursue Americans and Europeans for reparations for enslavement centuries ago than to consider the condition of men and women alive today?

Reparations

The question of reparations has become so central to discussion of slavery and the slave trade that it is impossible to ignore. Across Europe, debates are under way and solutions are being discussed. The responsibility of European and American nations is clear. What this book has attempted to explain is that African enslavement was so much more extensive than the trade across the Atlantic. The historic rights and wrongs, the politics of payments and apologies, are for others to consider. What is worth drawing from the evidence presented here is the context within which the debates take place.

These are some of the issues that arise:

- Why has the discussion about reparations been exclusively about the Trans-Atlantic slave trade? As indicated, this accounted for perhaps 20 per cent or 25 per cent of Africa's historic enslavement.
- The slave trade to Arabia, or controlled by Arab nations, was at least as large as that undertaken by the Europeans or Americans. It began very much earlier and continued into the 1960s or 1970s. Should these Arab nations not also be approached for reparations, if this debate is to encompass the whole gamut of enslavement?
- Equally, the responsibility of India, as a destination for the slave armies that fought in regions like the Deccan, long before Britain controlled the subcontinent, needs to be considered. So too should the role of the Ottomans, who traded in over 1 million African slaves. What is the responsibility of their successors, the Turkish state?

- British families (and the nation as a whole) have been singled out as beneficiaries of enslavement. The huge payments by the government to families who lost their 'property' when slaves were emancipated are frequently cited as unjust, particularly when compared with the enslaved, who received nothing at all. At the same time, the equally substantial cost of maintaining Royal Naval fleets off the west and east coasts of Africa to fight slavery is seldom mentioned.[15] Nor is the loss of 17,000 sailors who manned the Atlantic fleet, with an unknown number having died serving in the Indian Ocean.
- Indigenous African slavery raises extraordinarily complex problems. If the earliest evidence of slavery is etched into the rocks along the Nile, what responsibility does Egypt have to the peoples of Sudan and Ethiopia? Equally, should the Oromo, and other southern Ethiopians, look to the highland kingdoms of Ethiopia for recompense for their enslavement? Can the Hausa turn to the Fulani to ask for reparations for what the Sokoto Caliphate inflicted upon them?
- Finally, questions could be raised about the over a million Europeans who were captured by the Barbary states, offshoots of the Ottoman Empire. Might Italy, France and Spain, or even Denmark, Ireland and Britain, seek redress for their sufferings?

To all these questions I can see no easy answer, yet this past cannot be ignored. Finding a just and equitable means of addressing this history is likely to remain with humanity for generations.

This book has attempted to show the extraordinary length and scope of African slavery and how ingrained in many societies it has become. Much has yet to be revealed, and it will require careful research and the opening of archives that are currently closed for the full picture to be uncovered. The continent's people have suffered immensely over the centuries, and their plight has yet to end. Some of the pain has been inflicted by their own rulers, some by outside powers. All must accept their share of responsibility. Unless legal and political systems, domestic and international, can free slaves from their shackles, slavery will remain an enduring scar upon the conscience of humankind.

NOTES

PREFACE

1. Museum of the African Revolution, https://www.amrevmuseum.org/meet-elizabeth-freeman-performance. Accessed 27 February 2025.
2. Martin Plaut, *Dr Abdullah Abdurahman: South Africa's First Elected Black Politician*, Jacana Media, 2020.

INTRODUCTION

1. Trevor Burnard, 'The Atlantic Slave Trade', in Gad Heuman and Trevor Burnard (eds), *The Routledge History of Slavery*, Routledge, 2011, p. 91.
2. These figures are from reputable sources but are of course open to challenge. Measuring slavery is notoriously difficult: the information is partial and fragmentary. Beyond the Trans-Atlantic, there is still a huge amount of work to do. Even in the Atlantic, there are problems with the figures. For example, should one use the figures for the number of men and women who were embarked on ships, or the numbers who disembarked at their destination? David Eltis and David Richardson, in their highly regarded *Atlas of the Transatlantic Slave Trade*, show that in the period 1501–1867, 12,521,000 embarked but only 10,703,000 disembarked. Even here, after decades of research, there is a substantial degree of uncertainty, with the authors accepting that between 18 and 19 per cent are estimates. The issue is further complicated by the fact that the numbers who embarked are lower than the numbers of slaves captured, some of whom died or escaped before being sold by African elites to the European slave traders. All these figures should therefore be treated as estimates: ball-park numbers that give an indication of scale and nothing more. David Eltis and David Richardson, *Atlas of the Transatlantic Slave Trade*, Yale University Press, 2010, Map 11, pp. 18–19.
3. United Nations, 'Mali: Ban slavery by law, say top rights experts', UN News, 8 May 2023, https://news.un.org/en/story/2023/05/1136437. Accessed 27 February 2025.
4. Robert O. Collins, 'The African Slave Trade to Asia and the Indian Ocean Islands', *African and Asian Studies*, Vol. 5, Nos 3–4, 2006,

pp. 326–327. Note: The calculations can vary substantially depending on how enslavement is considered. Are the totals the numbers captured, the totals shipped from Africa, or the survivors who arrived at their destination? These figures are meant only as an indication of the scale of slavery, not the total number of men and women who have been enslaved.

5. David Eltis and David Richardson, *Atlas of the Transatlantic Slave Trade*, Yale University Press, 2010, Table 2, p. 23.

6. Ralph A. Austen, 'The Trans-Saharan Slave Trade: A Tentative Census', in Henry A. Gemery and Jan S. Hogendorn (eds), *The Uncommon Market: Essays in the Economic History of the Atlantic Slave Trade*, Academic Press, 1979, Table 2.8, p. 66. This figure includes a 20 per cent mortality rate en route.

7. Paul E. Lovejoy, *Slavery, Commerce and Production in the Sokoto Caliphate of West Africa*, Red Sea Press, 2005, p. 3.

8. Ehud R. Toledano, 'Enslavement in the Ottoman Empire in the Early Modern Period', in David Eltis and Stanley Engerman (eds), *The Cambridge World History of Slavery, Vol. 3: AD 1420–AD 1804*, Cambridge University Press, 2011, p. 26.

9. Robert Davis, *Christian Slaves, Muslim Masters: White Slavery in the Mediterranean, the Barbary Coast, and Italy, 1500–1800*, Palgrave Macmillan, 2003, p. 23. These figures are contested. However, as Bernard Capp points out, Davis does not include Morocco in his calculations, and slaves were taken before and after these dates. Capp concludes: '[N]o-one doubts that the numbers were huge.' Bernard Capp, *British Slaves and Barbary Corsairs, 1580–1750*, Oxford University Press, 2022, p. 17.

10. Behnaz A. Mirzai, *A History of Slavery and Emancipation in Iran: 1800–1929*, University of Texas Press, 2017, p. 64.

11. Giulia Bonacci and Alexander Meckelburg, 'Slavery and the Slave Trade in Ethiopia and Eritrea', *Oxford Research Encyclopedia of African History*, 31 January 2023, p. 10. This suggests a figure of 300,000–500,000. These are figures for a single year, and it is important to remember that Ethiopian slavery spanned many centuries.

12. Mekuria Bulcha, 'The Red Sea Slave Trade: Captives' Treatment in the Slave Markets of North-East Africa and the Islamic Societies of the Middle East', in Kwesi Kwaa Prah (ed.), *Reflections on Arab-Led Slavery of Africans*, Centre for Advanced Studies of African Society, 2005, p. 108.

13. Afua Hirsch, '"We are all mixed": Henry Louis Gates Jr on race, being arrested and working towards America's redemption', *Observer*, 10 March 2024, https://www.theguardian.com/books/2024/mar/10/henry-louis-gates-jr-black-box-writing-race-arrested-beers-with-obama. Accessed 27 February 2025.

14. Jane Austen, *Mansfield Park*, Penguin Classics, 2012 [1814].

15. See, for example, 'Church Commissioners' research identifies historic links to transatlantic chattel slavery', The Church of England, 16 June 2022, https://www.churchofengland.org/media/press-releases/church-commissioners-research-identifies-historic-links-transatlantic-chattel. Accessed 27 February 2025.

16. Yacine Daddi Addoun, '"So That God Frees the Former Masters from Hell Fire:" Salvation Through Manumission in Nineteenth Century Ottoman Algeria', in Ana Lucia Araujo, Mariana P. Candido and Paul E. Lovejoy (eds), *Crossing Memories: Slavery and African Diaspora*, Africa World Press, 2011, p. 237.

17. *Ibid.*, p. 237.

18. Donald Rayfield, *'A Seditious and Sinister Tribe': The Crimean Tatars and Their Khanate,* Reaktion Books, 2024, p. 157.

19. For example, although there are references to Ethiopian slavery, there are no entries on the subject in the following: Gad Heuman and Trevor Burnard (eds), *The Routledge History of Slavery*, Routledge, 2011; Seymour Drescher and Stanley Engerman (eds), *A Historical Guide to World Slavery*, Oxford University Press, 1998; Junius Rodriguez, *The Historical Encyclopedia of World Slavery*, Vol. 1, A–K, ABC-Clio, 1997.

20. Robert Harms, *Land of Tears: The Exploration and Exploitation of Equatorial Africa*, Basic Books, 2019, p. 6.

21. Thomas Pakenham, *The Scramble for Africa: 1876–1912*, Weidenfeld and Nicholson, 1991, p. 16.

22. T. C. McCaskie, 'Cultural Encounters: Britain and Africa in the Nineteenth Century', in Andrew Porter (ed.), *The Oxford History of the British Empire, Vol. III: The Nineteenth Century*, Oxford University Press, 1999, p. 666.

23. Christopher Fyfe, 'Freed Slave Colonies in West Africa', in John Flint (ed.), J. D. Fage and Roland Oliver (series eds), *The Cambridge History of Africa, Vol. 5: From c. 1790 to c. 1870*, Cambridge University Press, 1976, p. 170.

24. G. N. Sanderson, 'The European Partition of Africa: Origins and Dynamics', in G. N. Sanderson (ed.), J. D. Fage and Roland Oliver (series eds), *The Cambridge History of Africa, Vol. 6: From 1870 to 1905*, Cambridge University Press, 1985, p. 99.

25. Basil Davidson, *The African Slave Trade: Precolonial History, 1450–1850*, Little, Brown and Co., 1961, p. 81.

26. Bill Freund, *The Making of Contemporary Africa: The Development of African Society since 1800*, Indiana University Press, 1984, pp. 51–52.

27. Jeremy Black, *A Brief History of Slavery: A New Global History*, Robinson, 2011, p. 96.

28. Bronwen Everill, 'What About Slavery?', in Alan Lester (ed.), *The Truth About Empire: Real Histories of British Colonialism*, Hurst and Co., 2024, pp. 50–51.

29. Collins, 'The African Slave Trade to Asia', *op. cit.*, pp. 325–326.

30. *Ibid.*, p. 326.

31. Akosua Adoma Perbi, *A History of Indigenous Slavery in Ghana: From the 15th to the 19th Century*, Sub-Saharan Publishers, Accra, 2004, p. 16. Note: Ancient Ghana was a kingdom north of the current-day state of the same name, while the term Sudan extends well beyond modern-day Sudan and includes much of the Sahel region.

32. *Ibid.*, p. 16.

33. Lovejoy, *Slavery, Commerce and Production in the Sokoto Caliphate of West Africa*, *op. cit.*, pp. 1–3.

34. Batswana slavery is controversial and some question its existence. See the discussion by Barry Morton, 'Servitude, Slave Trading, and Slavery in the Kalahari', in Elizabeth A. Eldredge and Fred Morton (eds), *Slavery in South Africa: Captive Labour on the Dutch Frontier*, Westview Press, 1994, pp. 215–250.

35. Mark Leopold, 'Slavery in Sudan, Past and Present', *African Affairs*, Vol. 102, 2003, p. 653.

36. Ngũgĩ wa Thiong'o, *Something Torn and New: An African Renaissance*, Basic Books, 2009, p. 16.

37. Richard B. Allen, 'Suppressing a Nefarious Traffic: Britain and the Abolition of Slave Trading in India and the Western Indian Ocean', *The William and Mary Quarterly*, Vol. 66, No. 4, 2009, p. 873.

38. *Ibid.*, p. 873.

39. *Ibid.*, pp. 873–874. Allen is not alone in his concern. See, for example, P. Finkelman and J. C. Miller: 'Compared with the Atlantic trade, none of this Indian Ocean flow of captive labor, legal or illegal, has been well researched, and there are no conclusive quantitative studies of its volume.' P. Finkelman and J. C. Miller (eds), *MacMillan Encyclopedia of World Slavery*, MacMillan, 1998, p. 851.

40. Office of the Historian, US State Department, 'Barbary Wars, 1801–1805 and 1815–1816', https://history.state.gov/milestones/1801-1829/barbary-wars. Accessed 27 February 2025.

41. David Brion Davis, *Slavery and Human Progress*, Oxford University Press, 1986, p. 379.

42. Human Rights Watch Backgrounder, 'Conditions of Slavery in Sudan's Civil War', 15 March 2002, https://www.hrw.org/news/2002/03/15/conditions-slavery-sudans-civil-war. Accessed 31 January 2025.

43. Fred Harter, '"They told us—you are slaves": survivors give harrowing testimony of Darfur's year of hell', *The Guardian*, 30 December 2023,

https://www.theguardian.com/global-development/2023/dec/30/survivors-give-harrowing-testimony-of-darfur-sudan-year-of-hell. Accessed 27 February 2025.

44. Frederick Cooper, 'The Problem of Slavery in African Studies', *The Journal of African History*, Vol. 20, No. 1, 1979, p. 103.

45. 'The Slave Trade Archives Project was launched in 1999 with the aim of improving access to, and safeguarding of, original documents related to the transatlantic slave trade and slavery throughout the world … The first phase is limited to the Atlantic Slave Trade.' No further phases are mentioned. UNESCO, 'Slave Trade Archives', https://www.unesco.org/en/articles/slave-trade-archives. Accessed 27 February 2025.

46. Chouki El Hamel, '"Race", Slavery and Islam in Maghribi Mediterranean Thought: The Question of the Haratin in Morocco', *The Journal of North African Studies*, Vol. 7, No. 3, 2002, p. 45.

47. Richard Pankhurst, 'The History of Bareya, Sanqella and Other Ethiopian Slaves from the Borderlands of the Sudan', *Sudan Notes and Records*, Vol. 58, 1977, p. 1.

48. Perbi, *A History of Indigenous Slavery in Ghana*, *op. cit.*, p. 2.

49. *Ibid.*, p. 4.

50. Gwyn Campbell and Edward A. Alpers, 'Introduction: Slavery, Forced Labour and Resistance in Indian Ocean Africa and Asia', *Slavery & Abolition: A Journal of Slave and Post-Slave Studies*, Vol. 25, No. 2, August 2004, p. ix.

51. Robert Collins and James Burns, *A History of Sub-Saharan Africa*, Cambridge University Press, 2007, p. 204.

52. *Ibid.*, p. 204.

53. Quoted by Perbi, *A History of Indigenous Slavery in Ghana*, *op. cit.*, p. 7.

54. 'Slavery Convention', Geneva, 25 September 1926, UN Audiovisual Library of International Law, https://legal.un.org/avl/ha/sc/sc.html. Accessed 27 February 2025.

55. Modern slaves are said to number some 120,000 in the UK alone. Global Slavery Index/Country Study, 'Modern Slavery in United Kingdom', 2023, https://www.walkfree.org/global-slavery-index/country-studies/united-kingdom. Accessed 27 February 2025.

56. Paul Lovejoy, Igor Kopytoff and Frederick Cooper, 'Indigenous African Slavery', *Historical Reflections*, Vol. 6, No. 1, Summer 1979, p. 59.

PART 1: THE TRANS-SAHARAN SLAVE TRADE

1. Robert O. Collins, 'Slavery in the Sudan in History', *Slavery & Abolition: A Journal of Slave and Post-Slave Studies*, Vol. 20, No. 3, 1999, p. 69.

2. *Ibid.*, p. 69.

3. Donavyn Coffey, 'Could the Sahara ever be green again?', Live Science, 27 September 2020, https://www.livescience.com/will-sahara-desert-turn-green.html. Accessed 27 February 2025.

4. Raymond Mauny, 'Trans-Saharan Contacts and the Iron Age in West Africa', in J. D. Fage (ed.), J. D. Fage and Roland Oliver (series eds), *The Cambridge History of Africa, Vol. 2: From c. 500 BC to AD 1050*, Cambridge University Press, 1978, p. 287.

5. Matthew Gordon, 'Slavery in the Islamic Middle East', in Craig Perry *et al.* (eds), *The Cambridge World History of Slavery, Vol. 2: AD 500–AD 1420*, Cambridge University Press, 2021, p. 347.

6. There is no clarity as to the events or exact dates of the crossing into the Iberian Peninsula. See, for example, Nicola Clarke, 'Medieval Arabic Accounts of the Conquest of Cordoba: Creating a Narrative for a Provincial Capital', *Bulletin of the School of Oriental and African Studies, University of London*, Vol. 74, No. 1, 2011; Murray Dahm, 'Arab Sources on the Conquest of al-Andalus', *Medieval Warfare*, Vol. 1, No. 3, 2011.

7. Collins, 'The African Slave Trade to Asia', *op. cit.*, p. 331.

1.   ROUTES ACROSS THE SAHARA

1. Paul E. Lovejoy, *Transformations in Slavery: A History of Slavery in Africa*, Cambridge University Press, 2012, p. 35.

2. John Wright, 'The Wadai-Benghazi Slave Route', in Elizabeth Savage (ed.), *The Human Commodity: Perspectives on the Trans-Saharan Slave Trade*, Frank Cass, 1992, pp. 174–184.

3. *Ibid.*, p. 181.

4. John Wright, *The Trans-Saharan Slave Trade*, Routledge, 2007, p. 34.

5. P. L. Wickins, *An Economic History of Africa from the Earliest Times to Partition*, Oxford University Press, 1981, pp. 149–150.

6. Anne Haour, 'The Early Medieval Slave Trade of the Sahel', in Paul Lane and Kevin MacDonald (eds), *Slavery in Africa: Archaeology and Memory*, Oxford University Press, 2011, p. 62.

7. Frank Snowden, *Blacks in Antiquity: Ethiopians in Greco-Roman Experience*, Harvard University Press, 1970, p. 122.

8. Robert Harms, 'Introduction: Indian Ocean Slavery in the Age of Abolition', in Robert Harms, Bernard K. Freamon and David W. Blight (eds), *Indian Ocean Slavery in the Age of Abolition*, Yale University Press, 2013, p. 4. Harms suggests this route may even by this date have been sailed for centuries.

9. *Ibid.*, p. 4.

10. John Madden, 'Slavery in the Roman Empire: Numbers and Origins', *Classics Ireland*, Vol. 3, 1996, pp. 113–114.

11. Paul Lane, 'Slavery in Africa c. 500–1500 CE: Archaeological and Historical Perspectives', in Craig Perry *et al.* (eds), *The Cambridge World History of Slavery, Vol. 2: AD 500–AD 1420*, Cambridge University Press, 2021, p. 531.

12. Robert Morkot, 'The Darb el-Arbain, the Kharg Oasis and its forts, and other desert routes', *Archaeological Research in Roman Egypt: Journal of Roman Archaeology Supplement*, No. 19, December 1993, pp. 82–94.

13. Bernard K. Freamon, 'Straight, No Chaser: Slavery, Abolition, and Modern Islamic Thought', in Harms *et al.* (eds), *Indian Ocean Slavery in the Age of Abolition*, *op. cit.*, p. 67.

14. Quoted in David Edwards, 'Slavery and Slaving in the Medieval and Post-Medieval Kingdoms of the Middle Nile', in Paul Lane and Kevin MacDonald (eds), *Slavery in Africa: Archaeology and Memory*, Oxford University Press, 2011, p. 96.

15. John Swanson, 'The Myth of Trans-Saharan Trade During the Roman Era', *The International Journal of African Historical Studies*, Vol. 8, No. 4, 1975, pp. 582–600.

16. Joshua J. Mark, 'Roman Expeditions in Sub-Saharan Africa', World History Encyclopedia, 7 February 2020, https://www.worldhistory.org/article/1496/roman-expeditions-in-sub-saharan-africa. Accessed 27 February 2025.

17. Raymond Mauny, 'Trans-Saharan Contacts and the Iron Age in West Africa', in J. D. Fage (ed.), J. D. Fage and Roland Oliver (series eds), *The Cambridge History of Africa, Vol. 2: From c. 500 BC to AD 1050*, Cambridge University Press, 1978, p. 290.

18. Robert O. Collins, 'The Nilotic Slave Trade: Past and Present', *Slavery & Abolition: A Journal of Slave and Post-Slave Studies*, Vol. 13, No. 1, 1992, p. 140.

19. *Ibid.*, 140.

20. Terence Walz, *Trade between Egypt and Bilad as-Sudan, 1700–1820*, Institut Français d'Archéologie Orientale, 1978, p. 20.

21. William Y. Adams, 'The First Colonial Empire: Egypt in Nubia, 3200–1200 B.C.', *Comparative Studies in Society and History*, Vol. 26, No. 1, 1984, p. 36.

22. Mutwakil A. Amin, 'Ancient Trade and Trade Routes Between Egypt and the Sudan, 4000 to 700 B.C.', *Sudan Notes and Records*, Vol. 51, 1970, p. 23. Adams, 'The First Colonial Empire', *op. cit.*, p. 40.

23. Donald B. Redford, *From Slave to Pharaoh: The Black Experience of Ancient Egypt*, Johns Hopkins University Press, 2004, p. 6.

24. Wallis Budge, *The Literature of the Ancient Egyptians*, J. M. Dent & Sons, 1914, p. 100. Available at: https://www.gutenberg.org/files/15932/15932-h/15932-h.htm#Pg_100. Accessed 25 February

2025. It is suggested that even earlier evidence of slavery can be found from the reign of Pharaoh Djer, c. 2900 BCE, with images of a Nubian chief bound to the prow of an Egyptian ship with his followers being carried off to slavery. Robert Collins, 'Slavery in the Sudan in History', *Slavery & Abolition: A Journal of Slave and Post-Slave Studies*, Vol. 20, No. 3, 1999, p. 69.

25. Carl Seaver, 'Debunking the Myth That Slaves Built the Pyramids', History Defined, https://www.historydefined.net/debunking-the-myth-that-slaves-built-the-pyramids. Accessed 27 February 2025.

26. Collins, 'The Nilotic Slave Trade', *op. cit.*, p. 140.

27. R. W. Beachey, *The Slave Trade of Eastern Africa*, Rex Collings, 1976, p. 121.

28. P. M. Holt and M. W. Daly, *A History of the Sudan: From the Coming of Islam to the Present Day*, 5th edition, Longman, 2000, p. 15.

29. *Ibid.*, p. 16.

30. Abbès Zouache, 'Remarks on the Blacks in the Fatimid Army, Tenth–Twelfth Century CE', *Northeast African Studies*, Vol. 19, No. 1, 2019, p. 29.

31. Jere L. Bacharach, 'African Military Slaves in the Medieval Middle East: The Cases of Iraq (869–955) and Egypt (868–1171)', *International Journal of Middle East Studies*, Vol. 13, No. 4, November 1981, pp. 471–495.

2. THE ARAB CONQUEST AND ENSLAVEMENT

1. James Walvin, *A Short History of Slavery*, Penguin Books, 2007, p. 29.

2. J. O. Hunwick, 'Black Slaves in the Mediterranean World: Introduction to a Neglected Aspect of the African Diaspora', in Elizabeth Savage (ed.), *The Human Commodity: Perspectives on the Trans-Saharan Slave Trade*, Frank Cass, 1992, p. 7.

3. Archaeologists found the remains of a church and Christian graves dating from the fifth century CE. Kazimierz Michalowski, 'The Spreading of Christianity in Nubia', in Gamal Mokhtar (ed.), *General History of Africa, II: Ancient Civilizations of Africa*, UNESCO, 1981, p. 329.

4. P. L. Shinnie, 'Christian Nubia', in J. D. Fage (ed.), J. D. Fage and Roland Oliver (series eds), *The Cambridge History of Africa, Vol. 2: From c. 500 BC to AD 1050*, Cambridge University Press, 1978, pp. 565–567.

5. *Ibid.*, p. 566.

6. The term 'Sudan' is used here in its old-fashioned meaning, covering much of the Sahel and not indicating the land that is today Sudan or South Sudan.

7. Terence Walz, 'Egyptian-Sudanese Trade in the Ottoman Period to 1882', *Oxford Research Encyclopedia of African History*, 2018, p. 3.

8. P. M. Holt and M. W. Daly, *A History of the Sudan: From the Coming of Islam to the Present Day*, 5th edition, Longman, 2000, p. 17.

9. Jere L. Bacharach, 'African Military Slaves in the Medieval Middle East: The Cases of Iraq (869–955) and Egypt (868–1171)', *International Journal of Middle East Studies*, Vol. 13, No. 4, November 1981, p. 478.

10. *Ibid.*, p. 488.

11. *Ibid.*, p. 488.

12. Stephan Conermann, 'Slavery in the Mamluk Sultanate', in Craig Perry et al. (eds), *The Cambridge World History of Slavery, Vol. 2: AD 500–AD 1420*, Cambridge University Press, 2021, pp. 391–392.

13. *Ibid.*, p. 390.

14. Michael Winter, *Egyptian Society Under Ottoman Rule: 1517–1798*, Routledge, 1992, p. 15.

15. Robert O. Collins, 'The Nilotic Slave Trade: Past and Present', *Slavery & Abolition: A Journal of Slave and Post-Slave Studies*, Vol. 13, No. 1, 1992, p. 140.

16. *Ibid.*, p. 141.

17. Terence Walz, *Trade between Egypt and Bilad as-Sudan, 1700–1820*, Institut Français d'Archéologie Orientale, 1978, p. 26.

18. *Ibid.*, p. 27.

19. Collins, 'The Nilotic Slave Trade', *op. cit.*, p. 140.

20. *Ibid.*, p. 142.

21. Ismael M. Montana, 'Slavery in the Middle East and North Africa', in Damian A. Pargas and Juliane Schiel (eds), *The Palgrave Handbook of Global Slavery throughout History*, Palgrave Macmillan, 2023, p. 467.

22. Jok Madut Jok, *War and Slavery in Sudan*, University of Pennsylvania Press, 2001, p. 21.

23. *Ibid.*, p. 21.

24. R. S. O'Fahey, 'Slavery and Society in Dar Fur', in John Ralph Willis (ed.), *Slaves and Slavery in Muslim Africa, Vol. 2: The Servile Estate*, Frank Cass, 1985, p. 83.

25. Nehemia Levtzion, *Ancient Ghana and Mali*, Methuen & Co., 1973, p. 9.

26. Raymond Mauny, 'Trans-Saharan Contacts and the Iron Age in West Africa', in J. D. Fage (ed.), *The Cambridge History of Africa, Vol. 2, op. cit.*, p. 291.

27. E. Savage, 'Berbers and Blacks: Ibāḍī Slave Traffic in Eighth-Century North Africa', *The Journal of African History*, Vol. 33, No. 3, 1992, pp. 351–368.

28. *Ibid.*, p. 353.

29. *Ibid.*, p. 362. 'The aim of this article is to illustrate the process whereby certain Berber tribes during the eight century A. D. substituted slaves

from the Bilad al-Sudan for Berber slaves from North Africa.' *Ibid.*, p. 368.

30. Amr ibn al-As, who led the conquest of Egypt, concluded a treaty with the town of Barqa in 642, in present-day Libya, levying a tribute of 3,000 dinars on them and instructing them that they could sell any children they wished to, to fulfil the terms of the bargain. *Ibid.*, p. 357.

31. Isabel Toral, 'The Umayyad Dynasty and the Western Maghreb: A Transregional Perspective', *Medieval Worlds*, No. 16, 2022, p. 98.

32. Adam Gaiser, 'Slaves and Silver across the Strait of Gibraltar: Politics and Trade between Umayyad Iberia and Khārijite North Africa', *Medieval Encounters*, No. 19, 2013, p. 65.

33. Toral, 'The Umayyad Dynasty and the Western Maghreb', *op. cit.*, p. 98.

34. William D. Phillips, *Slavery in Medieval and Modern Iberia*, University of Pennsylvania Press, 2014, p. 17.

35. Debra Blumenthal, 'Slavery in Medieval Iberia', in Craig Perry *et al.* (eds), *The Cambridge World History of Slavery, Vol. 2: AD 500–AD 1420*, Cambridge University Press, 2021, p. 512.

36. Adam Gaiser, 'Slaves and Silver across the Strait of Gibraltar, *op. cit.*, p. 64.

37. Phillips, *Slavery in Medieval and Modern Iberia*, *op. cit.*, p. 21.

38. 'Spain and the Human Diaspora in 1492', *Islamic Encounters: America, Europe, and the Middle East before 1835* (JCB Digital Catalogue), https://www. brown.edu/Facilities/John_Carter_Brown_Library/exhibitions/ islamic/pages/spain.html#:~:text=Between%201492%20and%20 1610%2C%20some,Tunis%2C%20Morocco%2C%20and%20Tripoli. Accessed 27 February 2025.

39. Blumenthal, 'Slavery in Medieval Iberia', *op. cit.*, pp. 516–517.

40. Eloy Martín-Corrales, *Muslims in Spain, 1492–1814: Living and Negotiating in the Land of the Infidel*, Brill, 2021, p. 2.

41. *Ibid.*, p. 9.

3. TURNING TOWARDS THE SOUTH

1. Patrick J. Munson, 'Archaeology and the Prehistoric Origins of the Ghana Empire', *The Journal of African History*, Vol. 21, No. 4, 1980, p. 465.

2. Nehemia Levtzion, *Ancient Ghana and Mali*, Methuen & Co., 1973, p. 54.

3. Barbara Cooper, 'The Sahel in West African History', *Oxford Research Encyclopedia of African History*, 2018, p. 1.

4. E. Savage, 'Berbers and Blacks: Ibāḍī Slave Traffic in Eighth-Century North Africa', *The Journal of African History*, Vol. 33, No. 3, 1992, p. 351.

5. J. Alexander, 'Islam, Archaeology and Slavery in Africa', *World Archaeology*, Vol. 33, No. 1, 2001, p. 46.

6. Nehemia Levtzion, 'The Sahara and the Sudan from the Arab Conquest of the Maghrib to the Rise of the Almoravids', in J. D. Fage (ed.), J.D. Fage and Roland Oliver (series eds), *The Cambridge History of Africa, Vol. 2: From c. 500 BC to AD 1050*, Cambridge University Press, 1978, pp. 665ff.

7. *Ibid.*, p. 670.

8. Allan Fisher and Humphrey Fisher, *Slavery and Muslim Society in Africa: The Institution in Saharan and Sudan Africa and the Trans-Saharan Trade*, Hurst & Co., 1970, p. 10.

9. Ann McDougall, 'The View from Awdaghust: War, Trade and Social Change in Southwestern Sahara, from the Eighth to the Fifteenth Century', *The Journal of African History*, Vol. 26, No. 1, 1985, p. 12.

10. Paul E. Lovejoy, *Transformations in Slavery: A History of Slavery in Africa*, Cambridge University Press, 2012, p. 25.

11. *Ibid.*, p. 26.

12. Ralph A. Austen, *Trans-Saharan Africa in World History*, Oxford University Press, 2010, p. 32.

13. Ralph T. Ware, 'Slavery in Islamic Africa, 1400–1800', in David Eltis and Stanley Engerman (eds), *The Cambridge World History of Slavery, Vol. 3: AD 1420–AD 1804*, Cambridge University Press, 2011, p. 52.

14. David Gakunzi, 'The Arab-Muslim Slave Trade: Lifting the Taboo', *Jewish Political Studies Review*, Vol. 29, Nos 3–4, 2018, p. 41.

15. Lovejoy, *Transformations in Slavery*, *op. cit.*, p. 35.

16. Albert Adu Boahen, *British Penetration of the Sahara and Western Sudan, 1788–1861*, PhD thesis, SOAS University of London, 1959, p. 351.

17. *Ibid.*, p. 383.

18. Lovejoy, *Transformations in Slavery*, *op. cit.*, p. 32.

19. *Ibid.*, p. 35. Others put the figure at six out of ten. Gakunzi, 'The Arab-Muslim Slave Trade', *op. cit.*, p. 41.

20. Lovejoy, *Transformations in Slavery*, *op. cit.*, p. 26.

21. *Ibid.*, p. 26.

22. Alexander, 'Islam, Archaeology and Slavery in Africa', *op. cit.*, p. 47.

23. Austen, *Trans-Saharan Africa in World History*, *op. cit.*, p. 31.

4.   GOLD, SALT AND SLAVES

1. Ann McDougall, 'The View from Awdaghust: War, Trade and Social Change in Southwestern Sahara, from the Eighth to the Fifteenth Century', *The Journal of African History*, Vol. 26, No. 1, 1985, p. 13.

2. Ray A. Kea, 'Expansions and Contractions: World-Historical Change and the Western Sudan World-System (1200/1000 B.C.–1200/1250 A.D.)', *Journal of World-Systems Research*, Vol. 10, No. 3, 2004, p. 733.

3. *Ibid.*, p. 729.

4. *Ibid.*, p. 727.

5. *Ibid.*, p. 744.

6. *Ibid.*, p. 799.

7. *Ibid.*, p. 799.

8. Ibn Khaldun's *History of the Berbers*, quoted in J. D. Fage, 'Ancient Ghana: A Review of the Evidence', *Transactions of the Historical Society of Ghana*, Vol. 3, No. 2, 1957, p. 11.

9. UNESCO, 'Timbuktu', https://whc.unesco.org/en/list/119. Accessed 27 February 2025.

10. Naima Mohamud, 'Is Mansa Musa the richest man who ever lived?', BBC News, 10 March 2019, https://www.bbc.co.uk/news/world-africa-47379458. Accessed 27 February 2025.

11. Tahar Abbou, 'Mansa Musa's Journey to Mecca and Its Impact on Western Sudan', Conference Paper: Routes of Hajj in Africa, International University of Africa, Khartoum, August 2020, https://www.researchgate.net/publication/343392595_Mansa_Musa's_Journey_to_Mecca_and_Its_Impact_on_Western_Sudan. Accessed 27 February 2025.

12. *Ibid.*

13. Ralph A. Austen, *Trans-Saharan Africa in World History*, Oxford University Press, 2010, p. 24.

14. Abbou, 'Mansa Musa's Journey to Mecca', *op. cit.*

15. S. M. Cissoko, 'The Songhay from the 12th to the 16th Century', in D. T. Niane, *General History of Africa, Vol. 4: Africa from the Twelfth to the Sixteenth Century*, UNESCO, 1984, p. 187.

16. Seymour Drescher and Stanley Engerman (eds), *A Historical Guide to World Slavery*, Oxford University Press, 1998, p. 33.

17. M. Abitbol, 'The End of the Songhay Empire', in B. A. Ogot (ed.), *General History of Africa, Vol. 5: Africa from the Sixteenth to the Eighteenth Century*, UNESCO, 1992, p. 303.

18. Paul E. Lovejoy, *Transformations in Slavery: A History of Slavery in Africa*, Cambridge University Press, 2012, p. 29.

19. *Ibid.*, p. 30.

20. Barbara Cooper, 'The Sahel in West African History', *Oxford Research Encyclopedia of African History*, 2018, p. 6.

21. Lovejoy, *Transformations in Slavery*, *op. cit.*, p. 30.

22. Austen, *Trans-Saharan Africa in World History*, *op. cit.*, p. 49.

23. J. Alexander, 'Islam, Archaeology and Slavery in Africa', *World Archaeology*, Vol. 33, No. 1, 2001, p. 49.

24. David Brion Davis, quoted in John Wright, *The Trans-Saharan Slave Trade*, Routledge, 2007, p. 22.

25. *Ibid.*, p. 24.

26. Leo Africanus, *The History and Description of Africa done into English by John Pory*, edited by Robert Brown, Hakluyt Society, 1896, Vol. 3, p. 235.

PART 2: THE INDIAN OCEAN AND BEYOND

1. Markus Vink, '"The World's Oldest Trade": Slavery and Slave Trade in the Indian Ocean in the Seventeenth Century', *Journal of World History*, Vol. 14, No. 2, 2003, p. 132.

2. 'Trans-Atlantic Slave Trade—Database', SlaveVoyages.org, https://www.slavevoyages.org/voyage/database. Accessed 27 February 2025. An Indian Ocean database is gradually being produced: 'Indian Ocean and Maritime Asia Slave Trade Databases', International Institute of Social History, https://datasets.iisg.amsterdam/dataverse/IOMASTD. Accessed 24 November 2024.

3. Shihan de Silva Jayasuriya, 'Indians of African Descent: Emerging Roles and New Identities', *Journal of African Diaspora Archaeology and Heritage*, Vol. 4, No. 1, March 2015, p. 1.

4. Bernard K. Freamon, 'Straight, No Chaser: Slavery, Abolition, and Modern Islamic Thought', in Robert Harms, Bernard K. Freamon and David W. Blight (eds), *Indian Ocean Slavery in the Age of Abolition*, Yale University Press, 2013, p. 62.

5. Robert O. Collins, 'The African Slave Trade to Asia and the Indian Ocean Islands', *African and Asian Studies*, Vol. 5, Nos 3–4, 2006, pp. 326–327.

6. Edward A. Alpers, 'Recollecting Africa: Diasporic Memory in the Indian Ocean World', *African Studies Review*, Vol. 43, No. 1, April 2000, pp. 84–85.

7. Jan Knappert, 'East Africa and the Indian Ocean', in Jeffrey C. Stone (ed.), *Africa and the Sea: Proceedings of a Colloquium at the University of Aberdeen, March 1984*, Aberdeen University African Studies Group, 1985, p. 124.

8. Edward Pollard and Okeny Charles Kinyera, 'The Swahili Coast and the Indian Ocean Trade Patterns in the 7th–10th Centuries CE', *Journal of Southern African Studies*, Vol. 43, No. 5, 2017, p. 927.

9. Beatrice Nicolini, 'Little Known Aspects of the History of Muscat and Zanzibar During the First Half of the Nineteenth Century', *Proceedings of the Seminar for Arabian Studies*, Vol. 27, 1997, p. 195.

10. Lindsay Doulton, *The Royal Navy's Anti-Slavery Campaign in the Western Indian Ocean, c. 1860–1890: Race, Empire and Identity*, PhD thesis, University of Hull, 2010, p. 20.

11. Jonathan Miran, 'Red Sea Slave Trade', *Oxford Research Encyclopedia of African History,* 2022.

12. Richard B. Allen, *European Slave Trading in the Indian Ocean: 1500–1850*, Ohio University Press, 2014, p. 27.

13. Abdul Sheriff, *Slaves, Spices and Ivory in Zanzibar: Integration of an East African Commercial Empire into the World Economy, 1770–1873*, James Currey, 1987, pp. 8–11.

5.   SLAVERY BEFORE THE ARRIVAL OF THE EUROPEANS

1. Michael N. Pearson, *The Indian Ocean*, Routledge, 2003, p. 51.

2. Peter Frankopan, *The Silk Roads: A New History of the World*, Bloomsbury, 2015, pp. 15–16.

3. Pearson, *The Indian Ocean, op. cit.*, p. 52.

4. UNESCO Silk Roads Programme, 'Did You Know? The Port Trade Centre of Arikamedu and Roman Exchange with the Indian Subcontinent', https://en.unesco.org/silkroad/content/did-you-know-port-trade-centre-arikamedu-and-roman-exchange-indian-subcontinent. Accessed 27 February 2025.

5. Pearson, *The Indian Ocean, op. cit.*, p. 53.

6. K. R. Dark, 'Globalizing Late Antiquity: Models, Metaphors and the Realities of Long-Distance Trade and Diplomacy', *Reading Medieval Studies*, Vol. XXXII, 2006, p. 6.

7. Susan Whitfield, *Silk, Slaves, and Stupas: Material Culture of the Silk Road*, University of California Press, 2018, pp. 261–262. Of course, it is highly unlikely that any slave or trader traversed the entire route.

8. *Ibid.*, pp. 262–263.

9. *Ibid.*, pp. 262–263.

10. E. G. Pulleyblank, 'The Origins and Nature of Chattel Slavery in China', *Journal of the Economic and Social History of the Orient*, Vol. 1, No. 2, April 1958, p. 219.

11. Edward H. Schafer, *The Golden Peaches of Samarkand: A Study of T'ang Exotics*, University of California Press, 1963, p. 43.

12. Jiří Jákl, 'Black Africans on the Maritime Silk Route in Old Javanese Epigraphical and Literary Evidence', *Indonesia and the Malay World*, Vol. 45, No. 133, 2017, p. 335.

13. M. Reda Bhacker, *Trade and Empire in Muscat and Zanzibar: The Roots of British Domination*, Routledge, 1992, p. 9.

14. Jákl, 'Black Africans on the Maritime Silk Route', *op. cit.*, p. 335.

15. Don J. Wyatt, *The Blacks of Premodern China*, University of Pennsylvania Press, 2010, p. 56.

16. Jákl, 'Black Africans on the Maritime Silk Route', *op. cit.*, p. 336.

17. *Ibid.*, p. 343.

18. Shihan de Silva Jayasuriya, 'Indians of African Descent: Emerging Roles and New Identities', *Journal of African Diaspora Archaeology and Heritage*, Vol. 4, No. 1, March 2015, p. 17.

19. Edward Dreyer, *Zheng He: China and the Oceans in the Early Ming Dynasty, 1405–1433*, Pearson Longman, 2007, p. 33.

20. Patrick Federl, 'The Instrumental Use of Zheng He's Travels in Official Sino-African Relations' Discourse', *Asiadémica: revista universitaria de estudios sobre Asia Oriental*, Vol. 11, 2018, pp. 59–60.

21. For a detailed discussion of the voyages and the first contacts between Chinese and Africans, see Don J. Wyatt, *The Blacks of Premodern China*, University of Pennsylvania Press, 2010.

22. This interpretation is challenged by Michael N. Pearson, who concludes that, overall, Chinese merchants and the state played only a small and transient role in the Indian Ocean, since these voyages of discovery did not lead to more sustained trade or conquest. Pearson, *The Indian Ocean*, *op. cit.*, p. 91. He also maintains that the admiral made a total of six expeditions, not seven.

23. Li Anshan, *China and Africa in Global Context: Encounters, Policy, Cooperation and Migration*, Routledge, 2022, p. 13.

24. James L. Watson, 'Transactions in People: The Chinese Market in Slaves, Servants, and Heirs', in James L. Watson (ed.), *Asian and African Systems of Slavery*, Basil Blackwell, 1980, p. 223.

25. Rekha Rani Sharma, 'Slavery in the Mauryan Period (C. 300 BC–C. 200 BC)', *Journal of the Economic and Social History of the Orient*, Vol. 21, No. 2, May 1978, p. 194.

26. R. R. Chauhan, *Africans in India: From Slavery to Royalty*, Asian Publication Services, 1995, p. 18.

27. Ann M. Pescatello, 'The African Presence in Portuguese India', *Journal of Asian History*, Vol. 11, No. 1, 1977, p. 27.

28. De Silva Jayasuriya, 'Indians of African Descent', *op. cit.*, p. 6.

29. Ali Anooshahr, 'Military Slavery in Medieval North India', in Craig Perry *et al.* (eds), *The Cambridge World History of Slavery, Vol. 2: AD 500–AD 1420*, Cambridge University Press, 2021, p. 379.

30. Shihan de Silva Jayasuriya, *The African Diaspora in Asian Trade Routes and Cultural Memories*, Edwin Mellen Press, 2010, p. 2. Abdul Sheriff, *Slaves, Spices and Ivory in Zanzibar: Integration of an East African Commercial Empire into the World Economy, 1770–1873*, James Currey, 1987, p. 13.

31. See Mark Horton, 'Artisans, Communities, and Commodities: Medieval Exchanges between Northwestern India and East Africa', *Ars Orientalis*, Vol. 34, 2004, pp. 62–80.

32. Richard M. Eaton, 'The Rise and Fall of Military Slavery in the Deccan, 1450–1650', in Indrani Chatterjee and Richard M. Eaton (eds), *Slavery and South Asian History*, Indiana University Press, 2006, p. 118.

33. *Ibid.*, p. 117.

34. Pescatello, 'The African Presence in Portuguese India', *op. cit.*, p. 27.

35. H. A. R. Gibb, *Ibn Battuta: Travels in Asia and Africa, 1325–1354*, George Routledge & Sons, 1929, p. 224.

36. *Ibid.*, pp. 229–230.

37. *Ibid.*, p. 260.

38. Pearson, *The Indian Ocean*, *op. cit.*, p. 71.

39. Renata Czekalska and Agnieszka Kuczkiewicz-Fraś, 'From Africans in India to African Indians', *Politeja*, No. 42, 2016, p. 194.

40. *Ibid.*, p. 199.

41. Anooshahr, 'Military Slavery in Medieval North India', *op. cit.*, p. 379.

42. Sanjay Subrahmanyam, 'Between Eastern Africa and Western India, 1500–1650: Slavery, Commerce and Elite Formation', *Comparative Studies in Society and History*, Vol. 61, No. 4, 2019, p. 820.

43. Varun Gupta, 'Who is Malik Ambar? The African Slave Turned Indian Mercenary Kingmaker', The Collector, 6 October 2021, https://www.thecollector.com/who-is-malik-ambar-african-slave-turned-mercenary-kingmaker. Accessed 27 February 2025.

44. Omar H. Ali, *Malik Ambar: Power and Slavery Across the Indian Ocean*, Oxford University Press, 2016, p. 2.

45. *Ibid.*, p. 116.

46. *Ibid.*, p. 120.

47. *Ibid.*, p. 124.

48. De Silva Jayasuriya, 'Indians of African Descent', *op. cit.*, p. 7.

49. Eaton, 'The Rise and Fall of Military Slavery in the Deccan', *op. cit.*, p. 126.

50. Ali, *Malik Ambar*, *op. cit.*, p. 91.

51. Eaton, 'The Rise and Fall of Military Slavery in the Deccan', *op. cit.*, p. 127.

52. *Ibid.*, p. 127.

53. Anooshahr, 'Military Slavery in Medieval North India', *op. cit.*, p. 379.

54. Chauhan, *Africans in India*, *op. cit.*, p. 236.

55. Eaton, 'The Rise and Fall of Military Slavery in the Deccan', *op. cit.*, p. 129.

56. De Silva Jayasuriya, 'Indians of African Descent', *op. cit.*, p. 9.

57. Niall Finneran, 'The Invisible Archaeology of Slavery in the Horn of Africa?', in Paul Lane and Kevin MacDonald (eds), *Slavery in Africa: Archaeology and Memory*, Oxford University Press, 2011, p. 239.

58. Howard Temperley, 'The Delegalization of Slavery in British India', in Howard Temperley (ed.), *After Slavery: Emancipation and its Discontents*, Frank Cass, 2000, p. 177.

59. De Silva Jayasuriya, 'Indians of African Descent', *op. cit.*, p. 11.

60. Shihan de Silva Jayasuriya, 'African Slavery in Asia: Epistemologies Across Temporalities and Space', *Kansai University Economic Review*, Vol. 72, Special Issue, March 2023.

61. Shadi Khan Saif, 'Sheedis: The Lost African Tribe in Pakistan', Fair Planet, 2 March 2020, https://www.fairplanet.org/dossier/beyond-slavery/sheedis-the-lost-african-tribe-in-pakistan. Accessed 27 February 2025.

62. *Ibid.*

63. Joseph E. Harris, 'Africans in Asian History', in Joseph E. Harris (ed.), *Global Dimensions of the African Diaspora*, Howard University Press, 1993, p. 325.

64. Behnaz A. Mirzai, *A History of Slavery and Emancipation in Iran, 1800–1929*, University of Texas Press, 2017, pp. 53–73.

65. Ronald Segal, *Islam's Black Slaves: A History of Africa's Other Black Diaspora*, Atlantic Books, 2001, p. 121.

66. Behnaz A. Mirzai, 'Qajar Haram: Imagination or Reality?', in Behnaz A. Mirzai, Ismael Musah Montana and Paul E. Lovejoy (eds), *Slavery, Islam and Diaspora*, Africa World Press, 2009, p. 85.

67. Mirzai, *A History of Slavery and Emancipation in Iran*, *op. cit.*, p. 64.

68. *Ibid.*, p. 54.

69. *Ibid.*, p. 60.

70. 'برده داری در خلیج فارس' [Slavery in the Persian Gulf], *Donya-e-Eqtesad*, 8 October 2013, https://donya-e-eqtesad.com/%D8%A8%D8. Accessed 27 February 2025.

71. Mirzai, *A History of Slavery and Emancipation in Iran*, *op. cit.*, p. 64.

72. 'برده داری در خلیج فارس', *Donya-e-Eqtesad*, *op. cit.*

73. Alexandre Popovic, *The Revolt of African Slaves in Iraq in the 3rd/9th Century*, Marcus Wiener, 1999, p. 20.

74. Mekuria Bulcha, 'The Red Sea Slave Trade: Captives' Treatment in the Slave Markets of North-East Africa and the Islamic Societies of the Middle East', in Kwesi Kwaa Prah (ed.), *Reflections on Arab-Led Slavery of Africans*, Centre for Advanced Studies of African Society, 2005, p. 108.

75. Jere L. Bacharach, 'African Military Slaves in the Medieval Middle East: The Cases of Iraq (869–955) and Egypt (868–1171)', *International Journal of Middle East Studies*, Vol. 13. No. 4, November 1981, p. 473.

76. *Ibid.*, p. 473.

77. Pearson, *The Indian Ocean*, *op. cit.*, p. 85.

78. Junius Rodriguez, 'Zanj Slave Revolts (869–883 CE)', in Junius Rodriguez (ed.), *Encyclopedia of Slave Resistance and Rebellion, Vol. 2 (O–Z)*, Greenwood Press, 2007, pp. 585–587.

79. Robert Harms, 'Introduction: Indian Ocean Slavery in the Age of Abolition', in Robert Harms, Bernard K. Freamon and David W. Blight (eds), *Indian Ocean Slavery in the Age of Abolition*, Yale University Press, 2013, p. 4.

80. Thomas Ricks, 'Slaves and Slave Traders in the Persian Gulf, 18th and 19th Centuries: An Assessment', in William Clarence-Smith (ed.), *The Economies of the Indian Ocean Slave Trade in the Nineteenth Century*, Frank Cass, 1989, pp. 61ff.

81. Haggai Erlich, 'Arabia', in Siegbert Uhlig (ed.), *Encyclopaedia Aethiopica, Vol. 1*, Harrassowitz Verlag, 2003, p. 294.

82. Wolbert Smidt, 'Red Sea Slave Trade in the 19th Century', in Siegbert Uhlig (ed.), *Encyclopaedia Aethiopica, Vol. 1*, *op. cit.*, p. 674.

83. Rosie Bsheer, *Archive Wars: The Politics of History in Saudi Arabia*, Stanford University Press, 2020, pp. 20–22.

84. Benjamin Reilly, 'Mutawalladeen and Malaria: African Slavery in Arabian Wadis', *Journal of Social History*, Vol. 47, No. 4, Summer 2004, p. 879.

85. *Ibid.*, p. 886.

86. Paul E. Lovejoy, *Transformations in Slavery: A History of Slavery in Africa*, Cambridge University Press, 2012, p. 156. A total of 347,000 slaves were sent from East Africa to Arabia, Persia and India in the nineteenth century.

87. Matthew S. Hopper, *Slaves of One Master: Globalization and Slavery in Arabia in the Age of Empire*, Yale University Press, 2015, p. 39.

88. Benjamin Reilly, 'Mutawalladeen and Malaria', *op. cit.*, p. 883.

89. *Ibid.*, p. 885.

90. Reuben Levy, *The Social Structure of Islam*, Cambridge University Press, 1962, pp. 83–84.

91. James Walvin, *A Short History of Slavery*, Penguin Books, 2007, p. 232.

92. Frederick Cooper, *Plantation Slavery on the East Coast of Africa*, Yale University Press, 1977, p. 34.

93. Thomas Vernet, 'Slave Trade and Slavery on the Swahili Coast, 1500–1750', in Mirzai *et al.*, *Slavery, Islam and Diaspora*, *op. cit.*, p. 41.

94. Cooper, *Plantation Slavery on the East Coast of Africa*, *op. cit.*, p. 32.

95. Beatrice Nicolini, 'The Western Indian Ocean as a Cultural Corridor: Makran, Oman and Zanzibar through Nineteenth Century European Accounts and Reports', *Middle East Studies Association Bulletin*, Vol. 37, No. 1, 2003, p. 22.

96. *Ibid.*, p. 25.

97. T. C. McCaskie, 'Cultural Encounters: Britain and Africa in the Nineteenth Century', in Andrew Porter (ed.), *The Oxford History of the British Empire, Vol. III: The Nineteenth Century*, Oxford University Press, 1999, p. 673.

98. Edward Alter Alpers, *The Role of the Yao in the Development of Trade in East-Central Africa, 1698–c.1850*, PhD thesis, University of London, 1966, p. 12.

99. Vernet, 'Slave Trade and Slavery on the Swahili Coast', *op. cit.*, p. 55.

100. Sheriff, *Slaves, Spices and Ivory in Zanzibar*, *op. cit.*, p. 202. The semi-official biography of Said bin Sultan by Allen James Fromherz gives the date of the transfer from Muscat to Zanzibar as 1832, although it says that the sultan 'was recalled to Oman several times to suppress revolts and deal with various emergencies.' Allen James Fromherz, *From Muscat to Zanzibar: Sayyid Said bin Sultan's Cosmopolitan Empire*, Sultan Qaboos Cultural Center, 2016, p. 2.

6.   EUROPEANS IN THE INDIAN OCEAN

1. Paul Lane, 'Slavery in Africa c. 500–1500 CE: Archaeological and Historical Perspectives', in Craig Perry *et al.* (eds), *The Cambridge World History of Slavery, Vol. 2: AD 500–AD 1420*, Cambridge University Press, 2021, p. 549.

2. Thomas Vernet, 'Slave Trade and Slavery on the Swahili Coast, 1500–1750', in Behnaz A. Mirzai, Ismael Musah Montana and Paul E. Lovejoy (eds), *Slavery, Islam and Diaspora*, Africa World Press, 2009, p. 48.

3. Basil Davidson, *Africa in History: Themes and Outlines*, Paladin Books, 1984, p. 89.

4. Christiane Bird, *The Sultan's Shadow: One Family's Rule at the Crossroads of East and West*, Random House, 2010, p. 176.

5. Vernet, 'Slave Trade and Slavery on the Swahili Coast', *op. cit.*, p. 60.

6. Philippe Beaujard, *The Worlds of the Indian Ocean: A Global History, Vol. II: From the Seventh Century to the Fifteenth Century CE*, Cambridge University Press, 2019, p. 602.

7. Richard B. Allen, *European Slave Trading in the Indian Ocean: 1500–1850*, Ohio University Press, 2014, p. 12.

8. Titas Chakraborty, 'Slavery in the Indian Ocean World', in Damian A. Pargas and Juliane Schiel (eds), *The Palgrave Handbook of Global Slavery throughout History*, Palgrave Macmillan, 2023, p. 342.

9. *Ibid.*, p. 342.

10. Bernard K. Freamon, 'Straight, No Chaser: Slavery, Abolition, and Modern Islamic Thought', in Robert Harms, Bernard K. Freamon and David W. Blight (eds), *Indian Ocean Slavery in the Age of Abolition*, Yale University Press, 2013, pp. 66–67.

11. *Ibid.*, p. 66.

12. Allen, *European Slave Trading in the Indian Ocean, op. cit.*, pp. 10–11.

13. Source: Richard B. Allen, *European Slave Trading in the Indian Ocean, op. cit.*, Table 5, p. 24. Notes: 'Arab, Muslim and Swahili Slave Exports' are the estimated slave exports by Arab, Muslim and Swahili traders to Arabia, Persia and India. 'European Slave Exports' are the estimated slave exports by European traders from eastern Africa and Madagascar to the Americas, India, the Mascarenes and South-East Asia.

14. '[T]he rulers of the autonomous port cities—such as Mombasa, Kilwa, Mogadishu, Aden, Hurmuz, Calicut and Melaka—were completely dependent on trade for their revenue: controlling only small areas of land, the usual Asian resource of a tax on land and its products was not available to them.' Michael N. Pearson, *The Indian Ocean*, Routledge, 2003, p. 115.

15. *Ibid.*, p. 115.

16. Allen, *European Slave Trading in the Indian Ocean, op. cit.*, pp. 8ff.

17. *Ibid.*, p. 11.

18. Beaujard, *The Worlds of the Indian Ocean, Vol. II, op. cit.*, p. 602.

19. *Ibid.*, p. 604.

20. Pearson, *The Indian Ocean, op. cit.*, p. 128.

21. *Ibid.*, p. 137.

22. Frederick Cooper, *Plantation Slavery on the East Coast of Africa*, Yale University Press, 1977, p. 32.

23. Beatrice Nicolini, 'The Western Indian Ocean as a Cultural Corridor: Makran, Oman and Zanzibar through Nineteenth Century European Accounts and Reports', *Middle East Studies Association Bulletin*, Vol. 37, No. 1, 2003, p. 24.

24. Paul E. Lovejoy, *Transformations in Slavery: A History of Slavery in Africa*, Cambridge University Press, 2012, p. 229.

25. *Ibid.*, p. 223.

26. Saada Wahab, *The History of Indians in Zanzibar from the 1870s to 1963*, Göttingen University Press, 2022, p. 26.

27. *Ibid.*, p. 26.

28. Cooper, *Plantation Slavery on the East Coast of Africa, op. cit.*, p. 32.

29. *Ibid.*, p. 39.

30. Thomas Metcalf, *Imperial Connections: India in the Indian Ocean Arena, 1860–1920*, University of California Press, 2007, p. 166.

31. A. M. H. Sheriff, 'The Slave Mode of Production Along the East African Coast, 1810–1873', in John Ralph Willis (ed.), *Slaves and Slavery in Muslim Africa, Vol. 2: The Servile Estate*, Frank Cass, 1985, p. 171.

32. Richard B. Allen, 'The Mascarene Slave-Trade and Labour Migration in the Indian Ocean during the Eighteenth and Nineteenth Centuries', *Slavery & Abolition: A Journal of Slave and Post-Slave Studies*, Vol. 24, No. 2, 2003, p. 33.

33. Richard B. Allen, *European Slave Trading in the Indian Ocean: 1500–1850*, Ohio University Press, 2014, p. 10.

34. Allen, 'The Mascarene Slave-Trade and Labour Migration', *op. cit.*, p. 37.

35. *Ibid.*, p. 39.

36. Allen, *European Slave Trading in the Indian Ocean*, *op. cit.*, p. 11.

37. Gwyn Campbell, 'Madagascar and Mozambique in the Slave Trade of the Western Indian Ocean, 1800–1861', *Slavery & Abolition: A Journal of Slave and Post-Slave Studies*, Vol. 9, No. 3, 1988, p. 168.

38. Maurice Bloch, 'Modes of Production and Slavery in Madagascar: Two Case Studies', in James Watson (ed.), *Asian and African Systems of Slavery*, Basil Blackwell, 1980, pp. 100–134.

39. Markus Vink, '"The World's Oldest Trade": Slavery and Slave Trade in the Indian Ocean in the Seventeenth Century', *Journal of World History*, Vol. 14, No. 2, 2003, p. 139.

40. Allen, *European Slave Trading in the Indian Ocean*, *op. cit.*, p. 9.

41. Vink, '"The World's Oldest Trade"', *op. cit.*, p. 144.

42. 'Roughly 26 per cent of all slaves came from east Africa, a further 26 per cent from the Indian subcontinent, 25 per cent from Madagascar and the balance from the slave markets of the Indonesia archipelago—Macassar, Bima and Bali.' Gavin Young, 'Making Ugly/Preserving Self: Makonde and the Cape Slave Trade', Conference Paper: The 11th Stanford-University of California Law and Colonialism Symposium, 21 March 2009, https://www.academia.edu/961229/Making_ugly_Preserving_self. Accessed 28 February 2025.

43. Robert Shell, *Children of Bondage: A Social History of the Slave Society at the Cape of Good Hope, 1652–1838*, University Press of New England, 1994, pp. 40–41.

44. Antonia Malan and Nigel Worden, 'Constructing and Contesting Histories of Slavery at the Cape, South Africa', in Paul Lane and Kevin MacDonald (eds), *Slavery in Africa: Archaeology and Memory*, Oxford University Press, 2011, p. 393.

45. Company officials and European, Eurasian and Asian inhabitants of cities that the Company controlled owned the majority of the enslaved. Linda Mbeki and Matthias van Rossum, 'Private Slave Trade in the Dutch

Indian Ocean World: A Study into the Networks and Backgrounds of the Slavers and the Enslaved in South Asia and South Africa', *Slavery & Abolition: A Journal of Slave and Post-Slave Studies*, Vol. 38, No. 1, 2017, p. 96.

46. Fred Morton, 'Slavery and South African Historiography', in Elizabeth A. Eldredge and Fred Morton (eds), *Slavery in South Africa: Captive Labor on the Dutch Frontier*, Westview Press, 1994, p. 1.

47. Matthias van Rossum, 'Running Together or Running Apart?: Diversity, Desertion, and Resistance in the Dutch East India Company Empire, 1650–1800', in Marcus Rediker, Titas Chakraborty and Matthias van Rossum (eds), *A Global History of Runaways: Workers, Mobility, and Capitalism, 1600–1850*, University of California Press, 2019, p. 143.

48. Allen, *European Slave Trading in the Indian Ocean*, *op. cit.*, Table 1, p. 17. Allen calculates that between 1622 and 1804, Britain transported between 5,698 and 5,716 slaves across the Indian Ocean.

49. 'British occupation of the Cape', *Encyclopaedia Britannica*, https://www.britannica.com/place/South-Africa/British-occupation-of-the-Cape. Accessed 28 February 2025.

50. Vink, '"The World's Oldest Trade"', *op. cit.*, p. 172.

51. Fred Morton, 'Slavery in South Africa', in Eldredge and Morton (eds), *Slavery in South Africa*, *op. cit.*, pp. 251–253.

52. Dougie Oakes, *Illustrated History of South Africa: The Real Story*, Reader's Digest, 1988, p. 146.

7.   OMANI HEGEMONY

1. Beatrice Nicolini, 'The Western Indian Ocean as a Cultural Corridor: Makran, Oman and Zanzibar through Nineteenth Century European Accounts and Reports', *Middle East Studies Association Bulletin*, Vol. 37, No. 1, 2003, p. 24.

2. Ronald Segal, *Islam's Black Slaves: A History of Africa's Other Black Diaspora*, Atlantic Books, 2001, p. 148.

3. Captain Philip Howard Colomb, *Slave Chasing in the Indian Ocean: A Record of Naval Experiences*, Longmans, Green and Co., 1873, p. 396.

4. Abdul Sheriff, *Slaves, Spices and Ivory in Zanzibar: Integration of an East African Commercial Empire into the World Economy, 1770–1873*, James Currey, 1987, pp. 158–159.

5. Frederick Cooper, *Plantation Slavery on the East Coast of Africa*, Yale University Press, 1977, pp. 103–107.

6. Robert Harms, *Land of Tears: The Exploration and Exploitation of Equatorial Africa*, Basic Books, 2019, p. 22.

7. Cooper, *Plantation Slavery on the East Coast of Africa*, *op. cit.*, pp. 83, 84, 105, 106.

8. Nicolini, 'The Western Indian Ocean as Cultural Corridor', *op. cit.*, pp. 35–36.

9. Stuart Laing, *Tippu Tip: Ivory, Slavery and Discovery in the Scramble for Africa*, Medina Publishing, 2017, p. 4.

10. Francois Renault, 'The Structures of the Slave Trade in Central Africa in the 19th Century', in William Gervase Clarence-Smith (ed.), *The Economics of the Indian Ocean Slave Trade in the Nineteenth Century*, Frank Cass, 1989, p. 150.

11. Sheriff, *Slaves, Spices and Ivory in Zanzibar*, *op. cit.*, p. 187.

12. *Ibid.*, p. 187. R. W. Beachey, *The Slave Trade of Eastern Africa*, Rex Collins, 1976, p. 186.

13. Eginald Mihanjo, 'Life Among Enslaved Communities during the Slave Trade Era in East Africa, 1840s–1890s', in Kwesi Kwaa Prah (ed.), *Reflections on Arab-Led Slavery of Africans*, Centre for Advanced Studies of African Society, 2005, pp. 142–143.

14. Sheriff, *Slaves, Spices and Ivory in Zanzibar*, *op. cit.*, p. 163.

15. Paul E. Lovejoy, *Transformations in Slavery: A History of Slavery in Africa*, Cambridge University Press, 2012, p. 232.

16. Ismael M. Montana, 'Slavery in the Middle East and North Africa', in Damian A. Pargas and Juliane Schiel (eds), *The Palgrave Handbook of Global Slavery throughout History*, Palgrave Macmillan, 2023, p. 468.

17. Beachey, *The Slave Trade of Eastern Africa*, *op. cit.*, p. 186.

18. Cuneyt Yenigun and Yasir AlRahbi, 'The Omani Diaspora in East Africa', *International Journal of Innovation, Creativity and Change*, Vol. 15, No. 7, May 2021.

19. Matthew S. Hopper, *Slaves of One Master: Globalization and Slavery in Arabia in the Age of Empire*, Yale University Press, 2015, p. 43.

20. Adrian S. Wisnicki, 'Livingstone in 1871', edited by Debbie Harrison, in Adrian S. Wisnicki (dir.), *Livingstone's 1871 Field Diary*, Livingstone Online, University of Maryland Libraries, 2017, http://livingstoneonline.org/uuid/node/ee070bc7-7f68-4e61-962d-038e1703231a. Accessed 28 February 2025.

21. *Ibid.*

22. Harms, *Land of Tears*, *op. cit.*, p. 31.

23. *Ibid.*, p. 31.

24. Thomas Pakenham, *The Scramble for Africa: 1876–1912,* Weidenfeld and Nicholson, 1991, pp. 239ff.

25. *Ibid.*, p. 12.

26. *Ibid.*, p. 11.

27. Robert Weisbord, 'The King, the Cardinal and the Pope: Leopold II's Genocide in the Congo and the Vatican', *Journal of Genocide Research*, Vol. 5, No. 1, 2003, p. 36.

28. Laing, *Tippu Tip, op. cit.*, p. 196.

29. *Ibid.*, pp. 262–269.

30. Renault, 'The Structures of the Slave Trade', *op. cit.*, pp. 148–149.

31. *Ibid.*, p. 161.

32. Harms, *Land of Tears, op. cit.*, p. 46.

33. Sheriff, *Slaves, Spices and Ivory in Zanzibar, op. cit.*, p. 108.

34. Harms, *Land of Tears, op. cit.*, p. 196.

35. *Ibid.*, p. 196.

36. A. T. Atmore, 'Africa on the Eve of Partition', in G. N. Sanderson (ed.), J. D. Fage and Roland Oliver (series eds), *The Cambridge History of Africa, Vol. 6: From 1870 to 1905*, Cambridge University Press, 1985, p. 74.

37. Martin Ewans, *European Atrocity, African Catastrophe: Leopold II, the Congo Free State and its Aftermath*, Routledge Curzon, 2002, pp. 126–127.

38. *Ibid.*, p. 138.

39. *Ibid.*, p. 139. Laing, *Tippu Tip, op. cit.*, p. 265.

40. Robert B. Edgerton, *The Troubled Heart of Africa: A History of the Congo*, St Martin's Press, 2002, p. 96.

41. Laing, *Tippu Tip, op. cit.*, p. 268.

42. Edgerton, *op. cit.*, p. 103.

43. *Ibid.*, p. 104.

8. THE PORTUGUESE AND THE BRITISH

1. Allen F. Isaacman, *Mozambique: The Africanization of a European Institution, The Zambesi Prazos, 1750–1902*, University of Wisconsin Press, 1972, p. xi.

2. *Ibid.*, p. 18.

3. *Ibid.*, pp. 85ff.

4. *Ibid.*, pp. 83–84. Edward A. Alpers, *Ivory and Slaves in East Central Africa: Changing Pattern of International Trade to the Later Nineteenth Century*, Heinemann, 1975, pp. 229–233.

5. Gwyn Campbell, 'Madagascar and Mozambique in the Slave Trade of the Western Indian Ocean, 1800–1861', *Slavery & Abolition: A Journal of Slave and Post-Slave Studies*, Vol. 9, No. 3, 1988, p. 174.

6. *Ibid.*, p. 177.

7. Linell Chewins and Peter Delius, 'The Northeastern Factor in South African History: Reevaluating the Volume of the Slave Trade out of

Delagoa Bay and Its Impact on Its Hinterland in the Early Nineteenth Century', *The Journal of African History*, Vol. 61, No. 1, 2020, p. 95.

8. *Ibid.*, pp. 95–96.

9. Campbell, 'Madagascar and Mozambique in the Slave Trade', *op. cit.*, p. 179.

10. David Eltis and David Richardson, *Atlas of the Transatlantic Slave Trade*, Yale University Press, 2010, Map 110, p. 156.

11. *Ibid.*, p. 156.

12. Pedro Machado, 'A Forgotten Corner of the Indian Ocean: Gujarati Merchants, Portuguese India and the Mozambique Slave-Trade, c. 1730–1830', in Gwyn Campbell, *The Structure of Slavery in Indian Ocean Africa and Asia*, Frank Cass, 2004, pp. 20–21.

13. Abdul Sheriff, *Slaves, Spices and Ivory in Zanzibar: Integration of an East African Commercial Empire into the World Economy, 1770–1873*, James Currey, 1987, p. 108.

14. John Wright and Julian Cobbing, 'The Mfecane: Beginning the Inquest', Conference Paper: African Studies Seminar, African Studies Institute, University of the Witwatersrand, Johannesburg, 12 September 1988, p. 2.

15. Chewins and Delius, 'The Northeastern Factor in South African History', *op. cit.*, p. 109.

16. Paul E. Lovejoy, *Transformations in Slavery: A History of Slavery in Africa*, Cambridge University Press, 2012, p. 158.

17. Gaontatlhe Mautle, 'Bakgalagadi-Bakwena Relationship: A Case of Slavery, c.1840–c. 1920', *Botswana Notes and Records*, Vol. 18, 1986, pp. 19–31.

18. It has been argued that the humanitarian movement played only a limited role in ending slavery and that the development of capitalism and colonialism played a much greater part. This is not the place for an examination of this debate, but William Mulligan has argued convincingly against this perspective. See William Mulligan, 'British Anti-Slave Trade and Anti-Slavery Policy in East Africa, Arabia, and Turkey in the Late Nineteenth Century', in Brendan Simms and D. J. B. Trim (eds), *Humanitarian Intervention: A History*, Cambridge University Press, 2011, pp. 257–280.

19. Chaim D. Kaufmann and Robert A. Pape, 'Explaining Costly International Moral Action: Britain's Sixty-Year Campaign Against the Atlantic Slave Trade', *International Organisation,* Vol. 53, Issue 4, 1999, p. 631.

20. Richard B. Allen, 'Suppressing a Nefarious Traffic: Britain and the Abolition of Slave Trading in India and the Western Indian Ocean', *The William and Mary Quarterly*, Vol. 66, No. 4, 2009, p. 892.

21. Frederick Cooper, *Plantation Slavery on the East Coast of Africa*, Yale University Press, 1977, p. 45.

22. Lindsay Doulton, *The Royal Navy's Anti-Slavery Campaign in the Western Indian Ocean, c. 1860–1890: Race, Empire and Identity*, PhD thesis, University of Hull, 2010, p. 27.

23. Mulligan, 'British Anti-Slave Trade and Anti-Slavery Policy', *op. cit.*, p. 263.

24. Huw Lewis-Jones, 'The Royal Navy and the Battle to End Slavery', BBC Online, 17 February 2011, https://www.bbc.co.uk/history/british/abolition/royal_navy_article_01.shtml. Accessed 28 February 2025.

25. Paul Lane, 'Slavery and Slave Trading in Eastern Africa: Exploring the Intersections of Historical Sources and Archaeological Evidence', in Paul Lane and Kevin MacDonald (eds), *Slavery in Africa: Archaeology and Memory*, Oxford University Press, 2011, p. 301.

26. Raymond Howell, *The Royal Navy and the Slave Trade*, Croom Helm, 1987, p. 94.

27. Mulligan, 'British Anti-Slave Trade and Anti-Slavery Policy', *op. cit.*, p. 278.

28. Howell, *The Royal Navy and the Slave Trade*, *op. cit.*, p. 208.

29. Scott S. Reese, *Imperial Muslims: Islam, Community and Authority in the Indian Ocean, 1839–1937*, Edinburgh University Press, 2018, p. 112. The Akhdam were believed to be descendants of Ethiopian troops who had arrived during the Aksumite Kingdom's occupation of the region in the sixth century. The Jabarti were also from the Horn, but were thought to be from the Red Sea or Somali region.

30. Gwyn Campbell and Edward A. Alpers, 'Introduction: Slavery, Forced Labour and Resistance in Indian Ocean Africa and Asia', *Slavery & Abolition: A Journal of Slave and Post-Slave Studies*, Vol. 25, No. 2, August 2004, p. xxii.

31. United States Department of State, 'Saudi Arabia 2022 Human Rights Report', 20 March 2023, p. 57, https://www.state.gov/wp-content/uploads/2023/03/415610_SAUDI-ARABIA-2022-HUMAN-RIGHTS-REPORT.pdf. Accessed 28 February 2025.

32. *Ibid.* A 2022 report by the International Labour Organization, Walk Free and the International Organization for Migration states: 'Migrant domestic workers are another category of workers who in some countries can fall into situations tantamount to forced labour because of state laws restricting their rights and freedoms. Such situations have been noted in Oman, where the existence of a sponsorship system enables a relationship in which migrant workers, including domestic workers, are dependent on their sponsors/employers, and links the work permit of this category of workers to their sponsors. The system prevents migrant workers from

freely terminating their employment. In Saudi Arabia, where migrant domestic workers do not enjoy the same rights as other workers in the country, they can be subjected to economic and physical abuse and exploitation, the confiscation of passports by employers, and the de facto persistence of a sponsorship system.' *Global Estimates of Modern Slavery: Forced Labour and Forced Marriage*, International Labour Organization (ILO), Walk Free, and International Organization for Migration (IOM), September 2022, p. 57, https://researchrepository.ilo.org/esploro/outputs/report/995219569902676. Accessed 28 February 2025.

PART 3: INDIGENOUS SLAVERY

1. Martin Klein, 'West Africa', in Seymour Drescher and Stanley Engerman (eds), *A Historical Guide to World Slavery*, Oxford University Press, 1998, p. 34.
2. Paul E. Lovejoy, 'Indigenous African Slavery', *Historical Reflections/Réflexions Historiques*, Vol. 6, No. 1. 1979, p. 19.
3. Patrick Manning, *Slavery and African Life: Occidental, Oriental, and African Slave Trades*, Cambridge University Press, 1990, p. 143.

9.   ETHIOPIAN SLAVERY

1. Richard Pankhurst, 'The History of Bareya, Sanqella and Other Ethiopian Slaves from the Borderlands of the Sudan', *Sudan Notes and Records*, Vol. 58, 1977, p. 1.
2. Niall Finneran, 'The Invisible Archaeology of Slavery in the Horn of Africa?', in Paul Lane and Kevin MacDonald (eds), *Slavery in Africa: Archaeology and Memory*, Oxford University Press, 2011, p. 225. Given that India took predominantly male slaves as troops, this is perhaps questionable.
3. Sandra Shell, *Children of Hope: The Odyssey of the Oromo Slaves from Ethiopia to South Africa*, Ohio University Press, 2018.
4. Harold G. Marcus, *The Life and Times of Menelik II: Ethiopia 1844–1913*, Clarendon Press, 1975, p. 73.
5. This was by no means the last occasion when the British would free child slaves by capturing a dhow in the Red Sea. As late as 1922, a Royal Naval vessel made a similar seizure. Suzanne Miers, 'Britain and the Suppression of Slavery in Ethiopia', *Slavery & Abolition: A Journal of Slave and Post-Slave Studies*, Vol. 18, No. 3, p. 266.
6. Giulia Bonacci and Alexander Meckelburg, 'Revisiting Slavery and the Slave Trade in Ethiopia', *Northeast African Studies*, Vol. 17, No. 2, 2017, p. 5.

7. Abbès Zouache, 'Remarks on the Blacks in the Fatimid Army, Tenth–Twelfth Century CE', *Northeast African Studies*, Vol. 19, No. 1, 2019, p. 29. The Coptic patriarch in Alexandria supplied the bishop for Ethiopia from the fourth century onwards (until the 1950s), if sometimes reluctantly and after significant delays.

8. Mordechai Abir, 'The Ethiopian Slave Trade and Its Relation to the Islamic World', in John Ralph Willis (ed.), *Slaves and Slavery in Muslim Africa, Vol. 2: The Servile Estate*, Frank Cass, 1985, p. 123.

9. Giulia Bonacci and Alexander Meckelburg, 'Slavery and the Slave Trade in Ethiopia and Eritrea', *Oxford Research Encyclopedia of African History*, 31 January 2023, p. 2.

10. David W. Phillipson, *Foundations of an African Civilisation: Aksum and the Northern Horn, 1000 BC–AD 1300*, James Currey, 2012, Chapter 15, pp. 195–207.

11. G. W. Bowersock, *The Throne of Adulis: Red Sea Wars on the Eve of Islam*, Oxford University Press, 2013, p. 97.

12. Phillipson, *Foundations of an African Civilisation, op. cit.*, p. 209.

13. Youval Rotman, *Byzantine Slavery and the Mediterranean World*, Harvard University Press, 2009, p. 54.

14. Scott S. Reese, *Imperial Muslims: Islam, Community and Authority in the Indian Ocean, 1839–1937*, Edinburgh University Press, 2018, p. 112. Another African group to be found in Aden are the Jabarti, known in Aden records as the 'African sweeper class', who are of Somali, Sudanese or Ethiopian origin.

15. Harold G. Marcus, *A History of Ethiopia*, University of California Press, 1994, p. 13.

16. Magdalena Moorthy Kloss, 'Slavery in Medieval Arabia', in Damian A. Pargas and Juliane Schiel (eds), *The Palgrave Handbook of Global Slavery throughout History*, Palgrave Macmillan, 2023, p. 140.

17. *Ibid.*, p. 140.

18. Paul Lane, 'Slavery in Africa, c. 500–1500 CE: Archaeological and Historical Perspectives', in Craig Perry *et al.* (eds), *The Cambridge World History of Slavery, Vol. 2: AD 500–AD 1420*, Cambridge University Press, 2021, pp. 547–548.

19. Craig Perry, 'Slavery and the Slave Trade in the Western Indian Ocean World', in Perry *et al.* (eds), *The Cambridge World History of Slavery, Vol. 2, op. cit.*, p. 147.

20. Marcus, *A History of Ethiopia, op. cit.*, p. 19.

21. *Ibid.*, p. 40.

22. Arab Faqīh, Shihāb al-Dīn Aḥmad ibn ʿAbd al-Qādir, *The Conquest of Abyssinia: 16ᵗʰ Century*, translated by Paul Lester Stenhouse, Red Sea Press, 2003, pp. 160–161.

23. *Ibid.*, p. 161.
24. Jonathan Miran, 'Red Sea Slave Trade', *Oxford Research Encyclopedia of African History*, 2022.
25. Ayda Bouanga, 'Gold, Slaves, and Trading Routes in Southern Blue Nile (Abbay) Societies, Ethiopia, 13th–16th Centuries', *Northeast African Studies*, Vol. 17, No. 2, 2017, p. 44.
26. Miran, 'Red Sea Slave Trade', *op. cit.*
27. Marcus, *A History of Ethiopia*, *op. cit.*, p. 55.
28. Abir, 'The Ethiopian Slave Trade and Its Relation to the Islamic World', *op. cit.*, p. 125.

10.   ETHIOPIA IN THE MODERN ERA

1. Mebratu Kelecha, 'How Ethiopia's past has shaped its present', LSE Blog, 28 April 2023, https://blogs.lse.ac.uk/africaatlse/2023/04/28/how-ethiopias-past-has-shaped-its-present. Accessed 28 February 2025.
2. Harold G. Marcus, *A History of Ethiopia*, University of California Press, 1994, p. 81.
3. R. W. Beachey, 'The Arms Trade in East Africa in the Late Nineteenth Century', *The Journal of African History*, 1962, Vol. 3, No. 3, p. 462.
4. Abdussamad H. Ahmad, 'Trading in Slaves in Bela-Shangul and Gumuz, Ethiopia: Border Enclaves in History, 1897–1938', *The Journal of African History*, Vol. 40, No. 3, 1999, p. 433.
5. Wondim Tiruneh Zeleke, 'Centralization Effort and Local Gumuz Response in North Western Ethiopia: The Lambicha Revolt and Its After Math (1960–1961)', *Journal of Environmental and Earth Science*, Vol. 8, No. 6, 2018, p. 49.
6. A. K. Adegehe, *Federalism and Ethnic Conflict in Ethiopia: A Comparative Study of the Somali and Benishangul-Gumuz Regions*, PhD thesis, University of Leiden, 2009, p. 114.
7. Alfredo González-Ruibal, 'Monuments of Predation: Turco-Egyptian Forts in Western Ethiopia', in Paul Lane and Kevin MacDonald (eds), *Slavery in Africa: Archaeology and Memory*, Oxford University Press, 2011, pp. 251–277.
8. Marcus, *A History of Ethiopia*, *op. cit.*, p. 94.
9. Ahmad, 'Trading in Slaves in Bela-Shangul and Gumuz', *op. cit.*, p. 437.
10. *Ibid.*, p. 441.
11. Patrick Gilkes and Martin Plaut, 'Great War Intrigues in the Horn of Africa', in Shiferaw Bekele *et al.* (eds), *The First World War from Tripoli to Addis Ababa (1911–1924)*, Centre français des études éthiopiennes, 2018.
12. Marcus, *A History of Ethiopia*, *op. cit.*, p. 120.

13. Suzanne Miers, 'Britain and the Suppression of Slavery in Ethiopia', *Slavery & Abolition: A Journal of Slave and Post-Slave Studies*, Vol. 18, No. 3, p. 262.

14. Sterling Coleman, 'Gradual Abolition or Immediate Abolition of Slavery?: The Political, Social and Economic Quandary of Emperor Haile Selassie', *Slavery & Abolition: A Journal of Slave and Post-Slave Studies*, Vol. 29, No. 1, March 2008, p. 71.

15. Miers, 'Britain and the Suppression of Slavery in Ethiopia', *op. cit.*, p. 263.

16. Paul B. Henze, *Layers of Time: A History of Ethiopia*, Hurst & Co., 2000, p. 201.

17. Miers, 'Britain and the Suppression of Slavery in Ethiopia', *op. cit.*, p. 270.

18. Marcus, *A History of Ethiopia*, *op. cit.*, p. 134.

19. Coleman, 'Gradual Abolition or Immediate Abolition of Slavery?', *op. cit.*, p. 75.

20. Quoted in Coleman, 'Gradual Abolition or Immediate Abolition of Slavery?', *op. cit.*, p. 65.

21. Miers, 'Britain and the Suppression of Slavery in Ethiopia', *op. cit.*, p. 274.

22. Coleman, 'Gradual Abolition or Immediate Abolition of Slavery?', *op. cit.*, p. 79.

23. Author's personal collection.

24. Miers, 'Britain and the Suppression of Slavery in Ethiopia', *op. cit.*, p. 277.

25. *Ibid.*, p. 277.

26. *Ibid.*, p. 280. Some sources suggest even higher figures. A debate in Britain's House of Lords on 4 February 1942 alluded to no fewer than 139 slave raids into British territory in Sudan over 13 years and quoted a figure of as many as 2 million Ethiopian slaves out of a total population of 10 million. HL Deb, 4 February 1942, Vol 121, cc. 646–80, https://api.parliament.uk/historic-hansard/lords/1942/feb/04/abyssinia. Accessed 12 March 2025.

27. Zeleke, 'Centralization Effort and Local Gumuz Response', *op. cit.*, p. 49.

28. Richard Pankhurst, 'Ethiopian Slave Reminiscences of the Nineteenth Century', *Transafrican Journal of History*, Vol. 5, No. 1, 1976, pp. 98–110.

29. *Ibid.*, p. 100.

30. *Ibid.*, pp. 100–101.

31. *Ibid.*, p. 104.

32. *Ibid.*, p. 105.

33. *Ibid.*, pp. 106–107.

34. Zeleke, 'Centralization Effort and Local Gumuz Response', *op. cit.*, p. 49.

35. John Young, 'Along Ethiopia's Western Frontier: Gambella and Benishangul in Transition', *Journal of Modern African Studies*, Vol. 37, No. 2, 1999, p. 336.

36. Jamal Tigraway, Facebook, 29 November 2021, https://www.facebook. com/watch/?v=283653760216997&rdid=LZPSxTJLyVqG8Ohu. Accessed 28 February 2025.

37. Associated Press, 'Tigray, Other Groups Form Alliance Against Ethiopian Leader', Voice of America, 5 November 2021, https://www. voanews.com/a/tigray-other-groups-form-alliance-against-ethiopian-leader/6301306.html. Accessed 25 February 2025. Abdi Latif Dahir and Lara Jakes, 'Eight Groups Join Tigray Rebels Vowing to Oust Ethiopia's Leader', *The New York Times*, 5 November 2021, https:// www.nytimes.com/2021/11/05/world/africa/ethiopia-tigray-eight-groups.html. Accessed 25 February 2025.

38. Press conference seen live by the author, National Press Club, Washington, DC, 5 November 2021.

11.   THE SOKOTO CALIPHATE

1. Mohammed Bashir Salau, *Plantation Slavery in the Sokoto Caliphate: A Historical and Comparative Study*, University of Rochester Press, 2018, p. 20.

2. 'In the eighteenth century, the Imamates of Fuuta Bundu (1698–1699), Fuuta Jaalon (1726–1727) and Fuuta Toro (1769–1776), located in modern-day Guinea and Senegal, were established through revolution. Starting in 1804 and centered on Hausaland in contemporary northwestern Nigeria, the Sokoto jihad led to the formation of the largest state in precolonial sub-Saharan Africa, the Sokoto Caliphate (1804–1903), which at its greatest extent in the 1850s stretched westward to present-day Burkina Faso, north into modern Niger, east into contemporary Cameroon and south into modern southwestern Nigeria. It did so by conquering both Muslim and non-Muslim states.' Jennifer Lofkrantz, 'Slavery in Islamic West Africa', in Damian A. Pargas and Juliane Schiel (eds), *The Palgrave Handbook of Global Slavery throughout History*, Palgrave Macmillan, 2023, p. 479.

3. Paul E. Lovejoy, *Slavery, Commerce and Production in the Sokoto Caliphate of West Africa*, Red Sea Press, 2005, pp. 1–3.

4. Jeremy Black, *A Brief History of Slavery: A New Global History*, Robinson, 2011; James Walvin, *A Short History of Slavery*, Penguin Books, 2007.

5. H. A. S. Johnston, *The Fulani Empire of Sokoto*, Oxford University Press, 1967, p. 17. According to Al-Hajj Sekou Tall, described as one of the most important cultural figures on northern Mali and Burkina Faso: 'This subject is very controversial and has already caused enough ink to flow. This much is said to be certain: the Fulani are descended from white Semites on the Mediterranean coast.' Al-Hajj Sekou Tall, 'The Origins of the Fulani', in Christopher Wise (ed.), *The Desert Shore: Literatures of the Sahel*, Lynne Rienner Publishers, 2001, p. 15.

6. *Ibid.*, p. 18.

7. Mário Vicente *et al.*, 'Population History and Genetic Adaptation of the Fulani Nomads: Inferences from Genome-Wide Data and the Lactase Persistence Trait', *Genomics*, Vol. 20, 2019. Martina Čížková *et al.*, '*Alu* Insertion Polymorphisms in the African Sahel and the Origin of Fulani Pastoralists', *Annals of Human Biology*, Vol. 44, No. 6, 2017.

8. Vicente *et al.*, 'Population History and Genetic Adaptation of the Fulani Nomads', *op. cit.*, p. 12.

9. Čížková *et al.*, '*Alu* Insertion Polymorphisms in the African Sahel', *op. cit.*, p. 543.

10. Lawrence E. Cline, 'Jihadist Movements in the Sahel: Rise of the Fulani?', *Terrorism and Political Violence*, Vol. 35, No. 1, 2023, p. 177.

11. Johnston, *The Fulani Empire of Sokoto*, *op. cit.*, p. 25.

12. Benedetta Rossi, *From Slavery to Aid: Politics, Labour, and Ecology in the Nigerien Sahel, 1800–2000*, Cambridge University Press, 2015, p. 44.

13. *Ibid.*, p. 47.

14. Paul E. Lovejoy, 'The Bello-Clapperton Exchange: The Sokoto Jihad and the Transatlantic Slave Trade', in Wise (ed.), *The Desert Shore*, *op. cit.*, p. 208.

15. Salau, *Plantation Slavery in the Sokoto Caliphate*, *op. cit.*, p. 38.

16. Usman dan Fodio, quoted in Bruce S. Hall, *A History of Race in Muslim West Africa, 1600–1960*, Cambridge University Press, 2011, p. 103.

17. *Ibid.*, p. 103.

18. Salau, *Plantation Slavery in the Sokoto Caliphate*, *op. cit.*, p. 43.

19. John Edward Philips, 'Causes of the Jihad of Usman Dan Fodio: A Historiographical Review', *Journal for Islamic Studies*, Vol. 36, 2017, pp. 52–53.

20. *Ibid.*, p. 52.

21. M. T. M. Minna, 'Sultan Muhammad Bello and His Intellectual Contribution to the Sokoto Caliphate', PhD thesis, School of Oriental and African Studies, 1982, p. 14.

22. Joseph P. Smaldone, *Warfare in the Sokoto Caliphate: Historical and Sociological Perspectives*, Cambridge University Press, 1977, pp. 36–37.

23. Johnston, *The Fulani Empire of Sokoto*, *op. cit.*, p. 91.

24. *Ibid.*, p. 94.
25. Salau, *Plantation Slavery in the Sokoto Caliphate*, *op. cit.*, p. 51.
26. *Ibid.*, p. 57.

12. PLANTATIONS AND SLAVERY

 1. Paul E. Lovejoy, *Slavery, Commerce and Production in the Sokoto Caliphate of West Africa*, Red Sea Press, 2005, pp. 162–163.
 2. *Ibid.*, p. 1.
 3. *Ibid.*, pp. 157ff.
 4. Mohammed Bashir Salau, *Plantation Slavery in the Sokoto Caliphate: A Historical and Comparative Study*, University of Rochester Press, 2018, p. 72.
 5. Lovejoy, *Slavery, Commerce and Production in the Sokoto Caliphate of West Africa*, *op. cit.*, pp. 162–163.
 6. Moses Ochonu, 'Caliphate Expansion and Sociopolitical Change in Nineteenth-Century Lower Benue Hinterlands', *Journal of West African History*, Vol. 1, No. 1, 2015, pp. 148–149.
 7. H. A. S. Johnston, *The Fulani Empire of Sokoto*, Oxford University Press, 1967, p. 161.
 8. Lovejoy, *Slavery, Commerce and Production in the Sokoto Caliphate of West Africa*, *op. cit.*, p. 154. Others disagree. 'I argue that there were more similarities in plantation organization between the caliphate and the Americas than identified in earlier works.' Salau, *Plantation Slavery in the Sokoto Caliphate*, *op. cit.*, p. 165.
 9. Jennifer Lofkrantz, 'Slavery in Islamic West Africa', in Damian A. Pargas and Juliane Schiel (eds), *The Palgrave Handbook of Global Slavery throughout History*, Palgrave Macmillan, 2023, p. 487.
10. Salau, *Plantation Slavery in the Sokoto Caliphate*, *op. cit.*, pp. 106–107.
11. See Jennifer Lofkrantz, 'Ransoming Captives in the Sokoto Caliphate', in Behnaz A. Mirzai, Ismael Musah Montana and Paul E. Lovejoy (eds), *Slavery, Islam and Diaspora*, Africa World Press, 2009, Chapter 8, pp. 125–137.
12. Johnston, *The Fulani Empire of Sokoto*, *op. cit.*, p. 156.
13. Salau, *Plantation Slavery in the Sokoto Caliphate*, *op. cit.*, p. 107.
14. Sean Stilwell, *Slavery and Slaving in African History*, Cambridge University Press, 2014, p. 1.
15. Salau, *Plantation Slavery in the Sokoto Caliphate*, *op. cit.*, p. 108.
16. *Ibid.*, p. 108.
17. Lovejoy, *Slavery, Commerce and Production in the Sokoto Caliphate of West Africa*, *op. cit.*, p. 14.

18. Quoted in Paul E. Lovejoy, 'The Bello-Clapperton Exchange: The Sokoto Jihad and the Transatlantic Slave Trade', in Christopher Wise (ed.), *The Desert Shore: Literatures of the Sahel*, Lynne Rienner Publishers, 2001, p. 210.

19. Joseph P. Smaldone, *Warfare in the Sokoto Caliphate: Historical and Sociological Perspectives*, Cambridge University Press, 1977, pp. 71–72.

20. Darlene Clark Hine, William C. Hine and Stanley Harrold, *The African-American Odyssey*, Pearson Education, 5th edition, 2011, p. 33.

21. *Ibid.*, p. 72. 'Such wars or raids were conducted not only in fulfilment of a religious injunction but also to sustain the crucial institutions of slavery.'

22. Jennifer Lofkrantz, 'Slavery in Islamic West Africa', *op. cit.*, p. 483.

23. Johnston, *The Fulani Empire of Sokoto, op. cit.*, p. 161.

24. Salau, *Plantation Slavery in the Sokoto Caliphate, op. cit.*, p. 92. Salau cites the case of Adamawa, which formed an integral part of the Caliphate, to illustrate his point. 'Studies of the Adamawa emirate also reveal a pattern of war-making and slave-gathering within and fairly close to the emirate. Sources state that the jihad wars led by four Fulani clans in the Adamawa region not only led to the defeat of the non-Muslim groups which had dominated the region, but also resulted in the enslavement of many members of defeated non-Muslim groups, and in subsequent raids on independent non-Muslim populations on the frontiers of the state.'

25. *Ibid.*, p. 92.

13.   SLAVE TRADING AND THE END OF THE CALIPHATE

1. Camille Lefebvre, 'Hausa Diasporas and Slavery in Africa, the Atlantic, and the Muslim World', *Oxford Research Encyclopedia of African History*, 22 March 2023, p. 5.

2. *Ibid.*, p. 4.

3. David C. Tambo, 'The Sokoto Caliphate Slave Trade in the Nineteenth Century', *The International Journal of African Historical Studies*, Vol. 9, No. 2, 1976, p. 187.

4. H. A. S. Johnston, *The Fulani Empire of Sokoto*, Oxford University Press, 1967, p. 161.

5. Lefebvre, 'Hausa Diasporas and Slavery in Africa, the Atlantic, and the Muslim World', *op. cit.*, p. 8.

6. Moses Ochonu, 'Caliphate Expansion and Sociopolitical Change in Nineteenth-Century Lower Benue Hinterlands', *Journal of West African History*, Vol. 1, No. 1, 2015, p. 150.

7. Olatunji Ojo, 'The Slave Ship *Manuelita* and the Story of a Yoruba Community, 1833–1834', *Revista Tempo*, Vol. 23, No. 2, 2017, p. 363.

8. *Ibid.*, p. 364. Note the modern names of the cities have been used.

9. Paul E. Lovejoy, *Slavery, Commerce and Production in the Sokoto Caliphate of West Africa*, Red Sea Press, 2005, p. 15.

10. *Ibid.*, p. 55.

11. Isadora Moura Mota, 'On the Verge of War: Black Insurgency, the "Christie Affair", and British Antislavery in Brazil', *Slavery & Abolition: A Journal of Slave and Post-Slave Studies*, Vol. 43, No. 1, 2021.

12. Paul E. Lovejoy, 'The Bello-Clapperton Exchange: The Sokoto Jihad and the Transatlantic Slave Trade', in Christopher Wise (ed.), *The Desert Shore: Literatures of the Sahel*, Lynne Rienner Publishers, 2001, p. 212.

13. Mohammed S. Audu and Uzoma S. Osuala, 'The British Conquest and Resistance of Sokoto Caliphate, 1897–1903: Crisis, Conflicts and Resistance', *Historical Research Letter*, Vol. 22, 2015, p. 39.

14. Johnston, *The Fulani Empire of Sokoto*, *op. cit.*, p. 212.

15. Paul E. Lovejoy and Jan S. Hogendorn, *Slow Death for Slavery: The Course of Abolition in Northern Nigeria, 1897–1936*, Cambridge University Press, 1993, p. 19.

16. P. T. Terry, 'The Arab War on Lake Nyasa, 1887–1895: Part II (An Account of the Campaign Against the Slaver Mlozi)', *The Society of Malawi Journal*, Vol. 18, No. 2, 1965.

17. Lovejoy and Hogendorn, *Slow Death for Slavery*, *op. cit.*, p. 26.

18. Johnston, *The Fulani Empire of Sokoto*, *op. cit.*, p. 257.

19. Frederick D. Lugard, 'Northern Nigeria', *The Geographical Journal*, Vol. 23, No. 1, January 1904, p. 27.

20. Lovejoy and Hogendorn, *Slow Death for Slavery*, *op. cit.*, p. 41.

21. *Ibid.*, p. 53.

22. *Ibid.*, p. 32.

23. *Ibid.*, p. 31.

24. *Ibid.*, p. 38.

25. Jan Hogendorn and Paul Lovejoy, 'The Development and Execution of Frederick Lugard's Policies Toward Slavery in Northern Nigeria', *Slavery & Abolition: A Journal of Slave and Post-Slave Studies*, Vol. 10, No. 1, 1989, p. 10.

26. A. H. M. Kirk-Greene (ed.), *The Principles of Native Administration in Nigeria: Selected Documents, 1900–1947*, Oxford University Press, 1965, p. 44.

27. Lovejoy and Hogendorn, *Slow Death for Slavery*, *op. cit.*, p. 278.

28. *Ibid.*, p. 284.

29. Bruce S. Hall, *A History of Race in Muslim West Africa, 1600–1960*, Cambridge University Press, 2011, p. 220.

30. Benedetta Rossi, *From Slavery to Aid: Politics, Labour, and Ecology in the Nigerien Sahel, 1800–2000*, Cambridge University Press, 2015, p. 1. Ader lies just inside Niger, between Sokoto and Agadez.

31. Lawrence E. Cline, 'Jihadist Movements in the Sahel: Rise of the Fulani?', *Terrorism and Political Violence*, Vol. 35, No. 1, 2023.

32. *Ibid.*, p. 183.

33. Albert van Dantzig, 'Effects of the Atlantic Slave Trade on Some West African Societies', in J. E. Inikori (ed.), *Forced Migration: The Impact of the Export Slave Trade on African Societies*, Hutchinson University Library for Africa, 1982, p. 199.

34. *Ibid.*, p. 201.

PART 4: TRANS-ATLANTIC SLAVERY

1. A. J. R. Russell-Wood, 'Iberian Expansion and the Issue of Black Slavery: Changing Portuguese Attitudes, 1440–1770', *The American Historical Review*, Vol. 83, No. 1, February 1978, p. 16.

2. *Ibid.*, p. 16.

3. Paul E. Lovejoy, *Transformations in Slavery: A History of Slavery in Africa*, Cambridge University Press, 2012, Table 3.1, p. 46. Note that the figures for the Atlantic are much more accurate than those for the Islamic world.

4. Trevor Burnard, 'The Atlantic Slave Trade', in Gad Heuman and Trevor Burnard (eds), *The Routledge History of Slavery*, Routledge, 2011, p. 83.

14.   THE DEVELOPING TRADE

1. Adam Gaiser, 'Slaves and Silver across the Strait of Gibraltar: Politics and Trade between Umayyad Iberia and Khārijite North Africa', *Medieval Encounters*, No. 19, 2013, p. 65.

2. Paul E. Lovejoy, *Transformations in Slavery: A History of Slavery in Africa*, Cambridge University Press, 2012, p. 15.

3. Basil Davidson, *Africa in History: Themes and Outlines*, Paladin Books, 1984, p. 200.

4. P. L. Wickins, *An Economic History of Africa from the Earliest Times to Partition*, Oxford University Press, 1981, p. 152.

5. Darlene Clark Hine, William C. Hine and Stanley Harrold, *The African-American Odyssey*, Pearson Education, 5th edition, 2011, p. 33.

6. Toby Green, *The Rise of the Trans-Atlantic Slave Trade in Western Africa, 1300–1589*, Cambridge University Press, 2012, pp. 71–72.

7. Hine *et al.*, *The African-American Odyssey*, *op. cit.*, p. 33.

8. Lovejoy, *Transformations in Slavery*, *op. cit.*, pp. 36–37.

9. William D. Phillips, *Slavery in Medieval and Modern Iberia*, University of Pennsylvania Press, 2014, p. 22.

10. Debra Blumenthal, 'Slavery in Medieval Iberia', in Craig Perry *et al.* (eds), *The Cambridge World History of Slavery, Vol. 2: AD 500–AD 1420*, Cambridge University Press, 2021 p. 518.

11. Annemarie Jordan, 'Images of Empire: Slaves in the Lisbon Household and Court of Catherine of Austria', in T. F. Earle and K. J. P. Lowe (eds), *Black Africans in Renaissance Europe*, Cambridge University Press, 2005, p. 157.

12. Blumenthal, 'Slavery in Medieval Iberia', *op. cit.*, p. 518.

13. *Ibid.*, p. 518.

14. Richard Follett, 'The Demography of Slavery', in Gad Heuman and Trevor Burnard (eds), *The Routledge History of Slavery,* Routledge, 2011, p. 122. Rice was introduced to Spain by the Arabs or 'Moors' by the ninth century and was eaten in parts of Italy by the fifteenth century.

15. B. W. Higman, *A Concise History of the Caribbean*, Cambridge University Press, 2011, p. 76.

16. B. W. Higman, 'Demography and Family Structures', in David Eltis and Stanley Engerman (eds), *The Cambridge World History of Slavery, Vol. 3: AD 1420–AD 1804*, Cambridge University Press, 2011, p. 494.

17. Richard Graham, 'Another Middle Passage?: The Internal Slave Trade in Brazil', in Gad Heuman and Trevor Burnard (eds), *Slavery (Critical Concepts in Historical Studies), Vol. 1*, Routledge, 2014, p. 155.

18. *Ibid.*, p. 123.

19. Jack Gray, *Rebellions and Revolutions: China from the 1800s to 2000*, Oxford University Press, 2002, pp. 25–27. Jurgen Osterhammel, 'Britain and China: 1842–1914', in Andrew Porter (ed.), *The Oxford History of the British Empire, Vol. III: The Nineteenth Century*, Oxford University Press, 1999, pp. 146ff.

20. Hine *et al.*, *The African-American Odyssey*, *op. cit.*, p. 34.

21. Green, *The Rise of the Trans-Atlantic Slave Trade in Western Africa*, *op. cit.*, p. 84.

22. Herman L. Bennett, *African Kings and Black Slaves: Sovereignty and Dispossession in the Early Modern Atlantic*, University of Pennsylvania Press, 2019, p. 150.

23. Green, *The Rise of the Trans-Atlantic Slave Trade in Western Africa*, *op. cit.*, p. 79.

24. *Ibid.*, p. 78.

25. *Ibid.*, p. 90.

26. Hine *et al.*, *The African-American Odyssey*, *op. cit.*, p. 20.

27. Finn Fuglestad, *Slave Traders by Invitation: West Africa's Slave Coast in the Precolonial Period*, Hurst & Co., 2018, p. 1.

28. Joanne Chassot, '"Voyage Through Death / To Life Upon These Shores": The Living Death of the Middle Passage', *Atlantic Studies*, Vol. 12, No. 1, 2015, p. 90.

29. Fuglestad, *Slave Traders by Invitation*, *op. cit.*, p. 2.

30. *Ibid.*, p. 9.

31. Jeremy Black, *A Brief History of Slavery: A New Global History*, Robinson, 2011, p. 95.

32. *Ibid.*, p. 95.

33. Lovejoy, *Transformations in Slavery*, *op. cit.*, pp. 69ff.

34. *Ibid.*, pp. 72–73.

15. EUROPEAN POWERS AS SLAVING NATIONS

1. Source: Adapted from Maxine Berg and Pat Hudson, *Slavery, Capitalism and the Industrial Revolution*, Polity, 2023, Table 1.1, p. 14. Notes: 'Other powers' are the Netherlands, Spain and Uruguay, Northern Colonies/ United States and the Baltic states. Portugal includes Brazil.

2. Sean Stilwell, *Slavery and Slaving in African History*, Cambridge University Press, 2014, p. 105.

3. Joseph Miller, 'The Slave Trade in Congo and Angola', in Martin Kilson and Robert Rothberg (eds), *The African Diaspora: Interpretive Essays*, Harvard University Press, 1976, p. 83.

4. Jeremy Ball, 'The History of Angola', *Oxford Research Encyclopedia of African History*, 2017, p. 6.

5. Paul E. Lovejoy, *Transformations in Slavery: A History of Slavery in Africa*, Cambridge University Press, 2012, p. 74.

6. *Ibid.*, p. 75.

7. *Ibid.*, p. 74.

8. José C. Curto and Raymond R. Gervais, 'The Population History of Luanda during the Late Atlantic Slave Trade, 1781–1844', *African Economic History*, No. 29, 2001, p. 4.

9. Finn Fuglestad, *Slave Traders by Invitation: West Africa's Slave Coast in the Precolonial Period*, Hurst & Co., 2018, pp. 116–117.

10. Joseph Miller, *Way of Death: Merchant Capitalism and the Angolan Slave Trade, 1730–1830*, James Currey, 1988, Map 5.1, p. 148.

11. *Ibid.*, p. 234.

12. *Ibid.*, p. 285.

13. Curto and Gervais, 'The Population History of Luanda', *op. cit.*, p. 37.

14. Trevor Burnard, 'The Atlantic Slave Trade', in Gad Heuman and Trevor Burnard (eds), *The Routledge History of Slavery*, Routledge, 2011, p. 91.

15. *Ibid.*, p. 92.

16. Miller, *Way of Death*, *op. cit.*, p. 314.

17. Laird W. Bergad, *The Comparative Histories of Slavery in Brazil, Cuba, and the United States*, Cambridge University Press, 2007, p. 39.

18. Stuart B. Schwartz, 'Colonial Brazil, c. 1580–1750: Plantations and Peripheries', in Leslie Bethell (ed.), *The Cambridge History of Latin America, Vol. II*, Cambridge University Press, 1984, p. 424.

19. Bergad, *The Comparative Histories of Slavery*, *op. cit.*, p. 39.

20. Schwartz, 'Colonial Brazil, c. 1580–1750', *op. cit.*, p. 423.

21. Bergad, *The Comparative Histories of Slavery*, *op. cit.*, p. 156.

22. Paul E. Lovejoy, 'Background to Rebellion: The Origins of Muslim Slaves in Bahia', *Slavery & Abolition: A Journal of Slave and Post-Slave Studies*, Vol. 15, No. 12, 1994, pp. 151–180.

23. *Ibid.*, p. 171.

24. R. K. Kent, 'African Revolt in Bahia: 24–25 January 1835', *Journal of Social History*, 1970, pp. 334–356. João José Reis, 'Slave Resistance in Brazil: Bahia, 1807–1835', *Luso-Brazilian Review*, Vol. 25, No. 1, 1988, pp. 111–144.

25. Leslie Bethell, *Brazil: Essays on History and Politics*, University of London Press, 2018, p. 114.

26. *Ibid.*, p. 115.

27. Stephanie Smallwood, 'African Guardians, European Slave Ships, and the Changing Dynamics of Power in the Early Modern Atlantic', *The William and Mary Quarterly*, Vol. 64, No. 4, October 2007, p. 712.

28. Randy J. Sparks, 'Gold Coast Merchant Families, Pawning, and the Eighteenth-Century British Slave Trade', *The William and Mary Quarterly*, Vol. 70, No. 2, 2013, p. 321.

29. James Walvin, *A Short History of Slavery*, Penguin Books, 2007, p. 51.

30. Berg and Hudson, *Slavery, Capitalism and the Industrial Revolution*, *op. cit.*, p. 28.

31. Walvin, *A Short History of Slavery*, *op. cit.*, p. 55.

32. Darlene Clark Hine, William C. Hine and Stanley Harrold, *The African-American Odyssey*, Pearson Education, 5th edition, 2011, p. 40. It is worth noting in passing that Hine *et al.* quote the West Indian historian Eric Williams as asserting that the 'horrors of the Middle Passage have been exaggerated' by later abolitionist authors, who were pressing to end slavery. See p. 46.

33. David Eltis and David Richardson, *Atlas of the Transatlantic Slave Trade*, Yale University Press, 2010, p. 2.

34. David Richardson, 'Shipboard Revolts, African Authority, and the Atlantic Slave Trade', in Gad Heuman and Trevor Burnard (eds), *Slavery (Critical Concepts in Historical Studies), Vol. 1*, Routledge, 2014, p. 277.

35. *Ibid.*, p. 278.

36. Hine *et al.*, *The African-American Odyssey*, *op. cit.*, p. 46.

37. Smallwood, 'African Guardians, European Slave Ships', *op. cit.*, p. 680.

38. *Ibid.*, pp. 683–684.

39. *Ibid.*, p. 697.

40. John Henrik Clarke, 'Slave Revolts in the Caribbean Islands', *Présence Africaine,* No. 84, 1972. Gad Heuman, 'Slave Rebellions', in Gad Heuman and Trevor Burnard (eds), *The Routledge History of Slavery,* Routledge, 2011, p. 226.

41. William D. Phillips, *Slavery from Roman Times to the Early Transatlantic Trade,* Manchester University Press, 1985, p. 189.

42. Burnard, 'The Atlantic Slave Trade', *op. cit.*, p. 84.

43. Giorgio Riello, 'Cotton Textiles and the Industrial Revolution in a Global Context', *Past & Present,* Vol. 255, No. 1, May 2022.

44. Basil Davidson, *The African Slave Trade: Precolonial History, 1450–1850,* Little, Brown and Co., 1961, p. 242.

45. Barton C. Hacker, 'Firearms, Horses, and Slave Soldiers: The Military History of African Slavery', *ICON: Journal of the International Committee for the History of Technology,* Vol. 14, 2008, pp. 62–83.

46. J. E. Inikori, 'The Import of Firearms into West Africa, 1750–1807: A Quantitative Analysis', in J. E. Inikori (ed.), *Forced Migration: The Impact of the Export Slave Trade on African Societies,* Hutchinson University Library for Africa, 1982, p. 133.

47. Nathan Nunn, 'The Long-Term Effects of Africa's Slave Trades', *The Quarterly Journal of Economics,* Vol. 123, No. 1, February 2008, pp. 142–143.

48. Warren C. Whatley, 'Guns for Slaves: The 18th Century British Slave Trade in Africa', Working Paper: Department of Economics and CAAS, University of Michigan, 15 April 2008, p. 18, https://users.nber. org/~confer/2008/si2008/DAE/whatley.pdf. Accessed 1 March 2025.

49. Stilwell, *Slavery and Slaving in African History,* *op. cit.*, p. 101.

50. *Ibid.*, p. 101.

51. Patrick Manning, *Slavery and African Life: Occidental, Oriental, and African Slave Trades,* Cambridge University Press, 1990, p. 133.

52. *Ibid.*, p. 129.

53. Nunn, 'The Long-Term Effects of Africa's Slave Trades', *op. cit.*, p. 143.

16.   ABOLITION AND THE RETURN TO AFRICA

1. William M. Wiecek, 'Somerset: Lord Mansfield and the Legitimacy of Slavery in the Anglo-American World', *The University of Chicago Law Review,* Vol. 42, No. 1, 1974, p. 87.

2. Nick Rhodes, *William Cowper: Selected Poems,* Routledge, 2003, p. 84.

3. James Oldham, 'New Light on Mansfield and Slavery', *Journal of British Studies,* Vol. 27, No. 1, 1988, p. 45.

4. Jeremy Black, *A Brief History of Slavery: A New Global History*, Robinson, 2011, p. 102.

5. James Walvin, *A Short History of Slavery*, Penguin Books, 2007, pp. 86–89.

6. Trevor Burnard, 'A New Look at the Zong Case of 1783', *XVII–XVIII: Revue de la Société d'études anglo-américaines des XVIIᵉ et XVIIIᵉ siècles*, Vol. 76, 2019, p. 18.

7. UK Parliament, 'Parliament abolishes the slave trade', https://www.parliament.uk/about/living-heritage/transformingsociety/tradeindustry/slavetrade/overview/parliament-abolishes-the-slave-trade. Accessed 2 March 2025.

8. Christopher Lloyd, *The Navy and the Slave Trade*, Longmans, Green and Co., 1949, p. 3.

9. Peter Grindal, *Opposing the Slavers: The Royal Navy's Campaign against the Atlantic Slave Trade*, I.B. Tauris, 2016, p. 734.

10. *Ibid.*, p. 754.

11. Siân Rees, *Sweet Water and Bitter: The Ships that Stopped the Slave Trade*, Chatto & Windus, 2009, p. 4.

12. Black, *A Brief History of Slavery*, *op. cit.*, p. 186.

13. David Eltis and David Richardson, *Atlas of the Transatlantic Slave Trade*, Yale University Press, 2010, p. 286.

14. Anthony Sullivan, *Britain's War Against the Slave Trade: The Operations of the Royal Navy's West Africa Squadron, 1807–1867*, Frontline Books, 2020, p. 346.

15. Mary Wills, 'Royal Navy sailors were appalled by conditions on slave ships, but those they "rescued" rarely experienced true freedom', *The Conversation*, 6 March 2020, https://theconversation.com/royal-navy-sailors-were-appalled-by-conditions-on-slave-ships-but-those-they-rescued-rarely-experienced-true-freedom-126903. Accessed 2 March 2025.

16. Maxine Berg and Pat Hudson, *Slavery, Capitalism and the Industrial Revolution, Polity*, 2023, p. 195.

17. Michael Anson and Michael D. Bennett, 'The collection of slavery compensation, 1835–43', Bank of England, Staff Working Paper No. 1,006, November 2022, p. 1, https://www.bankofengland.co.uk/-/media/boe/files/working-paper/2022/the-collection-of-slavery-compensation-1835-43.pdf. Accessed 2 March 2025.

18. Claire Phelan, 'Africa Squadron', in Peter Hinks and John McKivigan (eds), *Encyclopedia of Antislavery and Abolition, Vol. 1 (A–I)*, Greenwood Press, 2007, p. 26.

19. Paul E. Lovejoy, *Transformations in Slavery: A History of Slavery in Africa*, Cambridge University Press, 2012, p. 140.

20. Royal Navy, 'Protector Honours Sailors Who Helped End African Slave Trade', 20 October 2021, https://www.royalnavy.mod.uk/news-and-latest-activity/news/2021/october/20/20211020-protector-slavery. Accessed 2 March 2025. This figure applies only to the West Coast naval forces.

21. Lindsay Doulton, *The Royal Navy's Anti-Slavery Campaign in the Western Indian Ocean, c. 1860–1890: Race, Empire and Identity*, PhD thesis, University of Hull, 2010, p. 7.

22. Eltis and Richardson, *Atlas of the Transatlantic Slave Trade, op. cit.*, p. 274. There are many other estimates, which are approximately in this area.

23. Raymond Howell, *The Royal Navy and the Slave Trade*, Croom Helm, 1987, p. 220.

24. Mary Wills, *The Royal Navy and the Suppression of the Atlantic Slave Trade, c. 1807–1867: Anti-Slavery, Empire and Identity*, PhD thesis, University of Hull, 2012, p. 3.

25. National Museum of the U.S. Navy, 'Anti-Slave Trade Patrols', 27 February 2023, https://www.history.navy.mil/content/history/museums/nmusn/explore/prior-exhibits/2020/anti-slave-trade-patrols.html. Accessed 2 March 2025.

26. Hannah Durkin, *Survivors: The Lost Stories of the Last Captives of the Atlantic Slave Trade*, William Collins, 2024, p. 19.

27. Henry B. Lovejoy and Richard Anderson, 'Introduction: "Liberated Africans" and Early International Courts of Humanitarian Effort', in Richard Anderson and Henry B. Lovejoy (eds), *Liberated Africans and the Abolition of the Slave Trade, 1807–1896*, University of Rochester Press, 2020, pp. 1–12.

28. Durkin, *Survivors, op. cit.*, 2024. Durkin has provided well-researched and very detailed material on how these men and women fared. The information here is from her work.

29. *Ibid.*, p. 2.

30. *Ibid.*, p. 6.

31. 'Africatown', *Encyclopaedia Britannica*, https://www.britannica.com/place/Africatown. Accessed 2 March 2025.

32. Lindsay Goulton, '"The Flag That Sets Us Free": Antislavery, Africans, and the Royal Navy in the Western Indian Ocean', in Robert Harms, Bernard K. Freamon and David W. Blight (eds), *Indian Ocean Slavery in the Age of Abolition*, Yale University Press, 2013, p. 101.

33. *Ibid.*, pp. 101–102.

34. H. Cockburn-Stewart to the Right Honourable J. Chamberlain, MP, Seychelles, 30 June 1897, The National Archives (United Kingdom), CO 167/708.

35. Goulton, "'The Flag That Sets Us Free'", *op. cit.*, pp. 111–112.

36. Eltis and Richardson, *Atlas of the Transatlantic Slave Trade*, *op. cit.*, Map 189, p. 289.

37. Andrew Pearson, *Distant Freedom: St Helena and the Abolition of the Slave Trade, 1840–1872*, Liverpool University Press, 2016, p. 3.

38. Chris Saunders, 'Liberated Africans at the Cape: Some Reconsiderations', in Anderson and Lovejoy (eds), *Liberated Africans and the Abolition of the Slave Trade*, *op. cit.*, p. 302.

39. *Ibid.*, p. 299.

40. *Ibid.*, p. 297. Joline Young, *An Uncomfortable Paradise: A History of Dispossession and Slavery in Simon's Town*, NagsPro Multimedia, 2023.

41. Preben Kaarsholm, 'The History of the Zanzibari Amakhuwa: Uprooting, Registration, and Inventions of Home in a Community of Liberated Africans', *Monsoon*, Vol. 2, No. 2, 2024, p. 5.

42. *Ibid.*, p. 5.

43. Black, *A Brief History of Slavery*, *op. cit.*, pp. 224–225.

44. Lovejoy, *Transformations in Slavery*, *op. cit.*, p. 249.

45. Michael Siva, 'Why did the Black Poor of London Not Support the Sierra Leone Resettlement Scheme?', *History Matters Journal*, Vol. 1, No. 2, 2021, pp. 25ff.

46. Kenneth Morgan, 'Sierra Leone', in Kevin Shillington (ed.), *Encyclopedia of African History, Vol. 3 (P–Z)*, Fitzroy Dearborn, 2005, p. 1352.

47. *Ibid.*, p. 1353.

48. *Ibid.*, p. 1353.

49. Eltis and Richardson, *Atlas of the Transatlantic Slave Trade, op. cit.*, p. 289.

50. Christopher Fyfe, 'Freed Slave Colonies in West Africa', in John Flint (ed.), J. D. Fage and Roland Oliver (series eds), *The Cambridge History of Africa, Vol. 5: From c. 1790 to c. 1870*, Cambridge University Press, 1976, p. 197.

51. Francois Ngolet, 'Libreville', in Kevin Shillington (ed.), *Encyclopedia of African History, Vol. 2 (H–O)*, Fitzroy Dearborn, 2005, p. 828.

52. John Yoder, 'Liberia', in Shillington (ed.), *Encyclopedia of African History, Vol. 2*, *op. cit.*, p. 819.

53. *Ibid.*, p. 818.

54. Sharla M. Fett, '"Fugitive Liberated Congoes": Recaptive Youth and the Rejection of Liberian Apprenticeships, 1858–61', in Anderson and Lovejoy (eds), *Liberated Africans and the Abolition of the Slave Trade*, *op. cit.*, p. 328.

55. Tom W. Shick, *Behold the Promised Land: A History of Afro-American Settler Society in Nineteenth-Century Liberia*, Johns Hopkins University Press, 1980, p. 91.

56. Robert W. July, *The Origins of Modern African Thought: Its Development in West Africa During the Nineteenth and Twentieth Centuries*, Faber & Faber, 1968, p. 90.

57. *Ibid.*, pp. 91–92.

58. Daniel B. Domingues da Silva and Edward A. Alpers, 'Abolition and the Registration of Slaves and *Libertos* in Portuguese Mozambique, 1856–76', *The Journal of African History*, Vol. 62, No. 3, 2022, pp. 377–393.

59. José C. Curto, 'Producing "Liberated" Africans in Mid-Nineteenth Century Angola', in Anderson and Lovejoy (eds), *Liberated Africans and the Abolition of the Slave Trade*, *op. cit.*, pp. 238–256.

60. *Ibid.*, p. 247.

61. Fred Morton, *Children of Ham: Freed Slaves and Fugitive Slaves on the Kenyan Coast, 1873 to 1907*, Westview Press, 1990, p. 52.

62. *Ibid.*, p. 55.

63. *Ibid.*, p. 57.

64. *Ibid.*, p. 61.

65. *Ibid.*, p. 65.

66. *Ibid.*, p. 67.

67. *Ibid.*, p. 72.

68. *Ibid.*, pp. 144, 170.

69. William Mulligan, 'British Anti-Slave Trade and Anti-Slavery Policy in East Africa, Arabia, and Turkey in the Late Nineteenth Century', in Brendan Simms and D. J. B. Trim (eds), *Humanitarian Intervention: A History*, Cambridge University Press, 2011, p. 280.

PART 5: THE OTTOMAN EMPIRE AND BARBARY SLAVERY

1. William Clarence-Smith and David Eltis, 'White Servitude', in David Eltis and Stanley Engerman (eds), *The Cambridge World History of Slavery, Vol. 3: AD 1420–AD 1804*, Cambridge University Press, 2011, p. 153. Attempting to reach definitive totals is fruitless, but anyone wishing to consider this further can read Professor Bernard Capp's examination of the calculations: Bernard Capp, *British Slaves and Barbary Corsairs, 1580–1750*, Oxford University Press, 2022, p. 17. See also: Robert C. Davis, 'Counting European Slaves on the Barbary Coast', *Past & Present*, No. 172, August 2001.

2. Capp, *British Slaves and Barbary Corsairs*, *op. cit.*, p. 17.

3. Kris Manjapra, *Black Ghost of Empire: The Long Death of Slavery and the Failure of Emancipation*, Penguin Books, 2022, pp. 76–77.

4. Yacine Daddi Addoun, '"So That God Frees the Former Masters from Hell Fire:" Salvation Through Manumission in Nineteenth Century

Ottoman Algeria', in Ana Lucia Araujo, Mariana P. Candido and Paul E. Lovejoy (eds), *Crossing Memories: Slavery and African Diaspora*, Africa World Press, 2011, pp. 254, 237.

17. THE OTTOMANS

1. Stanford J. Shaw, *History of the Ottoman Empire and Modern Turkey, Vol. 1*, Cambridge University Press, 1976, pp. 12–14.

2. Karen Barkey, 'The Ottoman Empire (1299–1923): The Bureaucratization of Patrimonial Authority', in Peter Crooks and Timothy Parsons (eds), *Empires and Bureaucracy in World History. From Late Antiquity to the Twentieth Century*, Cambridge University Press, 2016, p. 102.

3. Ehud R. Toledano, 'Enslavement in the Ottoman Empire in the Early Modern Period', in David Eltis and Stanley Engerman (eds), *The Cambridge World History of Slavery, Vol. 3: AD 1420–AD 1804*, Cambridge University Press, 2011, p. 25.

4. *Ibid.*, pp. 26–27.

5. *Ibid.*, p. 26.

6. Esma Durugönül, 'The Invisibility of Turks of African Origin and the Construction of Turkish Cultural Identity: The Need for a New Historiography', *Journal of Black Studies*, Vol. 33, No. 3, 2003, p. 282.

7. *Ibid.*, p. 289.

8. Reda Mowafi, *Slavery, Slave Trade, and Abolition Attempts in Egypt and the Sudan, 1820–1882*, Esselte Studium, 1981, p. 8.

9. Toledano, 'Enslavement in the Ottoman Empire', *op. cit.*, p. 33.

10. Bernard Lewis, *Race and Slavery in the Middle East: An Historical Enquiry*, Oxford University Press, 1990, p. 73.

11. Ehud R. Toledano, *The Ottoman Slave Trade and Its Suppression*, Princeton University Press, 1982, pp. 15–18.

12. *Ibid.*, p. 16.

13. *Ibid.*, p. 36.

14. *Ibid.*, p. 44.

15. Gábor Ágoston and Bruce Masters, *Encyclopedia of the Ottoman Empire*, Facts on File, 2009, p. 531.

16. Lewis, *Race and Slavery in the Middle East*, *op. cit.*, p. 74.

17. T. G. Otte, '"A Course of Unceasing Remonstrance": British Diplomacy and the Suppression of the Slave Trade in the East, 1852–1898', in Keith Hamilton and Patrick Salmon (eds), *Slavery, Diplomacy and Empire: Britain and the Suppression of the Slave Trade, 1807–1975*, Sussex Academic Press, 2009, p. 98.

18. *Ibid.*, p. 98.

19. Charles L. Wilkins, 'Slavery and Household Formation in Ottoman Aleppo, 1640–1700', *Journal of the Economic and Social History of the Orient*, Vol. 56, No. 3, 2013, p. 354.
20. *Ibid.*, p. 366.
21. *Ibid.*, p. 367.
22. Eve M. Troutt Powell, *Tell This in My Memory: Stories of Enslavement from Egypt, Sudan and the Ottoman Empire*, Stanford University Press, 2012, p. 131.
23. Toledano, *The Ottoman Slave Trade and Its Suppression, op. cit.*, pp. 52–53.
24. *Ibid.*, p. 54.
25. *Ibid.*, p. 248.

18. THE BARBARY CORSAIRS

1. Andrew Wheatcroft, *The Ottomans*, Viking, 1993, p. 65.
2. John E. Dotson, 'Foundations of Venetian Naval Strategy from Pietro II Orseolo to the Battle of Zonchio, 1000–1500', *Viator: Medieval and Renaissance Studies*, Vol. 32, 2001, pp. 113–125.
3. Khizr is known by several names, including Kheir el-Din.
4. Roger Crowley, *Empires of the Sea: The Final Battle for the Mediterranean, 1521–1580*, Faber & Faber, 2008, p. 33.
5. Alan Jamieson, *Lords of the Sea: A History of the Barbary Corsairs*, Reaktion Books, 2012, p. 34.
6. *Ibid.*, p. 36.
7. *Ibid.*, p. 37.
8. *Ibid.*, p. 38.
9. Gökçen Kalkan, 'Destruction of Penon Fortress and Stabilization of Ottoman Algeria', *Akademik Tarih ve Düşünce Dergisi*, Vol. 10, No. 5, 2019, p. 20.
10. Adrian Tinniswood, *Pirates of Barbary*, Vintage Books, 2011, p. 8.
11. Bernard Capp, *British Slaves and Barbary Corsairs, 1580–1750*, Oxford University Press, 2022, p. 10.
12. *Ibid.*, p. 10.
13. Gillian Weiss, *Captives and Corsairs: France and Slavery in the Early Modern Mediterranean*, Stanford University Press, 2011, p. 9.
14. Christine Isom-Verhaaren, *Allies with the Infidel: The Ottoman and French Alliance in the Sixteenth Century*, I. B. Tauris, 2011, pp. 116–119.
15. *Ibid.*, p. 3.
16. Weiss, *Captives and Corsairs, op. cit.*, p. 9.
17. *Ibid.*, p. 9.
18. *Ibid.*, p. 13.

19. Eloy Martín-Corrales, *Muslims in Spain, 1492–1814: Living and Negotiating in the Land of the Infidel*, Brill, 2021, p. 47.

20. Franca Pirolo, 'Social, Economic and Cultural Relations between the Ottoman Empire and the Barbary States in the Kingdom of Naples under the Hapsburgs and the Bourbons, 1707–1815', in Erminio Fonzo and Hilary A. Haakenson (eds), *Mediterranean Mosaic: History and Art*, ICSR Mediterranean Knowledge, 2019, p. 178.

21. *Ibid.*, p. 179.

22. Weiss, *Captives and Corsairs*, *op. cit.*, p. 16.

23. *Ibid.*, p. 17.

24. *Ibid.*, p. 7.

25. *Ibid.*, footnotes, pp. 226–227.

26. Kate Lowe, 'Introduction: The Black African Presence in Renaissance Europe', in T. F. Earle and K. J. P. Lowe (eds), *Black Africans in Renaissance Europe*, Cambridge University Press, 2005, p. 3.

27. 'Their number declined significantly in the second half of the seventeenth century, leaving only about one hundred and twenty-five thousand; it increased slightly in the eighteenth, however, to about one hundred fifty thousand.' Martín-Corrales, *Muslims in Spain*, *op. cit.*, p. 33.

28. *Ibid.*, pp. 31–32.

29. Eric Martone (ed.), *Encyclopedia of Blacks in European History and Culture, Vol. 1 (A–J)*, Greenwood Press, 2009, p. 88.

30. Eric Martone (ed.), *Encyclopedia of Blacks in European History and Culture, Vol. 2 (K–Z)*, Greenwood Press, 2009, p. 164.

31. Martín-Corrales, *Muslims in Spain*, *op. cit.*, p. 35.

32. *Ibid.*, p. 35.

33. *Ibid.*, p. 36.

34. William Clarence-Smith and David Eltis, 'White Servitude', in David Eltis and Stanley Engerman (eds), *The Cambridge World History of Slavery, Vol. 3: AD 1420–AD 1804*, Cambridge University Press, 2011, p. 155.

19. SLAVES OF THE BARBARY STATES

1. Nabil Matar, 'Introduction: England and Mediterranean Captivity, 1577–1704', in Daniel Vitkus (ed.), *Piracy, Slavery, and Redemption: Barbary Captivity Narratives from Early Modern England*, Columbia University Press, 2001, p. 8.

2. *Ibid.*, p. 7.

3. William Clarence-Smith and David Eltis, 'White Servitude', in David Eltis and Stanley Engerman (eds), *The Cambridge World History of Slavery, Vol. 3: AD 1420–AD 1804*, Cambridge University Press, 2011, p. 154.

4. Bernard Capp, *British Slaves and Barbary Corsairs, 1580–1750*, Oxford University Press, 2022, p. 12.

5. Alan Jamieson, *Lords of the Sea: A History of the Barbary Corsairs*, Reaktion Books, 2012, pp. 75ff.

6. *Ibid.*, p. 77.

7. Catherine M. Styer, *Barbary Pirates, British Slaves, and the Early Modern Atlantic World, 1570–1800*, PhD thesis, University of Pennsylvania, 2011, p. 178.

8. Ben Johnson, 'Barbary Pirates and English Slaves', Historic UK, 2017, https://www.historic-uk.com/HistoryUK/HistoryofEngland/Barbary-Pirates-English-Slaves. Accessed 2 March 2025.

9. Jo Esra, '"[H]eer Will Be Noe Fishing": 17ᵗʰ Century Barbary Piracy and the West Country Fisheries', *Troze*, Vol. 7, No. 1, March 2016, pp. 6–7.

10. Patrick J. Boyle, *The Archaeology of Lundy Pirates: A Case Study of Material Culture*, MPhil thesis, University of Bristol, 2016, pp. 39–40.

11. *Ibid.*, p. 38.

12. *Ibid.*, p. 39.

13. Henry Barnby, 'The Algerian Attack on Baltimore 1631', *The Mariner's Mirror*, Vol. 56, No. 1, 1970, p. 27.

14. Jamieson, *Lords of the Sea*, op. cit., p. 78.

15. Des Ekin, *The Stolen Village: A Thrilling Account of the 17th-century Raid on Ireland by the Barbary Pirates*, Fall River Press, 2008, p. 283.

16. *Ibid.*, p. 290.

17. *Ibid.*, p. 292.

18. *Ibid.*, p. 278.

19. Paolo Calcagno and Luca Lo Basso, 'The Barbary Obsession: The Story of the "Turk" through the Reports of Incursions in Liguria in the Sixteenth and Seventeenth Centuries', in Borja Franco Llopis and Laura Stagno (eds), *A Mediterranean Other: Images of Turks in Southern Europe and Beyond (15ᵗʰ–18ᵗʰ Centuries)*, Genova University Press, 2021, pp. 66–67.

20. Franca Pirolo, 'Social, Economic and Cultural Relations between the Ottoman Empire and the Barbary States in the Kingdom of Naples under the Hapsburgs and the Bourbons, 1707–1815', in Erminio Fonzo and Hilary A. Haakenson (eds), *Mediterranean Mosaic: History and Art*, ICSR Mediterranean Knowledge, 2019, p. 175.

21. Matar, 'Introduction: England and Mediterranean Captivity', *op. cit.*, p. 17.

22. Khalid Bekkaoui, *White Women Captives in North Africa: Narratives of Enslavement, 1735–1830*, Palgrave MacMillan, 2011, pp. 13–16.

23. *Ibid.*, p. 13.

24. Gillian Weiss, *Captives and Corsairs: France and Slavery in the Early Modern Mediterranean*, Stanford University Press, 2011, p. 149.

25. Tal Shuval, 'Households in Ottoman Algeria', *Turkish Studies Association Bulletin*, Vol. 24, No. 1, Spring 2000, pp. 62–63.

26. Clarence-Smith and Eltis, 'White Servitude', *op. cit.*, p. 154.

27. *Ibid.*, p. 154.

28. Matar, 'Introduction: England and Mediterranean Captivity', *op. cit.*, p. 19.

29. Christine E. Sears, '"Tyran[n]ical Masters Are the Turks": The Comparative Context of Barbary Slavery', in Mary Ann Fay (ed.), *Slavery in the Islamic World: Its Characteristics and Commonality*, Palgrave MacMillan, 2019, p. 172.

30. Capp, *British Slaves and Barbary Corsairs*, *op. cit.*, p. 58.

31. *Ibid.*, p. 116.

32. *Ibid.*, pp. 118–119.

33. Matar, 'Introduction: England and Mediterranean Captivity', *op. cit.*, p. 24.

34. Adrian Tinniswood, *Pirates of Barbary*, Vintage Books, 2011, p. 191.

35. Capp, *British Slaves and Barbary Corsairs*, *op. cit.*, p. 17.

36. *Ibid.*, p. 46.

37. Weiss, *Captives and Corsairs*, *op. cit.*, p. 20.

38. *Ibid.*, p. 21.

39. Capp, *British Slaves and Barbary Corsairs*, *op. cit.*, p. 46.

40. Matar, 'Introduction: England and Mediterranean Captivity', *op. cit.*, p. 37.

20. FIGHTING AND DOING DEALS WITH THE BARBARY STATES

1. Bernard Capp, *British Slaves and Barbary Corsairs, 1580–1750*, Oxford University Press, 2022, p. 183.

2. Caitlin M. Gale, *Beyond Corsairs: The British–Barbary Relationship During the French Revolutionary and Napoleonic Wars*, PhD thesis, Trinity College, 2016, Appendix 3, p. 265.

3. *Ibid.*, p. 254.

4. Erik Göbel, 'The Danish Algerian Sea Passes, 1747–1838: An Example of Extraterritorial Production of Human Security', *Historical Social Research*, Vol. 35, No. 4, 2010, p. 166.

5. *Ibid.*, p. 180.

6. Hans Christian Bjerg, 'Denmark and the Barbary States, 1745–1845', in Kjeld von Folsach, Torben Lundbæk and Peder Mortensen (eds), *The Arabian Journey: Danish Connections with the Islamic World Over a Thousand Years*, Prehistoric Museum Moesgård, 1996, p. 82.

7. National Museum of Denmark, 'Krigen mod Algier' [The war against Algiers], https://natmus.dk/historisk-viden/temaer/

militaerhistorie/danmarks-krige/krigen-mod-algier. Accessed 2 March 2025.

8. Paul Baepler, 'Introduction', in Paul Baepler (ed.), *White Slaves, African Masters: An Anthology of American Barbary Captivity Narratives*, University of Chicago Press, 1999, p. 6.

9. *Ibid.*, p. 8.

10. John C. Fredriksen, *The United States Navy: A Chronology, 1775 to the Present*, Bloomsbury Publishing, 2010, p. 21.

11. Frederick C. Leiner, *The End of Barbary Terror: America's 1815 War Against the Pirates of North Africa*, Oxford University Press, 2006, p. 20.

12. Baepler (ed.), 'Introduction', *op. cit.*, p. 20.

13. Adrian Tinniswood, *Pirates of Barbary*, Vintage Books, 2011, p. 284.

14. Alan Jamieson, *Lords of the Sea: A History of the Barbary Corsairs*, Reaktion Books, 2012, p. 201.

15. *Ibid.*, p. 201.

16. Naval History and Heritage Command, 'Barbary Wars: 1801–1805 and 1815', 22 February 2024, https://www.history.navy.mil/browse-by-topic/wars-conflicts-and-operations/barbary-wars.html. Accessed 2 March 2025.

17. William Clarence-Smith and David Eltis, 'White Servitude', in David Eltis and Stanley Engerman (eds), *The Cambridge World History of Slavery, Vol. 3: AD 1420–AD 1804*, Cambridge University Press, 2011, p. 153.

18. John Wright, *The Trans-Saharan Slave Trade*, Routledge, 2007, p. 59.

19. Clarence-Smith and Eltis, 'White Servitude', *op. cit.*, p. 153.

20. Thomas Willing Balch, 'French Colonization in North Africa', *The American Political Science Review*, Vol. 3, No. 4, November 1909.

21. Jacques Heers, *The Barbary Corsairs: Warfare in the Mediterranean, 1480–1580*, translated by Jonathan North, Frontline Books, 2017, p. 197.

22. Lotfi Ben Rejeb, 'Barbary's "Character" in European Letters, 1514–1830: An Ideological Prelude to Colonization', *Dialectical Anthropology*, Vol. 6, No. 4, June 1982, p. 346.

PART 6: SLAVERY TODAY

1. Richard Lobban, 'Slavery in the Sudan since 1989', *Arab Studies Quarterly*, Vol. 23, No. 2, 2001, p. 31.

2. Paul E. Lovejoy, *Transformations in Slavery: A History of Slavery in Africa*, Cambridge University Press, 2012, p. 283.

3. Kwesi Kwaa Prah, 'Introduction: Confronting Arab-Led Slavery of Africans', in Kwesi Kwaa Prah (ed.), *Reflections on Arab-Led Slavery of Africans*, Centre for Advanced Studies of African Society, 2005, p. 2.

21. CONTEMPORARY AFRICAN SLAVERY

1. Stephen J. King, 'Ending Hereditary Slavery in Mauritania: Bidan (Whites) and Black "Slaves" in 2021', Arab Reform Initiative, 26 August 2021, https://www.arab-reform.net/publication/ending-hereditary-slavery-in-mauritania-bidan-whites-and-black-slaves-in-2021/. Accessed 2 March 2025.

2. CIA World Factbook, 'Mauritania', https://www.cia.gov/the-world-factbook/countries/mauritania/#people-and-society. Accessed 2 March 2025. The government of Mauritania does not allow the collection of such data.

3. United Nations Human Rights Council, 'Visit to Mauritania: Report of the Special Rapporteur on contemporary forms of slavery, including its causes and consequences, Tomoya Obokata', 54th Session, A/HRC/54/30/Add.2, 21 July 2023, https://docs.un.org/en/A/HRC/54/30/ADD.2. Accessed 2 March 2025.

4. *Ibid.*, p. 7 (para. 29). Obokata's findings were echoed by a human rights report from the U.S. State Department, which explained how the 'black Moor' and 'white Moor' division operates: 'Racial and cultural tension and discrimination also arose from the geographic, linguistic, and cultural divides between Moors (Beydane and Haratine)—who, while historically representing a mix of Berber, Arab, and sub-Saharan descent, largely identified culturally and linguistically as Arab—and the sub-Saharan non-Arab minorities. Historically, the Beydane enslaved the Haratine population; Haratines continued to suffer from the legacy of centuries of slavery and present-day slavery practices. Beydane tribes and clans dominated positions in government and business far beyond their proportion of the population. As a group, the Haratines remained politically and economically weaker than the Beydane, although they represented the largest ethnocultural group in the country. The various sub-Saharan ethnic groups, along with the Haratines, remained underrepresented in leadership positions in government, industry, and the military.' United States Department of State, 'Mauritania 2023 Human Rights Report', 22 April 2024, pp. 27–28, https://mr.usembassy.gov/wp-content/uploads/sites/204/Mauritania-2023-Human-Rights-Report.pdf. Accessed 2 March 2025.

5. UNHRC, 'Visit to Mauritania', *op. cit.*, p. 11 (para. 54).

6. Amnesty International, 'Mauritania: A Future Free from Slavery', 7 November 2002, pp. 1–2, https://www.amnesty.org/en/wp-content/uploads/2021/06/afr380032002en.pdf. Accessed 3 March 2025.

7. United States Department of State, 'Country Report on Human Rights Practices 1993—Mauritania', 30 January 1994, https://

www.refworld.org/reference/annualreport/usdos/1994/en/25234. Accessed 2 March 2025.

8. UNHRC, 'Visit to Mauritania', *op. cit.*, pp. 3–4 (paras 6–9).

9. *Ibid.*, pp. 6–7 (para. 28).

10. Seif Kousmate, 'The unspeakable truth about slavery in Mauritania', *The Guardian*, 8 June 2018, https://www.theguardian.com/global-development/2018/jun/08/the-unspeakable-truth-about-slavery-in-mauritania. Accessed 3 March 2025.

11. *Ibid.*

12. Zekeria Ould Ahmed Salem, 'Bare-foot Activists: Transformation in the Haratine Movement in Mauritania', in Stephen Ellis and Ineke van Kessel (eds), *Movers and Shakers: Social Movements in Africa*, Brill, 2009, pp. 160–161.

13. *Ibid.*, p. 167.

14. David Malluche, 'Haratin Activism in Post-Slavery Mauritania: Abolition, Emancipation and the Politics of Identity', in Francisco Freire (ed.), *State, Society and Islam in the Western Regions of the Sahara: Regional Interactions and Social Change*, I. B. Tauris, 2022, p. 205.

15. *Ibid.*, p. 206.

16. Anti-Slavery International, 'Mauritania: Descent-Based Slavery', https://www.antislavery.org/what-we-do/mauritania. Accessed 3 March 2025.

17. Marie-France Cros, 'A Freed Slave's Son Fights Against Slavery; Biram Abeid: "The UN's Conventions Protect Slavery"', *La Libre Belgique*, translated by Unrepresented Nations and Peoples Organization, 10 June 2013, https://unpo.org/haratin-belgian-newspaper-slavery-still-exists. Accessed 3 March 2025.

18. U.S. Department of State, 'Mauritania 2023 Human Rights Report', *op. cit.*, pp. 2ff.

19. UNHRC, 'Visit to Mauritania', *op. cit.*, p. 17 (para. 91).

20. *Ibid.*, p. 18 (para. 93).

21. United Nations, 'Mali: Ban slavery by law, say top rights experts', UN News, 8 May 2023, https://news.un.org/en/story/2023/05/1136437. Accessed 27 February 2025.

22. *Ibid.*

23. Leslie Gross-Wyrtzen, '"There is No Race Here": Blackness, Slavery, and Disavowal in North Africa and North African Studies', *The Journal of North African Studies*, Vol. 28. No. 3, 2023, p. 646.

24. Bruce S. Hall, 'Bellah Histories of Decolonization, Iklan Paths to Freedom: The Meanings of Race and Slavery in the Late-Colonial Niger Bend (Mali), 1944–1960', *The International Journal of African Historical Studies*, Vol. 44, No. 1, 2011.

25. *Ibid.*, p. 62.

26. Baz Lecocq, 'The Bellah Question: Slave Emancipation, Race, and Social Categories in Late Twentieth-Century Northern Mali', *Canadian Journal of African Studies*, Vol. 39, No. 1, 2005, p. 45.

27. Baz Lecocq, *Disputed Desert: Decolonization, Competing Nationalisms and Tuareg Rebellions in Northern Mali*, Brill, 2010, pp. 181–226.

28. Hall, 'Bellah Histories of Decolonization', *op. cit.*, p. 85.

29. Bruce S. Hall, *A History of Race in Muslim West Africa, 1600–1960*, Cambridge University Press, 2011 p. 320.

30. Jean Sebastian Lecocq, *'That Desert Is Our Country': Tuareg Rebellions and Competing Nationalisms in Contemporary Mali (1946–1996)*, PhD thesis, University of Amsterdam, 2002, p. 301.

31. Tor A. Benjaminsen and Boubacar Ba, 'Fulani-Dogon Killings in Mali: Farmer-Herder Conflicts as Insurgency and Counterinsurgency', *African Security*, Vol. 14, No. 1, 2021, p. 8.

32. *Ibid.*, p. 9.

33. *Ibid.*, p. 12.

34. *Ibid.*, p. 19.

35. Galy Kadir Abdelkader (ed.), *Slavery in Niger: Historical, Legal and Contemporary Perspectives*, Anti-Slavery International and Association Timidira, 2004, p. 88, https://www.antislavery.org/wp-content/uploads/2017/01/full_english_slavery_in_niger.pdf. Accessed 3 March 2025.

36. Benedetta Rossi, 'African Post-Slavery: A History of the Future', *The International Journal of African Historical Studies*, Vol. 48, No. 2, 2015, pp. 322–323. 'Sources on Africa quote a variety of figures: the website Hadijatoumani.org states that 43,000 people are enslaved in Niger today. Without dismissing the gravity of present-day forms of slavery and human trafficking, headcounts in African contexts cannot be accepted uncritically. It is often unclear how the information provided in activist reports was obtained, from which sources, and whether those asking questions and those giving answers understood particular phenomena, and the terms used to describe them, in the same way.'

37. Abdelkader (ed.), *Slavery in Niger*, *op. cit.*, pp. 16–17.

38. Thomas A. Kelley, 'Unintended Consequences of Legal Westernization in Niger: Harming Contemporary Slaves by Reconceptualizing Property', *The American Journal of Comparative Law*, Vol. 56, No. 4, 2008, p. 1012.

39. Abdelkader (ed.), *Slavery in Niger*, *op. cit.*, p. 9.

40. *Ibid.*, p. 9.

41. Fred Harter, '"He bought me like a chicken": the struggle to end slavery in Niger', *The Guardian*, 28 June 2022, https://www.theguardian.

com/global-development/2022/jun/28/child-sex-trafficking-wahaya-girls-slavery-niger. Accessed 3 March 2025.

42. Rossi, 'African Post-Slavery', *op. cit.*, pp. 307–309.

43. Agence France Presse, 'Niger says it will adhere to slavery verdict', 28 October 2008.

44. Anti-Slavery International, 'Niger Condemned for Slavery', 27 October 2008, https://www.antislavery.org/latest/niger-condemned-slavery. Accessed 3 March 2025.

45. United States Department of State, 'Niger 2021 Human Rights Report', 12 April 2022, p. 30, https://www.state.gov/wp-content/uploads/2022/02/313615_NIGER-2021-HUMAN-RIGHTS-REPORT.pdf. Accessed 3 March 2025.

46. Kelley, 'Unintended Consequences of Legal Westernization in Niger', *op. cit.*, p. 1009.

47. Jennifer Lofkrantz, 'Slavery in Islamic West Africa', in Damian A. Pargas and Juliane Schiel (eds), *The Palgrave Handbook of Global Slavery throughout History*, Palgrave Macmillan, 2023, p. 479.

48. Kelley, 'Unintended Consequences of Legal Westernization in Niger', *op. cit.*, pp. 1014–1015.

49. Reda Mowafi, *Slavery, Slave Trade, and Abolition Attempts in Egypt and the Sudan, 1820–1882*, Esselte Studium, 1981, p. 11.

50. *Ibid.*, p. 34.

51. Zeinab Mohammed Salih, 'Viewpoint from Sudan—where black people are called slaves', BBC News, 26 July 2020, https://www.bbc.co.uk/news/world-africa-53147864. Accessed 3 March 2025.

52. Jok Madut Jok, *War and Slavery in Sudan*, University of Pennsylvania Press, 2001, p. 1. The book explores the subject extensively.

53. United Nations Security Council, 'Final report of the Panel of Experts on the Sudan', S/2024/65, 15 January 2024, p. 24 (para. 86).

54. Katharine Houreld and Hafiz Haroun, 'Sudanese militiamen carry out wave of abductions, seeking slaves and ransom', *Washington Post*, 23 February 2024, https://www.washingtonpost.com/world/2024/02/23/sudan-rsf-kidnapping-ransom-slaves. Accessed 3 March 2025.

55. Nima Elbagir *et al.*, '"They called me a slave": Witness testimony exposes alleged RSF-led campaign to enslave men and women in Sudan', CNN, 20 November 2023, https://edition.cnn.com/2023/11/16/africa/sudan-investigation-rsf-enslavement-intl-cmd/index.html. Accessed 3 March 2025. Salih, 'Viewpoint from Sudan', *op. cit.*

56. Fred Harter, '"They told us—you are slaves": survivors give harrowing testimony of Darfur's year of hell', *The Guardian*, 30 December 2023, https://www.theguardian.com/global-development/2023/dec/30/

survivors-give-harrowing-testimony-of-darfur-sudan-year-of-hell. Accessed 27 February 2025.

57. Nicholas Kristof, 'I Just Went to Darfur. Here Is What Shattered Me', *The New York Times*, 18 September 2024, https://www.nytimes. com/2024/09/18/opinion/darfur-sudan-famine.html. Accessed 26 February 2025.

58. Frontex, 'Monitoring and risk analysis', https://www.frontex.europa. eu/what-we-do/monitoring-and-risk-analysis/migratory-map. Accessed 3 March 2025.

59. United Nations Human Rights Council, 'Report of the Independent Fact-Finding Mission on Libya', 52nd Session, A/HRC/52/83, 3 March 2023, p. 9 (para. 52), https://reliefweb.int/report/libya/report-independent-fact-finding-mission-libya-ahrc5283-advance-edited-version-enar. Accessed 3 March 2025.

60. Nadia Al-Dayel, Aaron Anfinson and Graeme Anfinson, 'Captivity, Migration, and Power in Libya', *Journal of Human Trafficking*, Vol. 9, No. 3, 2023, pp. 280–281.

61. *Ibid.*

62. Nima Elbagir *et al.*, 'People for sale: Where lives are auctioned for $400', CNN, 15 November 2017, https://edition.cnn.com/2017/11/14/africa/libya-migrant-auctions/index.html. Accessed 3 March 2025.

63. *Ibid.*

64. Henry Kam Kah, '"Blood Money", Migrants' Enslavement and Insecurity in Africa's Sahel and Libya', *Africa Development*, Vol. 44, No. 1, 2019, pp. 33–34.

65. Interview by Klara Smits and Morgane Wirtz, face to face, June 2021, in Klara Smits and Mirjam Van Reisen, 'Deceived and Exploited: Classifying the Practice as Human Trafficking', in Mirjam Van Reisen *et al.* (eds), *Enslaved: Trapped and Trafficked in Digital Black Holes: Human Trafficking Trajectories to Libya*, Langaa, 2023, pp. 343–344.

66. Van Reisen *et al.* (eds), *Enslaved*, *op. cit.*, p. 332.

67. *Ibid.*, p. 644.

68. Al-Dayel *et al.*, 'Captivity, Migration, and Power in Libya', *op. cit.*, p. 292.

69. *Ibid.*, p. 292.

22. CAN AFRICAN SLAVERY BE FINALLY ENDED?

1. See Benedetta Rossi, 'African Post-Slavery: A History of the Future', *The International Journal of African Historical Studies*, 2015, Vol. 48, No. 2, pp. 303–324, for a detailed discussion of this question.

2. The International Scientific Committee of the Slave Route Project was established in September 1994 by UNESCO (27 C/Resolution 3.13 of

the General Conference). This is now described as the UNESCO 'Routes of Enslaved Peoples: Resistance, Liberty and Heritage', https://www.unesco.org/en/routes-enslaved-peoples. Accessed 3 March 2025.

3. UNESCO, 'The deep legacy of slavery, July–September 2024', *UNESCO Courier*, https://courier.unesco.org/en/articles/deep-legacy-slavery. Accessed 3 March 2025.

4. *Ibid.* Myriam Cottias is chair of the International Scientific Committee of the UNESCO programme 'Routes of Enslaved Peoples: Resistance, Liberty and Heritage'. Recognition of the memory of slavery began to emerge in the aftermath of the Second World War.

5. United Nations High Commissioner for Refugees, 'Third group of refugees evacuated to Rwanda from Libya with UNHCR support', Press Release, 25 November 2019, https://www.unhcr.org/news/news-releases/third-group-refugees-evacuated-rwanda-libya-unhcr-support. Accessed 3 March 2025.

6. African Union, 'African Union Action Plan towards Eradication of Child Labour and Modern Slavery on the Continent', Press Release, 14 February 2019, https://au.int/en/pressreleases/20190214/african-union-action-plan-towards-eradication-child-labour-and-modern-slavery. Accessed 3 March 2025.

7. African Committee of Experts on the Rights and Welfare of the Child, 'Concluding Observations and Recommendations by the African Committee of Experts on the Rights and Welfare of The Child (ACERWC) on the Initial Report of the Islamic Republic of Mauritania, on the Status of the Implementation of the African Charter on the Rights and Welfare of the Child', 2022, https://www.acerwc.africa/sites/default/files/2022-09/CO%20Mauritania%20ENG-1.pdf. Accessed 3 March 2025.

8. *Ibid.*, p. 4 (para. 17).

9. United Nations, 'World Conference Against Racism, Racial Discrimination, Xenophobia and Related Intolerance: Durban Declaration and Programme of Action', 1 January 2010, p. 1, https://www.ohchr.org/sites/default/files/Documents/Publications/Durban_text_en.pdf. Accessed 3 March 2025.

10. African Commission on Human and Peoples' Rights, 'Resolution on Africa's Reparations Agenda and The Human Rights of Africans in the Diaspora and People of African Descent Worldwide—ACHPR/Res.543 (LXXIII) 2022', 12 December 2022, https://achpr.au.int/index.php/en/adopted-resolutions/543-resolution-africas-reparations-agenda-and-human-rights-africans. Accessed 3 March 2025.

11. Rosie Bsheer, *Archive Wars: The Politics of History in Saudi Arabia*, Stanford University Press, 2020, pp. 20–22.

12. Shaun Flores, 'The Arab World Owes Reparations Alongside the Western World', *Common Sense*, 20 July 2021, https://www.tcsnetwork.co.uk/ the-veiled-genocide-the-arab-world-owes-reparations-alongside-the-western-world. Accessed 3 March 2025.

13. Declaration of the Conference on Arab-Led Slavery of Africans, quoted in Kwesi Kwaa Prah (ed.), *Reflections on Arab-Led Slavery of Africans*, Centre for Advanced Studies of African Society, 2005, pp. ix–xi.

14. Kwesi Kwaa Prah, 'Introduction: Confronting Arab-Led Slavery of Africans', in Prah (ed.), *Reflections on Arab-Led Slavery of Africans*, *op. cit.*, p. 4.

15. Anthony Sullivan, *Britain's War Against the Slave Trade: The Operations of the Royal Navy's West Africa Squadron, 1807–1867*, Frontline Books, 2020, p. 346.

SELECT BIBLIOGRAPHY

Books and Edited Volumes

Ali, Omar H., *Malik Ambar: Power and Slavery Across the Indian Ocean*, Oxford University Press, 2016.

Allen, Richard B., *European Slave Trading in the Indian Ocean: 1500–1850*, Ohio University Press, 2014.

Anderson, Richard, and Henry B. Lovejoy (eds), *Liberated Africans and the Abolition of the Slave Trade, 1807–1896*, University of Rochester Press, 2020.

Austen, Ralph A., *Trans-Saharan Africa in World History*, Oxford University Press, 2010.

Beachey, R. W., *The Slave Trade of Eastern Africa*, Rex Collings, 1976.

Beaujard, Philippe, *The Worlds of the Indian Ocean: A Global History, Vol. II: From the Seventh Century to the Fifteenth Century CE*, Cambridge University Press, 2019.

Bekkaoui, Khalid, *White Women Captives in North Africa: Narratives of Enslavement, 1735–1830*, Palgrave MacMillan, 2011.

Black, Jeremy, *A Brief History of Slavery: A New Global History*, Robinson, 2011.

Bsheer, Rosie, *Archive Wars: The Politics of History in Saudi Arabia*, Stanford University Press, 2020.

Capp, Bernard, *British Slaves and Barbary Corsairs, 1580–1750*, Oxford University Press, 2022.

Chauhan, R. R., *Africans in India: From Slavery to Royalty*, Asian Publication Services, 1995.

Clarence-Smith, William (ed.), *The Economies of the Indian Ocean Slave Trade in the Nineteenth Century*, Frank Cass, 1989.

Cooper, Frederick, *Plantation Slavery on the East Coast of Africa*, Yale University Press, 1977.

Davidson, Basil, *The African Slave Trade: Precolonial History, 1450–1850*, Little, Brown and Co., 1961.

———— *Africa in History: Themes and Outlines*, Paladin Books, 1984.

Davis, Robert, *Christian Slaves, Muslim Masters: White Slavery in the Mediterranean, the Barbary Coast, and Italy, 1500–1800*, Palgrave Macmillan, 2003.

Drescher, Seymour, and Stanley Engerman (eds), *A Historical Guide to World Slavery*, Oxford University Press, 1998.

Durkin, Hannah, *Survivors: The Lost Stories of the Last Captives of the Atlantic Slave Trade*, William Collins, 2024.

Edgerton, Robert B., *The Troubled Heart of Africa: A History of the Congo*, St Martin's Press, 2002.

Eldredge, Elizabeth A. and Fred Morton (eds), *Slavery in South Africa: Captive Labour on the Dutch Frontier*, Westview Press, 1994.

Eltis, David, and David Richardson, *Atlas of the Transatlantic Slave Trade*, Yale University Press, 2010.

Eltis, David, and Stanley Engerman (eds), *The Cambridge World History of Slavery, Vol. 3: AD 1420–AD 1804*, Cambridge University Press, 2011.

Fage, J. D. (ed.), *The Cambridge History of Africa, Vol. 2: From c. 500 BC to AD 1050*, Cambridge University Press, 1978.

Flint, John (ed.), *The Cambridge History of Africa, Vol. 5: From c. 1790 to c. 1870*, Cambridge University Press, 1976.

Fuglestad, Finn, *Slave Traders by Invitation: West Africa's Slave Coast in the Precolonial Period*, Hurst & Co., 2018.

Gibb, H. A. R., *Ibn Battuta: Travels in Asia and Africa, 1325–1354*, George Routledge & Sons, 1929.

Hall, Bruce S., *A History of Race in Muslim West Africa, 1600–1960*, Cambridge University Press, 2011.

Harms, Robert, *Land of Tears: The Exploration and Exploitation of Equatorial Africa*, Basic Books, 2019.

Harms, Robert, Bernard K. Freamon, and David W. Blight (eds), *Indian Ocean Slavery in the Age of Abolition*, Yale University Press, 2013.

Heuman, Gad, and Trevor Burnard (eds), *The Routledge History of Slavery*, Routledge, 2011.

———— *Slavery (Critical Concepts in Historical Studies), Vol. 1*, Routledge, 2014.

Hine, Darlene Clark, William C. Hine, and Stanley Harrold, *The African-American Odyssey*, Pearson Education, 5th edition, 2011.

Holt, P. M., and M. W. Daly, *A History of the Sudan: From the Coming of Islam to the Present Day*, 5th edition, Longman, 2000.

Hopper, Matthew S., *Slaves of One Master: Globalization and Slavery in Arabia in the Age of Empire*, Yale University Press, 2015.

Howell, Raymond, *The Royal Navy and the Slave Trade*, Croom Helm, 1987.

Inikori, J. E. (ed.), *Forced Migration: The Impact of the Export Slave Trade on African Societies*, Hutchinson University Library for Africa, 1982.

Isaacman, Allen F., *Mozambique: The Africanization of a European Institution, The Zambesi Prazos, 1750–1902*, University of Wisconsin Press, 1972.

Johnston, H. A. S., *The Fulani Empire of Sokoto*, Oxford University Press, 1967.

Jok, Jok Madut, *War and Slavery in Sudan*, University of Pennsylvania Press, 2001.

Laing, Stuart, *Tippu Tip: Ivory, Slavery and Discovery in the Scramble for Africa*, Medina Publishing, 2017.

Lane, Paul, and Kevin MacDonald (eds), *Slavery in Africa: Archaeology and Memory*, Oxford University Press, 2011.

Levtzion, Nehemia, *Ancient Ghana and Mali*, Methuen & Co., 1973.

Lewis, Bernard, *Race and Slavery in the Middle East: An Historical Enquiry*, Oxford University Press, 1990.

Lovejoy, Paul E., *Slavery, Commerce and Production in the Sokoto Caliphate of West Africa*, Red Sea Press, 2005.

——— *Transformations in Slavery: A History of Slavery in Africa*, Cambridge University Press, 2012.

Lovejoy, Paul E. and Jan S. Hogendorn, *Slow Death for Slavery: The Course of Abolition in Northern Nigeria, 1897–1936*, Cambridge University Press, 1993.

Manning, Patrick, *Slavery and African Life: Occidental, Oriental, and African Slave Trades*, Cambridge University Press, 1990.

Marcus, Harold G., *A History of Ethiopia*, University of California Press, 1994.

Miller, Joseph, *Way of Death: Merchant Capitalism and the Angolan Slave Trade, 1730–1830*, James Currey, 1988.

Mirzai, Behnaz A., *A History of Slavery and Emancipation in Iran: 1800–1929*, University of Texas Press, 2017.

Mirzai, Behnaz A., Ismael Musah Montana, and Paul E. Lovejoy (eds), *Slavery, Islam and Diaspora*, Africa World Press, 2009.

Mowafi, Reda, *Slavery, Slave Trade, and Abolition Attempts in Egypt and the Sudan, 1820–1882*, Esselte Studium, 1981.

Pakenham, Thomas, *The Scramble for Africa: 1876–1912*, Weidenfeld and Nicholson, 1991.

Pargas, Damian A., and Juliane Schiel (eds), *The Palgrave Handbook of Global Slavery throughout History*, Palgrave Macmillan, 2023.

Pearson, Michael N., *The Indian Ocean*, Routledge, 2003.

Perbi, Akosua Adoma, *A History of Indigenous Slavery in Ghana: From the 15th to the 19th Century*, Sub-Saharan Publishers, Accra, 2004.

Perry, Craig, *et al.* (eds), *The Cambridge World History of Slavery, Vol. 2: AD 500–AD 1420*, Cambridge University Press, 2021.

Phillips, William D., *Slavery in Medieval and Modern Iberia*, University of Pennsylvania Press, 2014.

Plaut, Martin, *Dr Abdullah Abdurahman: South Africa's First Elected Black Politician*, Jacana Media, 2020.

Porter, Andrew (ed.), *The Oxford History of the British Empire, Vol. III: The Nineteenth Century*, Oxford University Press, 1999.

Prah, Kwesi Kwaa (ed.), *Reflections on Arab-Led Slavery of Africans*, Centre for Advanced Studies of African Society, 2005.

Reese, Scott S., *Imperial Muslims: Islam, Community and Authority in the Indian Ocean, 1839–1937*, Edinburgh University Press, 2018.

Rossi, Benedetta, *From Slavery to Aid: Politics, Labour, and Ecology in the Nigerien Sahel, 1800–2000*, Cambridge University Press, 2015.

Salau, Mohammed Bashir, *Plantation Slavery in the Sokoto Caliphate: A Historical and Comparative Study*, University of Rochester Press, 2018.

Sanderson, G. N. (ed.), *The Cambridge History of Africa, Vol. 6: From 1870 to 1905*, Cambridge University Press, 1985.

Savage, Elizabeth (ed.), *The Human Commodity: Perspectives on the Trans-Saharan Slave Trade*, Frank Cass, 1992.

Segal, Ronald, *Islam's Black Slaves: A History of Africa's Other Black Diaspora*, Atlantic Books, 2001.

Shell, Sandra, *Children of Hope: The Odyssey of the Oromo Slaves from Ethiopia to South Africa*, Ohio University Press, 2018.

Sheriff, Abdul, *Slaves, Spices and Ivory in Zanzibar: Integration of an East African Commercial Empire into the World Economy, 1770–1873*, James Currey, 1987.

Smaldone, Joseph P., *Warfare in the Sokoto Caliphate: Historical and Sociological Perspectives*, Cambridge University Press, 1977.

Stilwell, Sean, *Slavery and Slaving in African History*, Cambridge University Press, 2014.

Sullivan, Anthony, *Britain's War Against the Slave Trade: The Operations of the Royal Navy's West Africa Squadron, 1807–1867*, Frontline Books, 2020.

Toledano, Ehud R., *The Ottoman Slave Trade and Its Suppression*, Princeton University Press, 1982.

Walvin, James, *A Short History of Slavery*, Penguin Books, 2007.

Watson, James L. (ed.), *Asian and African Systems of Slavery*, Basil Blackwell, 1980.

Weiss, Gillian, *Captives and Corsairs: France and Slavery in the Early Modern Mediterranean*, Stanford University Press, 2011.

Whitfield, Susan, *Silk, Slaves, and Stupas: Material Culture of the Silk Road*, University of California Press, 2018.

Wickins, P. L., *An Economic History of Africa from the Earliest Times to Partition*, Oxford University Press, 1981.

Willis, John Ralph (ed.), *Slaves and Slavery in Muslim Africa, Vol. 2: The Servile Estate*, Frank Cass, 1985.

Wise, Christopher (ed.), *The Desert Shore: Literatures of the Sahel*, Lynne Rienner Publishers, 2001.

Wright, John, *The Trans-Saharan Slave Trade*, Routledge, 2007.

Wyatt, Don J., *The Blacks of Premodern China*, University of Pennsylvania Press, 2010.

Articles, Book Chapters and Unpublished Theses

Addoun, Yacine Daddi, '"So That God Frees the Former Masters from Hell Fire:" Salvation Through Manumission in Nineteenth Century Ottoman Algeria', in Ana Lucia Araujo, Mariana P. Candido and Paul E. Lovejoy (eds), *Crossing Memories: Slavery and African Diaspora*, Africa World Press, 2011.

Ahmad, Abdussamad H., 'Trading in Slaves in Bela-Shangul and Gumuz, Ethiopia: Border Enclaves in History, 1897–1938', *The Journal of African History*, Vol. 40, No. 3, 1999.

Al-Dayel, Nadia, Aaron Anfinson, and Graeme Anfinson, 'Captivity, Migration, and Power in Libya', *Journal of Human Trafficking*, Vol. 9, No. 3, 2023.

Alexander, J., 'Islam, Archaeology and Slavery in Africa', *World Archaeology*, Vol. 33, No. 1, 2001.

Allen, Richard B., 'Suppressing a Nefarious Traffic: Britain and the Abolition of Slave Trading in India and the Western Indian Ocean', *The William and Mary Quarterly*, Vol. 66, No. 4, 2009.

Bacharach, Jere L., 'African Military Slaves in the Medieval Middle East: The Cases of Iraq (869–955) and Egypt (868–1171)', *International Journal of Middle East Studies*, Vol. 13. No. 4, November 1981.

Bulcha, Mekuria, 'The Red Sea Slave Trade: Captives' Treatment in the Slave Markets of North-East Africa and the Islamic Societies of the Middle East', in Kwesi Kwaa Prah (ed.), *Reflections on Arab-Led Slavery of Africans*, Centre for Advanced Studies of African Society, 2005.

Campbell, Gwyn and Edward A. Alpers, 'Introduction: Slavery, Forced Labour and Resistance in Indian Ocean Africa and Asia', *Slavery & Abolition: A Journal of Slave and Post-Slave Studies*, Vol. 25, No. 2, August 2004.

Chewins, Linell and Peter Delius, 'The Northeastern Factor in South African History: Reevaluating the Volume of the Slave Trade out of Delagoa Bay and Its Impact on Its Hinterland in the Early Nineteenth Century', *The Journal of African History*, Vol. 61, No. 1, 2020.

Coleman, Sterling, 'Gradual Abolition or Immediate Abolition of Slavery?: The Political, Social and Economic Quandary of Emperor Haile Selassie', *Slavery & Abolition: A Journal of Slave and Post-Slave Studies*, Vol. 29, No. 1, March 2008.

Collins, Robert O., 'The Nilotic Slave Trade: Past and Present', *Slavery & Abolition: A Journal of Slave and Post-Slave Studies*, Vol. 13, No. 1, 1992.

———— 'Slavery in the Sudan in History', *Slavery & Abolition: A Journal of Slave and Post-Slave Studies*, Vol. 20, No. 3, 1999.

———— 'The African Slave Trade to Asia and the Indian Ocean Islands', *African and Asian Studies*, Vol. 5, Nos 3–4, 2006.

Doulton, Lindsay, *The Royal Navy's Anti-Slavery Campaign in the Western Indian Ocean, c. 1860–1890: Race, Empire and Identity*, PhD thesis, University of Hull, 2010.

Eaton, Richard M., 'The Rise and Fall of Military Slavery in the Deccan, 1450–1650', in Indrani Chatterjee and Richard M. Eaton (eds), *Slavery and South Asian History*, Indiana University Press, 2006.

Gaiser, Adam, 'Slaves and Silver across the Strait of Gibraltar: Politics and Trade between Umayyad Iberia and Khārijite North Africa', *Medieval Encounters*, No. 19, 2013.

Jákl, Jiří, 'Black Africans on the Maritime Silk Route in Old Javanese Epigraphical and Literary Evidence', *Indonesia and the Malay World*, Vol. 45, No. 133, 2017.

Jayasuriya, Shihan de Silva, 'Indians of African Descent: Emerging Roles and New Identities', *Journal of African Diaspora Archaeology and Heritage*, Vol. 4, No. 1, March 2015.

Kea, Ray A., 'Expansions and Contractions: World-Historical Change and the Western Sudan World-System (1200/1000 B.C.–1200/1250 A.D.)', *Journal of World-Systems Research*, Vol. 10, No. 3, 2004.

Kelley, Thomas A., 'Unintended Consequences of Legal Westernization in Niger: Harming Contemporary Slaves by Reconceptualizing Property', *The American Journal of Comparative Law*, Vol. 56, No. 4, 2008.

Martín-Corrales, Eloy, *Muslims in Spain, 1492–1814: Living and Negotiating in the Land of the Infidel*, Brill, 2021.

Matar, Nabil, 'Introduction: England and Mediterranean Captivity, 1577–1704', in Daniel Vitkus (ed.), *Piracy, Slavery, and Redemption: Barbary Captivity Narratives from Early Modern England*, Columbia University Press, 2001.

McDougall, Ann, 'The View from Awdaghust: War, Trade and Social Change in Southwestern Sahara, from the Eighth to the Fifteenth Century', *The Journal of African History*, Vol. 26, No. 1, 1985.

Miers, Suzanne, 'Britain and the Suppression of Slavery in Ethiopia', *Slavery & Abolition: A Journal of Slave and Post-Slave Studies*, Vol. 18, No. 3.

Mulligan, William, 'British Anti-Slave Trade and Anti-Slavery Policy in East Africa, Arabia, and Turkey in the Late Nineteenth Century', in Brendan Simms and D. J. B. Trim (eds), *Humanitarian Intervention: A History*, Cambridge University Press, 2011.

Nicolini, Beatrice, 'The Western Indian Ocean as a Cultural Corridor: Makran, Oman and Zanzibar through Nineteenth Century European Accounts and Reports', *Middle East Studies Association Bulletin*, Vol. 37, No. 1, 2003.

Ochonu, Moses, 'Caliphate Expansion and Sociopolitical Change in Nineteenth-Century Lower Benue Hinterlands', *Journal of West African History*, Vol. 1, No. 1, 2015.

Pankhurst, Richard, 'The History of Bareya, Sanqella and Other Ethiopian Slaves from the Borderlands of the Sudan', *Sudan Notes and Records*, Vol. 58, 1977.

——— 'Ethiopian Slave Reminiscences of the Nineteenth Century', *Transafrican Journal of History*, Vol. 5, No. 1, 1976.

Pescatello, Ann M., 'The African Presence in Portuguese India', *Journal of Asian History*, Vol. 11, No. 1, 1977.

Reilly, Benjamin, 'Mutawalladeen and Malaria: African Slavery in Arabian Wadis', *Journal of Social History*, Vol. 47, No. 4, Summer 2004.

Renault, Francois, 'The Structures of the Slave Trade in Central Africa in the 19th Century', in William Gervase Clarence-Smith (ed.), *The Economics of the Indian Ocean Slave Trade in the Nineteenth Century*, Frank Cass, 1989.

Rossi, Benedetta, 'African Post-Slavery: A History of the Future', *The International Journal of African Historical Studies*, 2015, Vol. 48, No. 2.

Savage, E., 'Berbers and Blacks: Ibāḍī Slave Traffic in Eighth-Century North Africa', *The Journal of African History*, Vol. 33, No. 3, 1992.

Smallwood, Stephanie, 'African Guardians, European Slave Ships, and the Changing Dynamics of Power in the Early Modern Atlantic, *The William and Mary Quarterly*, Vol. 64, No. 4, October 2007.

Vink, Markus, '"The World's Oldest Trade": Slavery and Slave Trade in the Indian Ocean in the Seventeenth Century', *Journal of World History*, Vol. 14, No. 2, 2003.

Zeleke, Wondim Tiruneh, 'Centralization Effort and Local Gumuz Response in North Western Ethiopia: The Lambicha Revolt and Its After Math (1960–1961)', *Journal of Environmental and Earth Science*, Vol. 8, No. 6, 2018.

LIST OF MAPS AND ILLUSTRATIONS

* * *

INDEX

INDEX